Code of Conduct

For Servants of the Most High God

Code of Conduct
For Servants of the Most High God

Second Edition

Roger VanDerWerken

Scripture quotations in this commentary, unless otherwise indicated, are taken from the Holy Bible, New International Version®. Copyright © 1973, 1978, 1984 by International Bible Society Used by permission of Zondervan Publishing House. All rights reserved.

Second Edition, 2010

Printed in the United States of America

Publishing services by Selah Publishing Group, LLC, Tennessee. The views expressed or implied in this work do not necessarily reflect those of Selah Publishing Group.

ISBN: 978-1-58930-057-6
Library of Congress Control Number: 2002102281

Contents

PART TWO/ELEVEN LEADERSHIP PRINCIPLES

PART THREE/ARMING YOURSELF FOR BATTLE

INTRODUCTION
(2ND EDITION)

The primary reason for a second edition is to take advantage of Selah Publishing Group's print on demand feature, which allows the publisher to print exactly the number of copies desired by the customer, thus eliminating any need for warehousing. While taking advantage of this new technology, I have also taken the liberty of improving the text. (In this endeavor, I would like to extend special thanks to Mrs. Kellie Duck for her assistance). The result is more concise, more inclusive, and more readable. In the eight-year span between editions, I stand even firmer by the principles elaborated in my work. As you read, may the Most High God bring anointing to you and your ministry.

Roger VanDerWerken
February 2010

INTRODUCTION

"But Abram said to the King of Sodom, I have raised my hand to the LORD, God Most High, Creator of heaven and earth."

GENESIS 14:22

In 1983, the guided missile frigate upon which I was stationed passed through the Straits of Hormuz to begin patrolling the waters of the Persian Gulf. It was Easter Sunday, and the bloody war between Iran and Iraq dominated newspaper headlines. Lt. Ken Calhoun and I approached our Commanding Officer, requesting permission to conduct an Easter sunrise service on the forecastle. At precisely 0600 hours (6:00 a.m.), the frigate headed into the wind and slowed to five knots. To our amazement, nearly one hundred men (out of a crew of 250) gathered between the five-inch gun and the anti-submarine rocket launcher in order to celebrate the resurrection of the Lord Jesus Christ. This was a day off for the crew, and we had expected a mere handful of sailors to join with us; but deep within the soul of every human being lies a hunger for God. After months away from home, these men were spiritually famished.

St. Augustine, one of the greatest theologians in Church history, once declared, "Thou has made us for Thyself and our hearts are restless until they rest in thee."[1] Like the great saint of old, I believe that human beings, who are made in the image of God, find no peace for their souls until they discover the peace that comes from God through faith in Jesus Christ. Military service often exacerbates the human restlessness of which Augustine speaks, but when a sailor, a Marine, an airman or a soldier places his or her faith in Christ, the leadership principles learned in the U.S. military can be very helpful in bringing about significant spiritual growth.

When you become a Christian, you are enlisting in the mightiest of all armies: the army of the Lord of Hosts. Jesus Christ, the Captain of our salvation, is leading the charge, and behind him are a multitude of heavenly beings prepared to do battle. Christ is our Commander-in-Chief; He gives commands, and expects trust, teamwork, and obedience. Our faithfulness in serving Him will deeply influence the outcome of the greatest of all battles, one waged for the eternal souls of men and women made in His image.

I enlisted in this mighty army on a warm Sunday morning in October 1979. Bishop George D. McKinney of the St. Stephen's Church of God in Christ in Southeast San Diego was in the pulpit that day, the sweat rolling off the top of his bald head, and on to his forehead. "I tell you, brothers and sisters, Jesus Christ is the only way to heaven." McKinney looked much like a black Vladimir Ilych Lenin as he preached that morning, but the words that flowed through this faithful pastor pierced my very soul. I knew that they were true. An old way of life ended, and a new one began.

---

[1]*Confessions,* St. Augustine.

Prior to coming under the command of Jesus Christ, I had the privilege of attending one of the premier military schools in the world, the United States Naval Academy in Annapolis, Maryland. Little did I know that much of the leadership learned from the talented men and women who taught at that institution would one day prove invaluable in my service to the Most High. I have been involved in ministry for twenty-three years. Some of it has been informal in nature: conducting Bible studies as a lay leader on board Navy ships, teaching Sunday School to elementary children, and leading Junior/Senior High youth groups. Some of it has been quite formal: three and one half years as the Associate Pastor of a small suburban church outside of Philadelphia, PA; six and one half years as the Senior Pastor of a vibrant evangelical church in Central New York State; and nearly three years as a Chaplain to a battalion of United States Marines. Currently, it is my privilege to serve as the Protestant Pastor of the Marine Memorial Chapel at Camp Pendleton, CA. In the Church I have met some of the most sincere and dedicated human beings who walk this earth. In seminary I was schooled in the finest of theological thought. The best preparation I ever had for pastoral leadership, however, occurred in the Armed Forces of the United States. This preparation began with Plebe Summer at the Academy, it continued through five years as a Surface Warfare Officer in the Navy, and is reinforced again as I observe the leadership techniques of United States Marines. I am not a combat veteran. I cannot speak with the authority of one who has experienced human warfare. Nonetheless, my military experience has been an invaluable training tool, equipping me for the spiritual battles that confront Christians everywhere.

The Church is at war with unseen powers of evil that roam freely throughout this world. Much more is required of the Body of Christ than "preaching the gospel" and "walking the talk." Strategic thinking, planning and leadership are needed in order to *"take captive every thought and make it obedient to Christ"* (2 Co. 10:5). The purpose of this book is to share the leadership techniques of the United States military with pastors, church leaders, and with anyone who has been called to recruit and equip spiritual warriors for service in the army of the Most High. As a rule, pastors and church leaders tend to be congenial men and women who want to be respected by their parishioners. There is a tendency to try and make everyone happy who sets foot in the church. However, much in the same way as the Officer of the Deck on a ship gives decisive orders to the helmsman or to the Engineering Officer of the Watch, orders that must be obeyed immediately for the safety of the ship; so Christ gives commands to His people that must be obeyed for the health of the entire Church. His orders may not bring short-term happiness, but if they are obeyed, abundant and eternal life will result. In order for the ship at sea to accomplish its mission, there are standards of behavior expected from all who are on board. Leaders must clearly define what those standards are, must impeccably follow them, and be willing, if necessary, to go into harm's way.

Part one of this book examines the "Code of Conduct for Members of the Armed Forces," taught to every person upon his/her entry into the military, and tailors it to those who surrender their hearts to Christ. Part two takes the eleven leadership principles of the United States Marine Corps, the most elite fighting force in the world, and reflects on how they would be of great value to Church leaders. Part three focuses on key Biblical texts that teach us how to arm ourselves for the mighty battles we face as believers. I have quoted amply from the Scriptures in order to secure a smooth transition of thought. The heavy use of Scripture is not intended to keep you from reading the Bible directly. Conversely, it is my hope that this work will drive you to an even deeper study of God's Holy Word.

Acknowledgements

It is said that the shyest among us influences over 10,000 people in the course of a lifetime. I am sure there have been at least that many who have impacted me. While at the U.S. Naval Academy, Navy Captain Sean Stackley and Mr. Gary Stahl befriended me in very special ways, long before I bowed my heart to the Most High. On board ship, Chaplain Jerry McNabb and Mr. Ken Calhoun both showed me, in very gentle ways, what it meant to "walk the talk" in hostile environments. I was honored to have Jerry baptize me, together with his son, in a San Francisco Bay area church. Later, he also officiated in joining my wife and I in marriage.

I salute the many faithful church pastors serving in the trenches of the Kingdom; yours is one of the most challenging jobs in the world. There are many parishioners who made my own pastorates a lot of fun. Mr. John Hoover's "Skeeter the Clown" brought joy to many, while the music of Mr. and Mrs. David Brown and Mr. David Fairbanks stirred the hearts of all who listened. I have met many wonderful military men and women whose lives exude leadership, especially those Commanding Officers under whom I had the privilege to serve. Without exception, I would have followed any of them into harm's way.

Leadership is critical for anyone who seeks to pastor a church. Rev. Tim Keller, currently pastoring at Redeemer Presbyterian Church mid-town Manhattan, warned me (while working as a professor of practical theology at the Westminster Theological Seminary) that there is much more to spiritual leadership than preaching good sermons. Rev. Dan Nicewonger, currently pastoring at the Church in the Acres in Springfield, MA, caused me to come to grips with that reality when we were serving together on staff at the Memorial Baptist Church in Cortland, New York. For that I thank him whole-heartedly.

There are several people I would like to thank for making this manuscript become a reality. Mrs. Sarah Beatty, a talented young editor, improved immensely upon my original work; Major Hal Angus, USMC, offered wise counsel and support; Mrs. Jeanne Vinci, my choice for "secretary of kindness," gently suggested many textual improvements; while Master Gunnery Sergeant Octavio Smith, Director of the Corporal's Course at Marine Corps Base Camp Pendleton, helped me locate sources for many of the Marine Corps creeds.

Finally, and most importantly, I salute my parents who worked hard instilling a "code of conduct" into a rather rebellious young man; my wife Jacque; and my children Christina, Beth, and Jordan. These tolerated a husband and a father whose mind was totally engaged in the writing of a book, often oblivious to the pressing realities of everyday life. I first met Jacque when she was working as a Navy Religious Programs Specialist at the Great Lakes Naval Base in North Chicago. She continues to "beat feet for Jesus" to this day.

Part One / The Code Of Conduct

Origins of the Code of Conduct

> *Q: Why didn't you say sir?*
>
> *A: Sir, sir is a subservient word surviving from the surly days in old Serbia when certain serfs, too ignorant to remember their lord's names, yet too servile to blaspheme them, circumvented the situation by surrogating the subservient word, sir, by which I now belatedly address a certain senior cirriped, who correctly surmised that I was syrupy enough to say sir after every word I said, sir.*[1]

When you raise your right hand and swear to "protect and defend the Constitution of the United States against all enemies foreign and domestic," your life is no longer your own; you are under the authority of the Constitution, the Bill of Rights, and the chain of command that is above you, ultimately serving at the pleasure of the Commander-in-Chief, the President of the United States. The transition from the

---

[1]*Reef Points 1975-76, The Annual Handbook of the Brigade of Midshipmen,* (Annapolis: United States Naval Academy), p. 269.

civilian world to that of the military is radical, and an intense indoctrination takes place that transforms the recruit from citizen to soldier. In the same manner, when you surrender your life to the Lordship of Jesus Christ, your life is no longer your own. The *Heidelberg Catechism*, a document that has great value to many Christians of the Reformed persuasion, puts it this way: "I am not my own, but belong — body and soul, in life and in death — to my faithful Savior Jesus Christ."[2]

As a Christian, you are submitting to the authority of apostolic teaching as embodied in the Scriptures (n. Acts 2:42; 16:4; 2 Ti. 3:16; 2 Pe. 1:21) and manifest in the local church (Mt. 16:19; 18:18; John 20:23; Heb. 13:17). Ultimately, you are under the authority of Jesus Christ, the King of kings, and the Lord of lords (1 Ti. 6:15; Rev. 1:5; 17:14; 19:16). But unlike the indoctrination that takes place for a "new join" in the Armed Forces, a "new join" in the Church — the mightiest of all armies — often flounders along with little or no guidance, never coming to understand the purpose and expectations of those who serve. A radical change is to take place when you follow Christ. The Bible says, *"Do not conform any longer to the pattern of this world, but be transformed by the renewing of your mind. Then you will be able to test and approve what God's will is — his good, pleasing and perfect will"* (Ro. 12:2). Unfortunately, many who come to Christ have no understanding what sort of transformation is to take place.

My indoctrination into military culture was transforming, to say the least. I had just returned from a year in the Netherlands as a participant in Rotary International's student exchange program. I had learned to speak Dutch fluently, my hair had grown quite long, and I had become interested

---

[2]Ecumenical Creeds & Reformed Confessions, (Grand Rapids, Michigan: Board of Publications of the Christian Reformed Church, 1979), p. 7.

in the socialist movement that was popular among European youth at the time. Needless to say, my introduction to life at the Naval Academy was culture shock at its finest. In July 1975, I flew into Baltimore-Washington International Airport, took a cab to Annapolis, and spent my last day as a civilian sleeping on a bunk in Rickets Hall. The next day, I was issued six sets of long, white, heavy cotton pants and blouses called "Working Uniform White Alphas," a pair of heavy black shoes called "boondockers," and a Dixie cup cap with a blue stripe around its rim. For the next two months, in the sweltering summer heat along the Chesapeake Bay, this was the uniform for 1,600 plebes who were to be indoctrinated into the military system.

We ran, marched, and drilled with M-1 rifles. We arose at 5:00 a.m. in order to participate in rigorous physical training led by Mr. Heinz Lenz, a retired U.S. Naval Officer of German descent. We learned to sail, shoot a Colt 45, and read Morse Code and semaphore. Above all else, we perspired. Of all the requirements placed on us that summer, the most demanding was the sheer memorization of volumes of information. We had to know the menu for the next two meals served in the wardroom. We had to know the contents of three major front-page newspaper articles, and one from the sports page. We had to know what movies were playing at the five different movie theaters in town. (It was fascinating that Stephen Spielberg's "Jaws" played that entire summer at the Circle Theater, a theme most appropriate for terrified plebes about to embark upon a great naval adventure). We had to know the names of the Company Commanders from each of the thirty-six companies, and which ones had watch on any given day. All of this information had to be recited from memory at a moment's notice when requested by anyone who was senior to us, and that was just about everyone in the entire world.

For anyone who has ever graduated from Annapolis, the term "Reef Points" will have special meaning. Technically, reef points are grommets used on a sailboat to shorten sail in stormy weather, preventing the vessel from capsizing. To the plebe at Annapolis, however, it is a little book measuring 5.5 inches by 4.5 inches, laminated with plastic. The 1975-76 edition had 294 pages. As plebes we were required to take this little book wherever we went, and since our uniform had no pockets, the proper way to carry *Reef Points* was to open it in the middle and tuck it in the waste line of our pants. The long blouse hid the book from view.

It was the responsibility of every midshipman first class to indoctrinate the plebe in all of the material found in it. In essence, we were required to memorize everything in the book. This included Navy songs; famous naval sayings; the history of the naval service; traditions of the U.S. Naval Academy and sister schools; organizational structure of the Department of Defense; ranks and insignia of all personnel in the Armed Forces; and the ships, aircraft and weapons of the U.S. Navy. One of the more difficult passages in *Reef Points* that we were required to memorize was the "Code of Conduct For Members of the Armed Forces of the United States." President Eisenhower presented this six-point document to the nation and to its military on April 17, 1955. Although it was primarily designed as "a code for prisoner-of-war conduct, the concepts expressed apply not only to the prisoner of war, but also to the American military man who is free to defend his country."[3] "The Code of Conduct For Members of the Armed Forces of the United States" as we memorized it in the hot summer of 1975, reads as follows:

---

[3]*Reef Points* p. 33.

Code of Conduct

For Members of the Armed Forces of the United States (1975)

I. I am an American fighting man. I serve in the forces which guard my country and our way of life. I am prepared to give my life in their defense.

II. I will never surrender of my own free will. If in command I will never surrender my men while they still have the means to resist.

III. If I am captured I will continue to resist by all means available. I will make every effort to escape and aid others to escape. I will accept neither parole nor special favors from the enemy.

IV. If I become a prisoner of war, I will keep faith with my fellow prisoners. I will give no information or take part in any action which might be harmful to my comrades. If I am senior, I will take command. If not, I will obey the lawful orders of those appointed over me and will back them up in every way.

V. When questioned, should I become a prisoner of war, I am bound to give only name, rank, service number, and date of birth. I will evade answering further questions to the utmost of my ability. I will make no oral or written statements disloyal to my country and its allies or harmful to their cause.

VI. I will never forget that I am an American fighting man, responsible for my actions, and dedicated to the principles which made my country free. I will trust in my God and in the United States of America.[4]

---

[4]*ibid.*, p. 34.

I resigned my commission as a Line Officer in the U.S. Navy in 1984, in order to pursue theological education. Following fourteen years of broken service (four as a seminary student, and ten as a civilian pastor), I once again joined the Navy, this time as a chaplain. At the Navy Chaplain School in Newport, Rhode Island, the Code was again a very significant part of our training. Some small but important changes had been made over the years. The Code, as it reads now, follows; changes are in italics:

Code of Conduct

For Members of the Armed Forces of the United States (1998)

I. *I am an American, fighting in the armed forces* which guard my country and our way of life. I am prepared to give my life in their defense.

II. I will never surrender of my own free will. If in command I will never surrender my men while they still have the means to resist.

III. If I am captured I will continue to resist by all means available. I will make every effort to escape and aid others to escape. I will accept neither parole nor special favors from the enemy.

IV. If I become a prisoner of war, I will keep faith with my fellow prisoners. I will give no information nor take part in any action which might be harmful to my comrades. If I am senior, I will take command. If not, I will obey the lawful orders of those appointed over me and will back them in every way.

V. When questioned, should I become a prisoner of war, *I am required to give* name, rank, service number, and date of birth. I will evade answering further questions to the utmost of my ability. I will make no oral or written statements disloyal to my country and its allies or harmful to their cause.

VI. I will never forget that *I am an American, fighting for freedom*, responsible for my actions, and dedicated to the principles which made my country free. I will trust in my God and in the United States of America.[5]

---

[5]*Marine Battle Skills Training Handbook, Book 1, PVT-GYSGT, General Military Subjects,* (Arlington, VA: Marine Corps Institute, January 1993), pp. 1-10-1, 1-10-2.

The changes are good ones, and they are closer to the universal truths we learn from experience and from the Scriptures. The first change to the Code occurred on November 3, 1977, when President Jimmy Carter amended Article V.[6] Professor Porter Halyburton of the Navy War College in Newport, Rhode Island, made this particular change come to life for our group of newly-appointed Navy Chaplains. Halyburton is a retired Commander in the United States Navy whose F-4B Phantom Jet was shot down by an enemy missile in Vietnam, on October 17, 1965. For the next seven and one half years, he was a prisoner of war (POW) in an enemy country.[7]

The professor speaks with authority whenever he teaches the Code of Conduct to students attending the various schools at the Naval Education and Training Command, and on one warm afternoon in October 1998, he held the rapt attention of our class of fifteen. (To hold the attention of clergy is, in itself, no small feat!) During the afternoon session, Halyburton clarified something that is widely misunderstood: Article V requires the POW to give "name, rank, service number and date of birth," but he is certainly allowed to offer more information than these four items. The required items identify the captive as a member of the Armed Forces, and the information may save his/her life; but the POW is certainly allowed to communicate more than this: he can tell the enemy that he is not receiving enough to eat; she can remind him of the provisions of the Geneva Convention; he can offer volumes of irrelevant information. The questions that POWs are to evade answering are those that would prove helpful to the enemy cause. In addition, as Halyburton and other POWs know well, every man has his breaking point. The enemy can always get information from

---

[6]Executive Order 12017 "Amending the Code of Conduct for members of the Armed Forces of the United States," November 3, 1977.
[7]*Davidson Journal*, Fall 1989, p. 16.

you if he wants to. The purpose of the Code is to force him. Every man who returned from the "Hanoi Hilton" gave information against his will on at least one occasion - from James Stockdale, the most senior in rank - to everyone junior to him. The proud did not make it. The Code recognizes the frailty of human flesh and thus challenges us to "evade answering further questions to the utmost" of our abilities. To interpret Article V as saying that a POW can *only* give name, rank, service number and date of birth is to misunderstand its intent. The changes made to Article V in 1977, more clearly reflect the spirit of the original.

At the beginning of His ministry, when interrogated by the enemy, Jesus offered a significant amount of information that the Devil did not want to hear. When questioned about the possibility of turning stones to bread, our Lord answered, *"Man does not live on bread alone."* As to Satan's suggestion that all the kingdoms of this world would be offered to Him if He only bowed and worshipped, Jesus replied, *"Worship the Lord your God and serve him only."* When challenged to throw himself from the heights, our Lord answered, *"Do not put the Lord your God to the test"* (Luke 4:4, 8, 12). At the end of His ministry, while standing before the Governor of Judea, Jesus again offered information beyond what the enemy was seeking. When Pontius Pilate asked, *"Are you the king of the Jews,"* Jesus responded, *"Is that your own idea ...or did others talk to you about me?"* When Pilate asked, *"Am I a Jew ... It was your people and your chief priests who handed you over to me. What is it you have done?"* Jesus replied, *"My kingdom is not of this world. If it were, my servants would fight to prevent my arrest by the Jews. But now my kingdom is from another place"* (John 18:33-36). The type of resistance shown by Christ in the face of the enemy is precisely the kind expected by the Code of Conduct for members of the Armed Forces, and of Christians as we do battle against the world, the flesh, and the Devil.

Changes in Articles I and VI were made later, in order to reflect the more inclusive nature of the U.S. Military. The years I spent at the United States Naval Academy were quite turbulent to say the least. My class (1979) was the last all male class to graduate from the institution. During my plebe year (1975-76), the Academy was an all male organization; but the following year, eighty-one young women entered, ending a 131-year all-male tradition. In the years since, women have been incorporated into wardrooms and crews aboard warships and among the ground troops of Army and Marine forces. As our nation struggled to integrate its Armed Forces with respect to gender, the Code of Conduct experienced a corresponding change to reflect what was occurring.[8]

There remains to this day considerable debate over the role of women in the military, and there is also significant discussion over their position in the Church; but one thing remains very clear: the Bible and its preeminent focus - Jesus of Nazareth - both teach that women, as well as men, have invaluable roles as servants of the Most High. The very first person to whom Jesus revealed His messianic identity was a Samaritan woman (John 4:26). Jesus' female disciples were the only ones courageous enough to remain at the foot of the cross (Mt. 27:55-56; Mark 15:40-41; Luke 23:49; John 19:25-27), while women were the first among those used by God to declare the glory of the resurrection (Mt. 28:1; Mark 16:1; Luke 24:1; John 20:1). The Apostle Paul makes it very clear that the kingdom of God does not discriminate according to gender, *"There is neither ... male nor female, for you are all one in Christ Jesus"* (Gal. 3:28).

The military Code of Conduct as it now appears speaks truth to the heart of the soldier. The purpose of this present work is to take liberty with the "Code of Conduct for

---

[8]Sharon Hanley Disher's *First Class: Women Join the Ranks at the Naval Academy* (Naval Institute Press, 1998) offers profound insight into some of the changes that were taking place during this period.

Members of the Armed Forces," and establish a "Code of Conduct for Servants of the Most High God." As the military Code of Conduct is not the same type of document as the Constitution or the Bill of Rights, so this proposed spiritual Code is not meant to replace statements of faith, creeds or the Scripture proper. A member of the military has been sworn to uphold the Constitution and the Bill of Rights and has obligations to them, "even if the Code of Conduct had never been formulated as a high standard of general behavior." The military Code is an ethical guide, dealing with "the soldier's chief concerns as an American in combat;" concerns which "become critical when you must evade capture, resist while a prisoner, or escape from the enemy."[9]

In like manner, Christians are required to uphold their allegiance to Christ, to His Church, and to the Scriptures, even if such a document as the one I am proposing never existed. "Code of Conduct for Servants of the Most High God" is designed to serve as an ethical guide for Christians as we engage the enemy in battle. Unlike the enemies faced by men and women in the Armed Forces, ours are spiritual: *"For our struggle is not against flesh and blood, but against the rulers, against the authorities ... against the spiritual forces of evil in the heavenly realms"* (Eph. 6:12). The Code of Conduct For Servants of the Most High God is meant as a guide to resist the Devil and the ways of the flesh as we live out our lives in this world.

The document that follows describes who you are as a Christian, and sets a high standard for anyone who would take up the cross of Jesus Christ. Its six articles, if followed, will cause the mighty army of our Lord to make huge inroads in a culture desperately crying out for deliverance. Unlike

---

[9]Material taken from class notes, Navy Chaplain School Basic Course Class 99010. Based upon Executive Order 10631 of Aug. 17, 1955, as amended; and Dept. of Defense Directive 1300.7 of Dec. 23, 1988.

the military Code, this one is designed for those who are free. We were POWs until Christ liberated us from Satan's bondage. The Code is needed because we operate in enemy territory. Our nemesis is alive and well, binding fellow human beings in spiritual darkness, while often oppressing those of us who follow Christ. The Code is meant to instill courage until the day Christ returns in glorious victory.

Code of Conduct
For Servants of the Most High God

I. I am a Christian soldier. I serve in the Church of Jesus Christ, which proclaims the gospel and the message of God's love. I give my life to God and to His service.

II. I will never give up in the face of those forces that seek to suppress the gospel. As a leader, I will carry out my responsibilities and never lose hope.

III. When I sin against others or against God, I will confess it; I will repent, make restitution, and seek to have victory in that area of my life. I will not justify my sin or hold anger in my heart against another.

IV. In this warfare, I will be loyal to my church. I will be faithful to my brothers and sisters in Christ. I will support my church leaders and pastors. As a leader, I will take the initiative and be faithful to the gospel of Jesus Christ.

V. I will be a faithful witness to Christ in my dealings with those outside my church. I will support the Biblical witness of other churches in my community. I will not make disparaging remarks against my church or any other churches.

VI. I will never forget that I am a child of God, redeemed by the blood of Jesus Christ, responsible for my actions, dedicated to the cause of the gospel that has set me free. I will trust in God and in the person and work of His Son, Jesus Christ.

Why a Code of Conduct is Needed

> *"The art of war is of vital importance to the state. It is a matter of life and death, a road either to safety or to ruin. Hence under no circumstances can it be neglected."*
>
> Sun Tzu[1]

1. A Code of Conduct is needed because we are at war. We are at war with spiritual forces of evil, dark powers that seek to snuff out life as God created it. Behind these malevolent forces are unseen demonic personalities, hate-filled and hideous by nature. Their prince is a fallen angel called Lucifer, Satan, or the Devil. His message is death and his tactics powerful. We must engage him with all of the tools God has given.

Over the past two millennia, brilliant theologians have contributed to what is known as the doctrine of "Just War," criteria that leaders of the State should prayerfully consider prior to engaging their nation in armed combat. A just war

---

[1]Sun Tzu, *The Art of War,* James Clavell,editor, (New York, NY: Delacorte Press, 1983), p. 9.

consists of three parts: justice of war (*jus ad bellum*), justice in war (*jus in bello*), and justice after war (*jus post bellum*).[2] Servants of the Most High, engaged in spiritual warfare, can learn much from the guidance given to national leaders who direct the course of armed combat.

The seven criteria for the justice of war include (these are the items a head of state should consider prior to committing his nation to combat):

1. Engaged on order of competent authority.
2. Truly necessary for achievement of a just cause.
3. Carried out with right intention.
4. Proportionality of good over evil (i.e. the end result of a war leaves the world a better place).
5. Reasonable hope of success.
6. Last resort.
7. Declaration of war aims.

On a spiritual level, the justice of our war is clear:

1. Our competent authority is Christ.
2. Just cause: restore the earth to its original glory.
3. Right intent: crush the forces of spiritual evil and bring blessing to the human race.
4. Proportionally, the Kingdom of Heaven is infinitely better than the kingdoms of this world.
5. In following Christ, we are guaranteed victory.
6. Last resort: there is no other name under heaven by which we must be saved (Acts 4:12).
7. Declaration of war aims: to bring God's kingdom to the earth (Mt. 6:10).

---

[2]William V. O'Brien, *The Conduct of Just and Limited War*, NY: Praeger, 1981, ch. 1-2. James Turner Johnson and George Weigel, *Just War and the Gulf War,* Washington, DC: Ethics and Public Policy Center, 1991, pp. 21-29.

The two criteria for justice in war include (these are the issues soldiers on the battlefield must discern prior to engaging the enemy):

1. Proportionality (this proportionality forbids using excessive force to accomplish the mission).
2. Discrimination (soldiers must distinguish between combatant and non-combatant).

On a spiritual level Christians exercise justice in war by:

1. Being spiritually sensitive as we share our faith with others (i.e. those who are hungry might benefit more from a hot meal than from a theological treatise)
2. Recognizing the difference between those who have another perspective on the faith from those who have no faith at all. (People from other denominations may not necessarily need to be "converted").

The three criteria for justice after war include:

1. Repentance (victors are humble)
2. Honorable surrender
3. Restoration (remove the instruments of war)

On a spiritual level Christians display justice after war:

1. By acknowledging our own brokenness; we need to repent and seek forgiveness from God for our own sins on a continual basis
2. By recognizing the dignity of all human beings, especially those who have surrendered their hearts to Christ
3. By helping new believers remove temptations that war against their souls.

2. *A Code of Conduct is needed because war is exceedingly stressful.* United States Marines know this. Marine Corps leaders have identified nine elements commonly found in a combat environment.

1. Violent, unnerving sights and sounds.
2. Casualties.
3. Confusion and lack of information.
4. Feeling of isolation.
5. Communications breakdowns.
6. Individual discomfort and physical fatigue.
7. Fear, stress, and mental fatigue.
8. Continuous operations.
9. Homesickness[3]

Spiritually, the servant of the Most High can expect:

1. Sights that are unnerving as the gospel is brought to bear on a culture in rebellion against God.
2. Casualties: people thought to be brothers or sisters in the faith may fall away.
3. Confusion: misunderstanding about the mission.
4. Feelings of isolation: no one else in the neighborhood or on the job seems to be engaged.
5. Communication breakdowns: he does not speak the same language as the world.
6. Discomfort, fatigue: living for God is difficult.
7. Continuous operations: duty calls 24/7.
8. Fear or stress: as a result of living in a way that is very different from the rest of the world.
9. Homesickness: longing for the ultimate destination of heaven, or for the fellowship of the Church.

---

[3]*Marine Battle Skills Training Handbook, Book 1, PVT-GYSGT, General Military Subjects,* (Arlington, VA: Marine Corps Institute, January 1993), p. 1-8-3.

3. A Code of Conduct is needed to overcome fear. Marine leaders have identified four characteristics enabling their troops to succeed in this endeavor:

1. Morale.
2. Discipline.
3. Esprit de Corps.
4. Proficiency[4].

Christians are able to overcome fear by working as a team. If servants of the Most High agree together to follow the teachings of Jesus, morale increases and esprit de corps develops. Proficiency in the Scriptures aids immensely in this discipline and brings victory over the forces of evil.

4. A Code of Conduct is needed because of the extremely high casualty rates local churches experience due to "friendly fire." People who do not attend church often speak of Christians "killing their wounded" or of the local "First Fighting Church." Comments made by the "saints" can be downright rude. "We don't need your type around here;" "Why don't you take your show on the road?" (Directed at a music leader who volunteered his time leading a vibrant and meaningful time of worship); or "What are you doing here?" are some of the more astonishing remarks I have heard from upstanding church members on more than one occasion. People who smoke cigarettes, go to the club, sport tattoos, play cards, dance, wear long hair or jewelry, or struggle with their sexuality are often accosted and treated like second class citizens. Churches may spend more time fighting hundred-year-old theological battles than they do preaching the good news of Jesus Christ. Local houses of

---

[4]*Initial Stage Combat Skills Tasks,* (Arlington, VA: Marine Corps Institute, 1989), p. 11-7.

worship can become so politically partisan that anyone not of that persuasion feels completely alienated. Debates over creation vs. evolution or impassioned points of view on how the world will end can become so animated that the primary message of love and salvation is lost in the heat of the exchange. Idealistic young pastors, thrown into this type of scenario for the first time, suddenly discover the harsh realities of church politics and of raising enough money to meet the annual budget. People often leave the local church because of the shrapnel wounds of a fiery exchange that took place in the middle of the sanctuary, instead of behind the closed doors of the pastor's office.

5. A Code of Conduct is needed because wars need to be governed by laws. Marines have nine laws which govern war, and every recruit is required to memorize them prior to graduating from boot camp:

1. Marines fight only enemy combatants.
2. Marines do not harm enemies who surrender. They must disarm them and turn them over to their superior.
3. Marines do not kill or torture prisoners.
4. Marines collect and care for the wounded, whether friend or foe.
5. Marines do not attack medical personnel, facilities, or equipment.
6. Marines destroy no more than the mission requires.
7. Marines treat all civilians humanely.
8. Marines do not steal. Marines respect private property and possessions.
9. Marines should do their best to prevent violations of the law of war. They must report all vialations of the law of war to their superior.[5]

---

[5]*Marine Battle Skills Training Handbook, Book 1, PVT-GYSGT, General Military Subjects*, (Arlington, VA: Marine Corps Institute, January 1993), p. 1-1-19.

On a spiritual level, believers do not attack fellow believers. We are kind to all, especially to those who have surrendered their hearts to Christ. We do not overwhelm new believers with excessive theological jargon or try to impress them with the depth of our Bible knowledge. All human beings are made in the image of God and should be treated accordingly, regardless of religion. Christians care for each other and are accountable to each other, always behaving in such a way that brings honor to our Commander.

6. Finally, a Code of Conduct is needed because our God is a warrior God, battling against spiritual forces of evil. His Son, the Lord Jesus Christ, is the greatest of all warriors. The angels of heaven, also known as the "heavenly host" (or army), serve at the beck and call of the Almighty. We, as believers in Christ, form the human component of this great militia. Given the fact that the human element is the weakest link in the chain, it is highly appropriate that a Code of Conduct be established.

Almighty God as Divine Warrior

Throughout the Bible we read of a warrior God. When the Egyptian army trapped Moses at the Red Sea, he comforted the Israelite people:

> *"Do not be afraid. Stand firm and you will see the deliverance the LORD will bring you today. The Egyptians you see today you will never see again. The LORD will fight for you; you need only to be still"* (Ex. 14:13-14; c.f. Neh. 4:20).

Following the overwhelming defeat of the Egyptians, Miriam, the sister of Moses, broke out in song and dance:

> *"The LORD is my strength and my song; he has become my salvation ... The LORD is a warrior ... Pharaoh's chariots and his army he has hurled into the sea ... Your right hand, O LORD, shattered the enemy"* (Ex. 15:2-6).

Approaching death, Moses passed on these words to his successor Joshua, the man who was to lead the Israelites into the Promised Land:

> *"The LORD himself goes before you and will be with you; he will never leave you nor forsake you. Do not be afraid; do not be discouraged"* (Deut. 31:8).

To all of the Israelites Moses declared:

> *"Blessed are you, O Israel! Who is like you, a people saved by the LORD? He is your shield and helper and your glorious sword"* (Deut. 33: 29).

Joshua, just prior to the battle of Jericho, "*saw a man standing in front of him with a drawn sword in his hand.*" When the Israelite leader asked for identification, he was told: "*as commander of the army of the LORD I have now come*" (Josh. 5:13-14). Joshua's response was to fall face down on the ground out of reverence.

David, Israel's greatest king, had a warrior's heart and understood the nature of God to be that of Divine Warrior. As a young man, the future king challenged Goliath with the following:

> "*You come against me with sword and spear and javelin, but I come against you in the name of the LORD Almighty, the God of the armies of Israel, whom you have defied*" (1 Sam. 17:45).

As king, David frequently called upon God for military advice (1 Chr. 14:10), and was given victory everywhere he went (1 Chr. 18:6). The Psalms, many of which are attributed to King David, testify to the warrior-like nature of the LORD. Nearly every one speaks of the destruction of the wicked, the defeat of enemies, or of God's victory over evil. Of particular note are Psalms such as:

> "*May God arise, may his enemies be scattered; may his foes flee before him ... as wax melts before the fire, may the wicked perish before God ... Sing to God, sing praise to his name, extol him who rides on the clouds — his name is the LORD*" (Ps. 68:1-4).

> "*With your mighty arm you redeemed your people ... The waters saw you, O God, the waters saw you and writhed; the very depths were convulsed. The clouds poured down water, the skies resounded with thunder; your arrows flashed back and forth ... the earth trembled and quaked*" (Ps. 77: 15-18).

> *"The LORD reigns, let the earth be glad; let the distant shores rejoice. Clouds and thick darkness surround him ... Fire goes before him and consumes his foes on every side ... The mountains melt like wax before the LORD ... Let those who love the LORD hate evil."* (Ps. 97: 1-10).

> *"Part your heavens, O LORD, and come down; touch the mountains, so that they smoke. Send forth lightning and scatter the enemies; shoot your arrows and rout them. Reach down your hand from on high; deliver me and rescue me from the mighty waters, from the hands of foreigners whose mouths are full of lies, whose right hands are deceitful"* (Ps. 144: 5-8).

The Old Testament prophets also recognize God's warrior-like qualities. Isaiah writes:

> *"The LORD will march out like a mighty man, like a warrior he will stir up his zeal; with a shout he will raise the battle cry and will triumph over his enemies"* (42:13).

Jeremiah speaks of the LORD opening his arsenal and bringing out weapons of wrath (50:25), declaring that the name of the LORD is a war club, a weapon for battle (51:20). Ezekiel writes of God placing hooks in the jaws of the army of Gog (38:4), sending down fire on the land of Magog (39:6). Joel tells us that *"The LORD thunders at the head of his army"* (2:11); while Micah speaks of mountains melting before the His presence (1:4), and of the destruction of enemy horses and chariots (5:10-15). Habakkuk prays:

> *"Sun and moon stood still in the heavens at the glint of your flying arrows ... In wrath you strode through the earth ... You came out to deliver your people ... You crushed the leader of the land of wickedness ... With his own spear you pierced his head"* (3:11-14).

Zechariah writes of the LORD going out, fighting all the nations of the earth in a final day of battle (14:3). Nearly every Old Testament prophet uses the metaphor of war to describe the wrath of the true and the living God.

Many believe that the God of the Old Testament is wrath-filled, while the God of the New Testament is full of love and mercy. Do not be deceived by this: the same God has ruled over the affairs of humanity from the beginning; His attributes are changeless. He loves those who humble their hearts before Him, but will reveal His wrath toward those who reject Him. The warrior-like imagery so prevalent in the Old Testament continues into the New.

In preparing the way for Messiah's coming, John the Baptist warns the religious establishment to *"flee from the coming wrath"* (Mt. 3:7, Luke 3:7). In the Sermon on the Mount, Jesus declares that anyone who would call another man or woman "fool" was *"in danger of the fire of hell"* (Mt. 5:22). To those tempted by adultery or by greed He proclaims: *"It is better for you to lose one part of your body than for your whole body to go into hell"* (Mt. 5:30). In commissioning twelve disciples to preach the message of the Kingdom, Jesus says:

> *"Do not be afraid of those who kill the body but cannot kill the soul. Rather, be afraid of the one who can destroy both soul and body in hell"* (Mt. 10:28).

In many of the parables Jesus warns of the wrath of God. The wicked tenants would be given a wretched end (Mt. 21:41). The men who refused to come to the wedding feast were killed, and their city was burned down (Mt. 22:7). The worthless servant who did not use his God-given talents was to be thrown *"into the darkness, where there will be weeping and gnashing of teeth"* (Mt. 25:30).

In the most theological of the New Testament books, the Apostle Paul writes to the church in Rome:

> *"The wrath of God is being revealed from heaven against all the godlessness and wickedness of men who suppress the truth by their wickedness"* (Ro. 1:18).
>
> *"Do not take revenge, my friends, but leave room for God's wrath"* (Ro. 12:19).
>
> *"The God of peace will soon crush Satan under your feet"* (Ro. 16:20).

In 2 Corinthians, Paul writes: *"thanks be to God who always leads us in triumphal procession in Christ"* (2:14). The book of Revelation, in its essence, is a war depicting the smashing victory that the Most High God will bring upon the spiritual forces of evil in our world.[6] In light of the testimony of both Testaments, the words recorded by the author of Hebrews should be heeded most soberly: *"It is a dreadful thing to fall into the hands of the living God"* (Heb. 10:31).

---

[6]Recommended reading: *Captain's on the Bridge: The Book of Revelation from a Military Perspective,* by Roger VanDerWerken, (Selah Publishing Group, 2007)

Jesus Christ as Divine Warrior

The nature of God has not changed: the metaphor of divine warrior applies to the Son as well as to the Father, and Jesus is the greatest of all warriors. He is the one who destroys every last vestige of evil that afflicts humankind, sending it to the pit of an everlasting hell. He wages war against the very powers of evil that rear up their ugly heads against us and within us. As the following verses make clear, Christ has defeated the powers of sin and death, and grants overwhelming victory to all who follow Him.

Hundreds of years before His birth, the divinely anointed authors of Holy Scripture foresaw His coming. Christians understand Psalm 2 to be one of many Old Testament passages that point to Jesus:

> *'The kings of the earth take their stand and the rulers gather together against the LORD and against his Anointed One ... The One enthroned in heaven laughs ... Then he rebukes them in his anger and terrifies them in his wrath, saying "I have installed my King on Zion, my holy hill" ... Therefore, you kings, be wise; be warned, you rulers of the earth. Serve the LORD with fear and rejoice with trembling. Kiss the Son, lest he be angry and you be destroyed in your way, for his wrath can flare up in a moment'* (Ps. 2:2-17).

In another Psalm, widely quoted in the New Testament, we read:

> *'The LORD says to my Lord: "Sit at my right hand until I make your enemies a footstool for your feet." The LORD will extend your mighty scepter from Zion; you will rule in the midst of your enemies. Your troops will be willing on your day of battle ... The Lord is at your right hand; he will crush kings on the*

> *day of his wrath. He will judge the nations, heaping up the dead and crushing the rulers of the whole earth'* (Ps. 110:1-3, 5-6; c.f. Mt. 22:44; Acts 2:35; Heb. 1:13; 10:13).

The prophet Isaiah offers many stunning insights into the coming of our Lord. In one passage, frequently read during the Christmas season, he writes:

> *"Every warrior's boot used in battle and every garment rolled in blood will be destined for burning, will be fuel for the fire. For to us a child is born, to us a son is given, and the government will be on his shoulders"* (Is. 9:5-6).

In another passage he declares:

> *"A shoot will come up from the stump of Jesse ... The Spirit of the LORD will rest on him ... with righteousness he will judge the needy ... He will strike the earth with the rod of his mouth; with the breath of his lips he will slay the wicked"* (Is. 11:1-4).

The role of Christ becomes abundantly clear in the New Testament. He has command authority over the elements of nature (Mt. 8:26; 21:19), over the unseen spirit realm (Mark 1:24; 5:7; 9:25), and over the religious leaders of His day (Mark 11:15-16). In one parable Jesus teaches, "*no one can enter a strong man's house and carry off his possessions unless he first ties up the strong man" (Mark 3:27).* When He later stands in the synagogue and proclaims, "*The Spirit of the Lord is on me ... he has anointed me to preach good news to the poor ... to proclaim freedom for the prisoners ... to release the oppressed"* (Luke 4:18), or when He declares, "*All authority in heaven and on earth has been given to me"* (Mt. 28:18); a de facto announcement is made: the one able to bind the strong man is now here.

In the early days of His ministry Jesus said, *"I have come to bring fire on the earth"* (Luke 12:49). Later He announced that His return would be accompanied with the clouds of heaven, and with great power and glory (Mt. 24:30; 26:64). A judgment of the entire human race was to follow, and all who oppose Him would be sent to an *"eternal fire prepared for the devil and his angels"* (Mt. 25:41). This kind of language is not that of a meek and passive religious leader; these are the words of a great heavenly warrior who knows the power of evil and is able to crush it underfoot.

Both angels and humans understand the warrior-like authority of Jesus Christ. Gabriel the archangel, in announcing to Mary that she was to give birth to the Messiah, declares:

> *"He will be great and will be called the Son of the Most High. The Lord God will give him the throne of his father David, and he will reign over the house of Jacob forever; his kingdom will never end"* (Luke 1:32-33).

John the Baptist, chosen to prepare Israel for Messiah's coming, says to the people who met him at the river:

> *"I baptize you with water. But one more powerful than I will come, the thongs of whose sandals I am not worthy to untie. He will baptize you with the Holy Spirit and with fire"* (Luke 3:16).

On Palm Sunday, thousands of people who saw Jesus entering the city of Jerusalem riding on a donkey cry out:

> *"Hosanna (save us now!) ... Blessed is he who comes in the name of the Lord! Hosanna in the highest!"* (Mt. 21:9).

The Apostle Paul, whose life was dramatically changed as a result of an encounter with Jesus, writes:

> *"For the Lord himself will come down from heaven, with a loud command, with the voice of the archangel and with the trumpet call of God, and the dead in Christ will rise first"* (1 Th. 4:16).

He later declares:

> *"the lawless one will be revealed, whom the Lord Jesus will overthrow with the breath of his mouth and destroy by the splendor of his coming"* (2 Th. 2:8).

John, the author of Revelation, writes about how the kings of the earth will make war against the Lamb, *"but the Lamb will overcome them because he is the Lord of lords and King of kings"* (Rev. 17:14). He tells us that Jesus uses a sword to strike down the nations and that: *"He will rule them with an iron scepter."* (Rev. 19:15). Let there be no doubt, the Lord Jesus Christ is a warrior without peer, ruling over both heaven and earth.

His greatest victory, however, involves snatching life from the jaws of death. When Jesus called in a loud voice, *"Lazarus, come out!"* (John 11:43), a man who had been dead for three days came to life again. This was a foreshadowing of something much greater, for not long after the Lazarus miracle, a crucified Jesus also rose from the dead, destroying forever the mightiest weapon in Satan's arsenal. As the Apostle Paul so eloquently puts it:

> *"For as in Adam all die, so in Christ all will be made alive" (1 Co. 15:22); or "he must reign until he has put all his enemies under his feet. The last enemy to be destroyed is death"* (1 Co. 15:25-26).

and again,

> *'"Death has been swallowed up in victory." "Where, O death, is your victory? Where, O death is your sting?" ... thanks be to God! He gives us victory through our Lord Jesus Christ'* (1 Co. 15:54-57).

The greatest of all battles is waged between life and death; and the reward promised to those who come under the command of Jesus Christ, the heavenly warrior, is nothing less than life itself, abundant and eternal.

The Angels of Heaven as Divine Warriors

Angels also serve in the army of the Most High, and contrary to popular opinion, they are not pudgy-looking winged characters who shoot tiny arrows into the hearts of would be lovers. Angels are warriors who serve at the beck and call of the Almighty. Thousands of them surround the throne of God, prepared to go to war on His behalf. Biblical visions of angels are consistent throughout Scripture (n. 1 Ki. 22:19; Is. 6; Eze. 1; and Rev. 4-5), and the people who encounter them often find themselves trembling with fear.

Angels watch over the affairs of humanity. Michael guarded the Jewish people during the time of Babylonian captivity (Dan. 12:1); Gabriel spoke to Zechariah, announcing the birth of John the Baptist (Luke 1:19); Jesus spoke of guardian angels watching over the lives of small children (Mt. 18:10). He told Peter that, if needed, He was able to call upon twelve legions of angels to defend Himself (Mt. 26:52-53).[7]

In the Old Testament, two angels destroyed the cities of Sodom and Gomorrah (Gen. 19:13). Just one led the Israelites out of the land of Egypt and annihilated the armies of Pharaoh (Ju. 2:1). Another came to the defense of Hezekiah, king of Judah, and slaughtered 185,000 Assyrian soldiers (2 Ki. 19:35; Is. 37:36).

In the New Testament, an angel appeared to shepherds, in the field in order to announce the birth of Jesus. They were terrified at his presence (Luke 2:8). On Easter Sunday, an angel rolled back the stone covering the entrance to Christ's tomb, striking fear not only in the hearts of the

---

[7]According to Bible scholar John Broadus, "A full Roman legion at that day contained some six thousand men." *Commentary on the Gospel of Matthew*, John A. Broadus, (Valley Forge, PA: The American Baptist Publication Society, 1886), p. 542.

women who came to grieve, but also in the lives of the soldiers who were supposed to be guarding it (Mt. 28:2-5). At the end of the age, Jesus says:

> *"The Son of Man will send out his angels, and they will weed out of his kingdom everything that causes sin and all who do evil. They will throw them into the fiery furnace, where there will be weeping and gnashing of teeth"* (Mt. 13:41-42).

The book of Revelation tells us of a war in heaven, where "*Michael and his angels fought against the dragon,*" hurling him to the earth, and "*his angels with him*" (Rev. 12:7-9). Let there be no doubt; there is a huge war going on, and the angels of God serve nobly in the army of the Most High.

Human Beings as Divine Warriors

In addition to angels, God has also chosen human beings, made in His image, to be spiritual warriors. The reason life is so difficult today is because the very first man *failed* to be a warrior. Adam's mission was to "take care" of the Garden of Eden (Gen. 2:15). The Hebrew original means to "guard or defend," but when the serpent arrived, Adam was nowhere to be found. Eve was left to negotiate with the snake, and instead of slaying it, the first humans succumbed to its temptations, bringing condemnation upon the entire human race. Fortunately, God sent a second Adam who, at great cost, accomplished what the first man should have done at the very beginning (1 Co. 15:45). Ultimately, Christ defeated Satan at the cross, and will one day toss him into the lake of fire (Rev. 20:10). In the interim, God wants His people to be salt and light in a world that can be unsavory and dark. He wants us to use our talents and "occupy" the land until Jesus returns (Luke 19:13, KJV). Until then, we are involved in a military operation, spiritual in nature.

In the book of Genesis, God told Abraham that his *"descendants will take possession of the cities of their enemies"* (Gen. 22:17). Two generations later, the promise was repeated to Jacob (Gen. 28:4). The Old Testament nation of Israel engaged in war as we understand it today. God was at the head of the army, issuing commands. The Israelites set up their tents by division (Nu. 1:52); they encamped at the LORD's command and set out at the LORD's command. When they went into battle, they were to sound the trumpet in order to gain victory (Nu. 9:23; 10:9). At Mount Sinai, just prior to the invasion of Palestine, God speaks to Moses:

> *"See, I have given you this land. Go in and take possession of the land that the LORD swore he would give to your fathers — to Abraham, Isaac and Jacob — and to their descendants after them"* (Deut. 1:8).

Moses later gives instructions to his people:

> *"You will pursue your enemies, and they will fall by the sword before you. Five of you will chase a hundred, and a hundred of you will chase ten thousand ..."* (Lev. 26:7-8; c.f. Josh. 23:9-10).

God praises many in the Old Testament for their military abilities. Gideon (Ju. 6:12), Samson (Ju. 13:3-5), and King David (mentioned above) are among the more noteworthy. There are countless stories where God's people serve as mighty warriors (2 Ki. 1; Neh. 4:16; Ps. 45:3; Mic. 4:13; Zech. 10). One of the more interesting stories involves the prophet Elisha: the Arameans were threatening to destroy Israel. Their horses and chariots surrounded the city of Dothan. In the midst of the chaos, Elisha comforted his terrified servant: *"Don't be afraid ... Those who are with us are more than those who are with them."* He then prayed, *"O LORD, open his eyes so he may see."* When God opened the servant's eyes, *"he looked and saw the hills full of horses and chariots of fire."* As the enemy approached, Elisha prayed, *"Strike these people with blindness,"* and the Arameans were blinded (2 Ki. 6:16-18). Elisha was the human element in a divine drama that also involved God and His holy angels.

With the coming of Christ, the *nature* of our warfare has changed, but the *principles* have not. The enemy is no longer physical, but spiritual (Eph. 6:12). As descendants of Abraham (Gal. 3:29), Christians are to take possession of the cities and of the land that God has given. We bring the influence of Christ to bear upon the individuals and institutions that make up our culture. We are obedient to the commands of God. Metaphorically, five of us will chase a hundred non-believers, and a hundred will pursue 10,000. Thousands of holy angels surround us, and the world will become a better place as a result of our service.

The language of the New Testament is just as militaristic as that of the Old. Jesus told His followers that *"the kingdom of heaven has been forcefully advancing, and forceful men lay hold of it"* (Mt. 11:12); that *"whatever you bind on earth will be bound in heaven, and whatever you loose on earth will be loosed in heaven"* (Mt. 16:19; c.f. Mt. 18:18); and that *"you who have followed me will also sit on twelve thrones, judging the twelve tribes of Israel"* (Mt. 19:28). The Christian faith is not one that is passive; we are to engage the enemy on God's terms, employing techniques that are military-oriented in nature. Christ sends us out, expecting us to be wise as serpents but harmless as doves (Mt. 10:16); He commands us to love (John 13:34); He commissions us to make disciples of all nations (Mt. 28:18); and He empowers us with the presence of His Spirit (Acts 1:8).

The Apostle Paul, who wrote nearly half of the New Testament, clearly understood the military culture of the Roman Empire and often uses militaristic language in his writings. The following passages serve to illustrate:

> *"we are more than conquerors through him who loved us"* (Ro. 8:37).
>
> *"let us put aside the deeds of darkness and put on the armor of light"* (Ro. 13:12).
>
> *"Be on your guard; stand firm in the faith; be men of courage; be strong"* (1 Co. 16:13).
>
> *"We demolish arguments and every pretension that sets itself up against the knowledge of God, and we take captive every thought to make it obedient to Christ"* (2 Co. 10:5).

"Put on the full armor of God so that you can take your stand against the devil's schemes" (Eph. 6:11).

"Fight the good fight of the faith" (1 Ti. 6:12).

"Endure hardship with us like a good soldier of Christ Jesus" (2 Ti. 2:3).

Does the New Testament leave any doubt that we are involved in spiritual warfare? If believers fail to grasp this, we will miss out on one of the most important concepts of the Christian faith. We have a Commander who rules from the heavens, and there are millions who serve in His army. He gives commands and expects obedience. He commissions, equips, and empowers. For these reasons alone, a Code of Conduct is needed.

Many local churches and some denominations already have excellent catechetical processes that prepare believers for service in the army of the Most High. Other groups use well-written statements of faith, confessions, and creeds that summarize Biblical doctrine, but do very little to equip Christians for the spiritual battles they face. Some churches do nothing at all to prepare their troops for combat. Perhaps the six articles of this spiritual code will help all of us to serve with honor in the army of the Lord Jesus Christ. May His Church prosper and His Kingdom expand as a result of our faithfulness.

Article One

"I am Christian Soldier"

"On desperate ground, proclaim to your soldiers the hopelessness of saving their lives. The only chance of life lies in giving up all hope of it".

Sun Tzu[1]

I am a Christian soldier. I serve in the Church of Jesus Christ, which proclaims the gospel and the message of God's love. I give my life to God and to His service.

The commentary for Article I of the Code of Conduct For Members of the Armed Forces reads as follows: "All men and women in the Armed Forces have the duty at all times and under all circumstances to oppose the enemies of the United States and support its national interests. In training or in combat, alone or with others, while evading capture or enduring captivity, this duty belongs to each American defending our nation regardless of circumstances."[2]

---

[1]Sun Tzu, *The Art of War*, James Clavell,ed., (New York, NY: Delacorte Press, 1983), p. 67.

[2]Material taken from class notes, Navy Chaplain School Basic Course Class 99010. Based upon Executive Order 10631 of August 17, 1955, as amended; and Dept. of Defense Directive 1300.7 of Dec. 23, 1988.

In like manner, men and women who serve in God's army have a similar duty at all times and under all circumstances to oppose the enemies of Jesus Christ and support the work of His Church. The Bible tells us *"Let those who love the Lord hate evil"* (Ps. 97:10). Whether we are in church, in the workplace, alone or with others, while tempted by the enemy, or while living in the midst of a culture that has taken a stance against the true and the living God; this is our responsibility — to serve the Lord Jesus Christ regardless of circumstances.

Articles I and VI of the "Code of Conduct For Members of the Armed Forces," serve as bookends to the meat of the document. They are philosophical in nature, identifying who you are. In the same way, Articles I and VI of the "Code of Conduct For Servants of the Most High God" serve as philosophical bookends to the ethical code contained in Articles II-V.

I am a *Christian* soldier. God has stamped His identity on me; I cannot change who I am. I have been saved by grace, God has touched me by His Spirit, and in faith I believe. Jesus said, *"My sheep listen to my voice; I know them, and they follow me. I give them eternal life, and they shall never perish; no one can snatch them out of my hand" (John 10:27-28).*

In the military code the soldier is identified as an American. He is a citizen of the United States whether sleeping, working, eating or relaxing. The behavior of the soldier does not take away his identity; he is either a good ambassador of the American nation or a poor one. In the same way as the American soldier cannot suddenly decide to stop being a citizen of the United States, a Christian cannot decide to stop being a follower of Jesus Christ. As a citizen of God's Kingdom, the Christian is always on duty; the question is not, "Am I an ambassador of Christ?," but rather, "What kind of ambassador am I?"

I am distinctly Christian. *"There is no other name under heaven given to men by which we must be saved"* (Acts 4:12). There are not many roads leading to the top of the mountain; there is only one. Jesus said, *"I am the way and the truth and the life. No one comes to the Father except through me"* (John 14:6). Faith in Buddha will not make you a citizen of the kingdom of God. Trusting Confucius or Mohammed will not open the gates to heaven. Jesus is in a category all by Himself. Others may have offered profound insight into human nature or may have taught moral codes to live by, but no one else ever rose from the dead; no one else ever lived a perfect life. Jesus is at the head of the army to which I belong; His name is stamped upon me.

In the military, the chain of command is very clear. The captain of a ship at sea is the final authority. There is no other captain, no other person to whom I can appeal. If I disobey the lawful orders of my commanding officer and suggest that there is someone else on the ship of equal or greater authority, I could very well be in danger of non-judicial punishment under the Uniform Code of Military Justice. Restrictions, loss of pay, confinement to the brig, a three-day diet of bread and water, and dishonorable discharge from military service are all distinct possibilities. To suggest that there is some other name than that of Christ who would command my ultimate allegiance is to blaspheme the name of God, and fly in the face of everything the Bible teaches. The effectiveness with which I live the Christian life will be greatly hampered, and the question "Am I even part of the kingdom of God?" must be posed. *"Many will say to me ... 'Lord, Lord, did we not prophesy in your name ... and perform many miracles?' Then I will tell them plainly, 'I never knew you. Away from me, you evildoers!'"* (Mt. 7:22-23). Jesus – the One called Christ – He is my Captain. There is no other. I lift up His name. I am a *Christian* soldier.

I am a Christian *soldier*. This further clarifies your identity. In becoming a Christian, you have joined a great fighting force, the host of heaven. (n. *Human Beings as Divine Warriors*, pp. 52-55, above).

I *serve* ... This is the most important concept for leaders anywhere, and especially for those involved in the Church. We are humble. We subordinate ourselves to the cause, and focus on the mission at hand in order to achieve the goal. We do not use our positions of authority in order to advance our career or to take care of our own selfish interests. When Robert E. Lee, the great Confederate General, was asked to give advice to a new mother on the instruction of her infant son, he responded: "Teach him he must deny himself."[3] Jesus expressed it even more clearly: *"If anyone would come after me, he must deny himself and take up his cross and follow me. For whoever wants to save his life will lose it, but whoever loses his life for me will find it"* (Mt. 16:24-25). When James and John were seeking special privileges, Jesus told them in no uncertain terms:

> *"whoever wants to become great among you must be your servant, and whoever wants to be first must be your slave — just as the Son of Man did not come to be served, but to serve, and to give his life as a ransom for many"* (Mt. 20:26-28).

Leadership at any level involves service to others and to causes higher than self, and Christians have the most noble cause of all – that of bringing the message of eternal life to the world around them. The very best leaders begin as the best of followers, and always keep the concept of service par-

[3]H.W. Crocker III, ***Robert E. Lee On Leadership,*** (Rocklin, CA: Prima Publishing, 1999), p. 17.

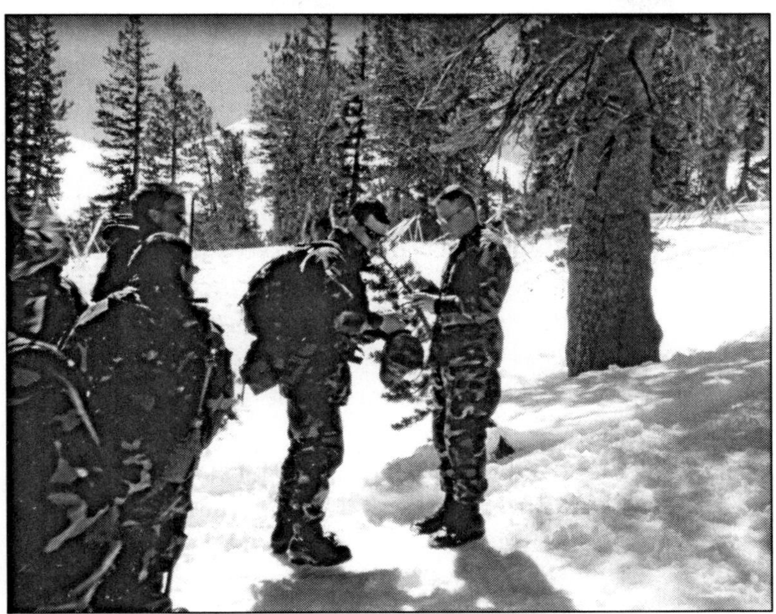

amount. To aspire to become a pastor, a deacon, an elder, an usher, or to any other position of authority within the Church is a noble goal; but it should automatically imply that the man or woman involved – above all else – desires to be a servant to Christ, to the mission of the local church, and to the people who come into his/her sphere of influence.

I serve in the *Church* of Jesus Christ ... To continue the military metaphor, Jesus is the great Commander, and the Church is His army. When Peter first realized that Jesus is the Messiah, our Lord replied, *"Blessed are you, Simon son of Jonah, for this was not revealed to you by man, but by my Father in heaven. And I tell you that you are Peter, and on this rock I will build my church, and the gates of Hades will not overcome it"* (Mt. 16:17-18). The word "Church," with a capital "C," transcends time and denomination. Its membership consists of people, like Peter, who confess that Jesus is *"the Christ, the Son of the living God"* (Mt. 16:16).

There are no preferred denominations: Christians serve nobly in Orthodox, Roman Catholic, and in Protestant communions. There are no eras in Church history more important than others: God has always had His people in place, spokespersons who faithfully herald the Divine cause. Spiritual warriors proclaimed the gospel message long ago in ancient Rome; they lifted up their voices in Medieval Europe; and they are not ashamed to declare the message of His Kingdom in the most remote corners of our modern world. The Church, under the leadership of our great Commander, is majestic and powerful, bringing a message of hope to oppressed peoples everywhere.

As Christian soldiers, we have a responsibility to serve in a local church; but we are always mindful that the "Church," in its universal sense, is far greater than the local body in which we are involved. While serving as Chaplain of the First Combat Engineer Battalion, my primary loyalty was to my battalion and its commander, but I also knew that the battalion in which I served came under a much larger entity called the First Marine Division. By being a faithful chaplain to the Marines of the First Combat Engineer Battalion, I served the General of the First Marine Division. I did not know the General on a personal level, but I know that the quality of work that took place in one of his 23 battalions served the cause of the whole. Someday we will all meet the Lord of the Church, but in the meantime we are faithful to Him through our hard work in the local church body where He has placed us.

Many suggest that one can be a faithful Christian and not even be involved in the work of a local church. This is as absurd a claim as stating that one can be a soldier without being affiliated with a military unit. If you are not working together with other warriors in the trenches – if you are not connected to a squad, a platoon, a company, a division or a department – you are not a soldier; you are a vigilante, a lone ranger, under no one's command. Such a status affords you no protection under the Geneva standards. In like manner, the person who states that he or she is a Christian but fails to come under the authority of a local church is ineffective as a spiritual warrior.

The entire New Testament speaks to the importance of the local church. The book of Acts records many fascinating accounts of how Spirit-filled men and women ministered in churches – places where believers gathered for worship, prayer, fellowship and study – all over the Roman Empire. The Apostle Paul wrote letters to members of churches in Rome, Corinth, Galatia, Ephesus, Philippi, Colossae, and Thessolonica. These writings make up nearly half of the New Testament. His letters to Timothy and Titus serve as instructions to younger men on how to pastor a church. Hebrews, James, and the letters of Peter and John circulated among all the churches known to have been in existence at the time. John, the author of Revelation, addressed his masterpiece to the seven churches in Asia Minor.

The local church is the conscience of the community in which it is located; it is the voice that appeals to the divine spark present in all human beings. The local church promotes righteousness, holiness, and life, while resisting evil with all of her resources. The church speaks for dignity and for respect of all human beings in ways that no other human organization is able. Christians point others to One who is far greater than anything this world has to offer, and our witness increases exponentially when we work in unison. It is both wrong and arrogant to downplay the importance of the local church, and it is essential that every servant of the Most High affiliate with fellow believers in order to put teeth into Christ's prayer *"Thy kingdom come. Thy will be done in earth, as it is in heaven"* (Mt. 6:10, KJV).

I serve in the Church of Jesus Christ, *which proclaims the gospel ...* The word "gospel" means "good news." Many who have had some sort of church background often believe that the word "gospel" is a type of literature one is apt to hear in a worship setting; but it is not that at all! The gospel is the fact that Jesus Christ died on a cross for our sins, was buried, and rose again on the third day (1 Co. 15:3-4). The gospel declares that anyone who places his/her trust in the person and in the work of Jesus Christ will have victory over sin, will be spared the ravages of eternal hellfire, and will live forever in the kingdom of God.

While the message of Christ is good news, the world in which we live – the kingdom of man – is filled with bad news of all types: death, pain, sorrow and misery. Nearly everything you read in the newspaper or watch on television news stations brings despair. Friends betray you, children let you down, and people who are complete strangers seek to bring harm. Your own willpower is so weak that it can be depressing. Even the Apostle Paul, one of the pillars of our faith writes, *"For I have the desire to do what is good, but I cannot carry it out. For what I do is not the good I want to do; no, the evil I do not want to do — this I keep on doing"* (Ro. 7:18-19). Everything that is living will eventually die. Every family member, friend, loved one, and acquaintance will be taken from you. Ultimately, you will pass through the valley of the shadow of death, all alone, unaccompanied by others.

But the gospel tells us that death is not the end. There is life beyond the grave for those who place their faith in Jesus Christ. Jesus destroyed the stranglehold that sin and death have held upon all creation since the time of Adam and Eve. The first four books of the New Testament (appropriately called the Gospels) tell this good news from the perspective of four different writers.

The Church is to proclaim this good news, but we live in a world where tremendous powers of evil seek to suppress its message. These dark powers employ their considerable resources marginalizing the gospel and ridiculing the people of God. If unsuccessful in silencing the Church, Satan and his legions endeavor to compartmentalize its message to the eleven o'clock hour on Sunday morning, neutering any sort of influence that might be brought to bear upon society at large. On one hand, the enemy seeks to suppress knowledge of the Most High, while on the other hand he tempts us to use His name in vile and blasphemous ways. People who talk coherently about any subject under the sun become strangely quiet or completely incoherent when the name of Jesus surfaces in everyday conversation. Representatives of the Church are often viewed by society as "not having the right stuff." Pastors are portrayed as effeminate, sexless beings not having a grip on reality, or as extremely wicked persons who clothe their actions behind a clergy collar. (While there are some who match these descriptions, the vast majority of pastors and priests are faithful ministers of the gospel who love the Lord and are dedicated to His cause).

As Christians, this should not take us by surprise. Although the Devil and his army want to stop us, we persevere in battle because our cause is just. We stand against these powers of darkness in the name of the Lord, and proclaim the message of hope and life given to us by our great Commander. We persevere in our cause in the same way that valiant soldiers in by-gone wars persevered in theirs.

In WWII, for example, all of Europe reeled under the oppression and genocide of the Nazi regime. Life was bleak. There seemed to be no hope, but the Allied Forces under the command of General Dwight David Eisenhower persevered in the face of tremendous opposition and brought liberation and life to those who were in darkness. All Europe rejoiced when the Axis Powers were driven back and freedom was restored. In like manner, the armies of the Lord Jesus Christ are called to proclaim the good news of life and freedom in our dark world. We come against those forces who would stop us, because the message we proclaim brings liberation and life. Jesus said, "*For God did not send his Son into the world to condemn the world, but to save the world through him. Whoever believes in him is not condemned, but whoever does not believe stands condemned already* ..." (John 3:17-18).

Human beings, although created in the image of God, live out their lives under a death penalty. The rebellion that permeates our hearts separates us from the love of God. The book of Revelation tells us "*If anyone's name was not found written in the book of life, he was thrown into the lake of fire*" (Rev. 19:15). Our responsibility, as spiritual warriors, is to tell others how to get their names written in that book. We have a passion for souls, and nothing should stop us from proclaiming the good news that Christ has for all people. Gospel proclamation – through worship, through the spoken word, and through righteous living – is the single most important activity for soldiers serving in the mighty army of God.

The vision and the mission of an organization are very helpful concepts to understand. One might say that the vision of the United States is to see our nation and our world living at peace, enjoying the rights of "life, liberty and the pursuit of happiness" as delineated in the *Declaration of Independence*. The mission of our Armed Forces is to ensure that the vision is achieved. For United States Marines, mission is everything. According to the 1999 Campaign Plan for the First Marine Division,

> Mission accomplishment is our first and foremost responsibility. It is our focus and our purpose; our objective and our goal. The mission is always paramount. Nothing ever takes precedence over

> the mission. The mission may vary at times. But at no time will it be a secondary responsibility. At times the mission may be to attack or defend, to deploy overseas or devote time to families at home, to endure harsh conditions or engage in a recreational event ... to augment the Camp Guard or take liberty or leave. Accomplish the mission — whatever the mission.

The Campaign Plan continues with yet a clearer definition of what that mission is:

> Our mission for now and the foreseeable future is to make war dirtier and uglier for our enemies. We will prosecute war as violently and as powerfully as necessary to convince our adversaries that peace is preferable to war. Peace on terms favorable to us is our ultimate objective. The power of war is at times the means to that end. We train for war in order to preserve peace.[4]

The vision of the Church — what we see when the journey is finished — is the liberation of the human soul from bondage. We want people to be free from the influence of the Evil One. Jesus came in order that we might have life, abundant and eternal (John 10:10). From beyond the pale of our senses, God sent His Son to take us out of the kingdom of darkness and bring us into the kingdom of light. As foot soldiers in God's army, our mission is to proclaim that message in this world. We are not to use violence as members of the Armed Forces might, but we are to bind these powers of darkness in the name of the Lord God Almighty, and offer the light of Jesus Christ. This is the main message; let us keep our focus.

---

[4] 1st Marine Division Campaign Plan 99-00, p. 10.

It is highly appropriate for the Church to be involved in social justice issues. It is important for local churches to better the communities in which God has placed them. To serve as a facilitator for organizations such as the Boy Scouts, Alcoholics Anonymous, or the Red Cross is an excellent way for a church to be involved in a local community. These types of programs, though, are always subordinated to the primary mission of proclaiming the good news of Jesus Christ. Programs such as these are always a means to the ultimate end of seeing people come to know Jesus Christ as Lord and Savior. William Booth, founder of the Salvation Army — one of the greatest social agencies of our time, was not even involved in social services until years after his organization was established. In 1874, Booth rejected the idea of sponsoring "rescue homes for fallen women, brigades to save drunkards and prisoners, and slum sisters to care for London's poor women and children" because such work "dissipated evangelists' energies and wasted limited funds."[5] By 1883, Booth realized that 'he needed new solutions to the problem of converting the "heathen,"' but still declared that "the way to help the prodigal son was not to build him a comfortable hut, or to give him an allowance from the parish, or provide for his education, but to get him to see and acknowledge his sin."'[6] Likewise, Walter Rauschenbusch, called "the real founder" of the "social gospel" movement by Reinhold Niebuhr, was 'an evangelist in the tradition of the great revivalists, seeking to win people to an experience of Christ and to put them to work in the interests of Christ's kingdom. He entered the ministry with a strong desire to "save souls" and this, in his own mind, continued to be a constant objective.'[7] The focus

---

[5]Norman H. Murdoch, *Origins of the Salvation Army*, (Knoxville: The University of Tennessee Press, 1994), p. 113.

[6]*ibid.*, p. 147.

[7]*Walter Rauschenbusch, Selected Writings*, edited by Winthrop S. Hudson, (New York: Paulist Press, 1984), p.4.

of Mother Theresa was always the proclamation of the gospel. When a reporter referred to her and her fellow sisters as social workers, she replied, "We are not social workers, we do this for Jesus."[8]

Employing the same kind of zeal with which United States Marines use in carrying out their mission of defending our nation, may we, as Servants of the Most High and as members of His Church, make the proclamation of the gospel of Jesus Christ our first and foremost responsibility.

I serve in the Church of Jesus Christ, which proclaims the gospel *and the message of God's love.* Among the last words that Jesus ever spoke to His followers were: *"go and make disciples of all nations, baptizing them in the name of the Father and of the Son and of the Holy Spirit, and teaching them to obey everything I have commanded you"* (Mt. 28:19-20). This is our mission, but it is one that is to be carried out with a love that is unconditional in nature.

In many ways, the English language is not as rich as the common Greek in which the New Testament was written. In English we use the expression "love" rather loosely. "I love pizza," for example, is on a whole different level than "I love my wife." The common Greek uses three different words for "love."[9] The word for the love of food, fine art, or of anything that stimulates our senses is "eros." Eros refers to external beauty, a beauty that causes a very strong emotional feeling. From this word comes the English "erotic."

The second type of love is "phileo," a strong tie that is cultivated by a group of people going through a similar experience. Phileo is the "esprit de corps" so typical of United

---

[8]Roger Finke and Rodney Stark, *The Churching of America 1776-1990, Winners and Losers in our Religious Economy,* (New Brunswick, New Jersey: Rutgers University Press, 1992), p. 266.

[9]Recommended reading: *The Four Loves* by C.S. Lewis.

States Marines. It describes the strong bond I have with my classmates from the Naval Academy, and with those from Chaplain School, a bond much stronger than "eros." Phileo inspires loyalty to a fellow human at any time and any place. Philadelphia, the city of brotherly love, draws its name from this word. In the Bible, passages such as: *"If you belonged to the world, it would love you as its own"* (John 15:19), and *"Be devoted to one another in brotherly love"* (Ro. 12:10) use the word "phileo."

The third type of love, called "agape," comes from within. It is unconditional in nature, dependent neither upon any particular quality of the beloved nor upon any sort of common bonding experience. "Agape" is the kind of love with which God wants to build His Church. When Jesus declared that the greatest of the commandments is to *'Love the Lord your God with all your heart and with all your soul and with all your mind' and 'Love your neighbor as yourself'* (Mt. 22:37, 39), the word He used was "agape." You need not appreciate any particular quality about the person with whom you are dealing, nor do you need a common experience with him/her. Agape simply means that you will treat the other person with dignity, respect, and kindness, regardless of how that person treats you. In his letter to the church in Corinth, the Apostle Paul offers us an excellent definition of agape love:

> *"Love is patient, love is kind. It does not envy, it does not boast, it is not proud. It is not rude, it is not self-seeking, it is not easily angered, it keeps no record of wrongs. Love does not delight in evil, but rejoices with the truth. It always protects, always trusts, always hopes, always perseveres"* (1 Co. 13:4-7).

One of the most astonishing things Jesus ever said employed the word "agape": *"You have heard that it was said, 'Love your neighbor and hate your enemy.' But I tell you: Love your enemies and pray for those who persecute you"* (Mt. 5:43-44). We may not like the things that our enemy does, but we are to afford him/her the dignity we show to any other human being. The word "agape" is used on many occasions in the New Testament; some of the more prominent occurrences include: John 15:12-13; Romans 8:35; Galatians 5:22; and Ephesians 5:25.

Agape is the kind of love that God shows to us, and as a result, He expects us to love others in the same way. There is nothing beautiful about our dark rebellion against the Creator that causes Him to love us. There are no mutually shared experiences that prompt our Lord to show affection. Nonetheless, the Bible tells us, *"While we were still sinners, Christ died for us"* (Ro. 5:8). As a result of the unconditional love that God shows to us, we reach out to others in the same way. As we battle against spiritual wickedness in high places, this ability to love is the greatest weapon in our arsenal. As servants of the Most High, we love the unlovable. Jesus commands us to show agape love to all; this, He says, is the greatest commandment. The Apostle Paul calls agape love the greatest of the spiritual gifts (1 Co. 13:13). When we arm ourselves with the love of God, the enemy is disarmed and thrown off balance.

I have witnessed something akin to agape love on many occasions in the Marine Corps. It is a respect shown for that brother Marine even when he is not keeping up with the rest of the platoon in a physical training exercise or conditioning hike. The entire platoon will cycle back and pick up those who are straggling. Words of encouragement inspire the one who has fallen out of formation, and as a result, platoon effectiveness and morale is very high. There is a pride in being associated with such a unit. But sometimes that love is not evident, and its absence is very noticeable. When leaders utter profanities, attack the dignity of other human beings, or allow undercurrents of racism to flow through the ranks; mission effectiveness is hampered, and morale plummets. On numerous occasions I have noticed how something as simple as calling cadence, when it crosses over the boundary of decency and respect, hampers the unity of a platoon.

The morale and effectiveness of the Church is likewise affected by attitude. If agape love is not evident in the meetings of the local church, very few people will be inspired to work in God's great army. If church membership is based upon racial background, political affiliation, socio-economic status, or upon adherence to theological minutia – and everyone else is made to feel extremely uncomfortable — that particular church will not be very effective in proclaiming the gospel. Jokes are often told of congregations where there is such a chill in the air that the ushers take up the offering on ice-skates! Unfortunately, there is often a lot of truth behind the levity. On one occasion I witnessed a debate that lasted hours into the night over whether a Korean congregation should be allowed to use a church facility owned by a predominately white congregation. The major argument against the proposal was that the smell of kimchee might waft through the building. On another occasion, a lady who had come to know Christ as Lord and Savior wanted to use a church classroom for a Narcotics Anonymous meeting. The major argument against the proposal was that "we don't want to be associated with those types of people." Fortunately, in both cases, wiser counsel prevailed; but attitudes were displayed that are absolutely counter-productive to the mission of the Church. God wants our churches to proclaim His message with an attitude like that which was found in

Jesus Christ, one which ministers to the poor as well as to the rich, to the sinner as well as to the morally upright, and to people of all nations of the world.

There may be some people you genuinely dislike. There may be others with whom you have nothing in common. God does not expect that you become best friends with everyone, but He does expect that you will show patience, kindness, humility and self-control to all. You are to honor all people, treat them with dignity, and look for the best in them. Paul's letter to the church in Philippi declares: "*whatever is true, whatever is noble, whatever is right, whatever is pure, whatever is lovely, whatever is admirable — if anything is excellent or praiseworthy — think about such things*" (Phil. 4:8). Generally you can find these qualities in others if you look for them. It is easy to love your friends; it is easy to love those who inspire you, or those with whom you share a common experience; but the real challenge for the Christian is to love those who are unlovable. If you treat others as human beings made in the image of God, you will find many wonderful qualities. If you treat others as incorrigible pagans, you will see the ugly side of human nature and inspire a behavior that corresponds to what you think about them. God displays agape love to us, and He expects His people to love others in the same way. As servants of this great God, and as members of His Church, we carry out our primary mission of proclaiming the good news of Jesus Christ and we do it with a love that is unconditional.

I give my life to God and to His service. The American fighting man is prepared to give his life for his country, and many have paid the supreme price. A visit to the cemetery in Normandy where thousands of crosses stand rank and file — marking the final resting places of those who died on its beaches — serves as a sober reminder of the sacrifices made. People from nearly every small town in America gather together on Memorial Day to remember those men and women who died in the service of their country. Granite markers with the names of those who gave their lives remind us of their supreme sacrifice.

We, who take the name of Christ, value service to Him even greater than life itself. Jesus declared that *"If anyone would come after me, he must deny himself and take up his cross and follow me"* (Mt. 16:24). "Taking up the cross" means that you are willing to die rather than deny the principles for which Jesus stood. The story of Telemachus, a 4th century Christian from Asia, serves to illustrate. Telemachus was on a visit to Rome and was caught up with a mob attending an event at the Coliseum. Gladiators stood on the playing field and saluted the Emperor with the words "We who are about to die salute you." When Telemachus realized that two men were about to battle together to the death for the amusement of the audience, he arose and cried out, "In the name of Christ, stop." Initially, Coliseum-goers thought he was part of the act, and they began to laugh; but when they realized he was serious, someone plunged a sword into him to silence him. A silence did indeed fall over the stadium that day. As Telemachus lay dying, the Coliseum began to empty, and the horrible spectacle of gladiatorial battles was forever ended. The courage of one man brought victory over the powers of evil, but Telemachus paid for it with his life.[10]

Another example of giving one's life to the service of God occurred during the trial of Martin Luther at the Diet of Worms in 1521. Luther was charged with heresy for suggesting that a human being makes peace with God simply by trusting in the person and work of Jesus Christ. A man's salvation had nothing to do with good deeds. Swiss guards stood rattling their swords as the Holy Roman Emperor threatened the great reformer with

[10]Michael Grant, *Gladiators* (New York, NY: Delacorte Press, 1967), p. 123.

death if he refused to recant. Having thought about his positions, Luther replied, "Here I stand. I can do no other. God help me! Amen." Luther was condemned. Emissaries from the German Elector Frederick abducted him in order to keep him from the Emperor's henchman, and Luther spent the remaining 25 years of his life under a death sentence.[11]

Thomas Cranmer, Archbishop of Canterbury, also gave his life in the service of God. During the reigns of Henry VIII and of his son Edward VI, Cranmer was instrumental in leading the Reformation in England, and was able to compose such powerful theological works as *The Book of Common Prayer*. Following Edward's reign, Queen Mary, a very zealous Roman Catholic, ascended to power. She had Cranmer imprisoned and insisted that the former Archbishop recant all Protestant leanings. Cranmer refused, and on March 21, 1556, he was burned at the stake. His last words were "Lord Jesus, receive my spirit!"[12]

Over the centuries, millions of believers have given their lives for the cause of Christ.[13] In the recent past, many of us witnessed the tragic assassination of the Rev. Dr. Martin Luther King, Jr., as he took his stand against the evils of racial prejudice. An assassin's bullet cut short his life, but the cause for which he stood flowed out of Christian convictions that were more precious than life itself.

It is unlikely that many of us will lay down our lives for the faith, but those who take the name "Christian" should be willing to stand for causes that are just. Edmund Burke, author of the massive *The History of the Decline and Fall of the*

---

[11]*Christian History*, (Carol Stream, IL: Christianity Today, Inc., Issue 34, volume. XI, no. 2, 1992), p. 16.

[12]*Christian History*, (Carol Stream, IL: Christianity Today, Inc., Issue 48, vol. XIV, no. 4, 1995), pp. 9-15.

[13]Recommended reading: *Foxe's Book of Martyrs* by John Foxe.

Roman Empire, once wrote to a friend, "The only thing necessary for the triumph of evil is for good men to do nothing."[14] It is as simple as that.

Nothing is more important than service to God. Anything we undertake is for His glory. Any pleasures we enjoy are centered in Him. As Christians, we serve in the mightiest of all armies; we have the most significant message in the world; and we serve the greatest Commander. The Apostle Paul writes, *"I am not ashamed of the gospel, because it is the power of God for the salvation of everyone who believes"* (Ro. 1:16). Joshua, the general who led the Israelites into the land of promise, declares, *"Now fear the LORD and serve him with all faithfulness ... But if serving the LORD seems undesirable to you, then choose for yourselves this day whom you will serve ... But as for me and my household, we will serve the LORD"* (Josh. 24:14-15). It is with this spirit that we, as servants of the Most High, give our lives to God and to His service.

---

[14]John Bartlett, *Bartlett's Familiar Quotations,* (Boston: Little, Brown and Company, Fourteenth Edition, Fourth Printing, 1968), p.454.

Article Two

"I Will Never Give Up"

I press toward the mark for the prize of the high calling of God in Christ Jesus.

Philippians 3:14

I will never give up in the face of those forces that seek to suppress the gospel. As a leader, I will carry out my responsibilities and never lose hope.

The commentary for Article II of the Code of Conduct For Members of the Armed Forces reads as follows: "As an individual, a member of the Armed Forces may never voluntarily surrender. When isolated and no longer able to inflict casualties on the enemy, the American soldier has an obligation to evade capture and rejoin friendly forces. Only when evasion by an individual is impossible and further fighting would lead only to death with no significant loss to the enemy should one consider surrender. With all reasonable means of resistance exhausted and with certain death the only alternative, capture does not imply dishonor."[1]

In 1972, a man by the name of Shoichi Yokoi turned up in a remote Guam jungle fighting a war that had ended 26 years earlier. Yokoi was a sergeant who joined the Japanese army in 1941. He was sent to northeastern China, and later to Guam during World War II. Japan occupied Guam during the war, and most of its 22,000 troops were killed when U.S. soldiers recaptured the island in 1944. But Yokoi never gave up. Adhering to the Imperial Army's code of "never surrender," he survived on a diet of nuts, berries, frogs, snails and rats. He wove materials from tree bark for clothing, and continued to resist capture. When two local hunters discovered him in January 1972, he was wearing a pair of burlap pants and a shirt made from the bark of a tree, living in a cave and still carrying the rifle issued to him at the beginning of the war. Upon his return to Tokyo, Yokoi's first words were: "It is with much embarrassment that I return." The words were broadcast nationally and instantly became a popular saying. Yokoi persevered in a cause in which he believed, and never gave up.[2]

The Armed Forces of the United States are not infallible. Our troops have suffered many humiliating defeats, and there have been conflicts where even the "justness" of the cause has been called into question. But Christians, who serve in the army of the Lord Jesus Christ, follow a leader who is infallible and always on the side of justice. In fact, our Commander has already crushed the serpent's head; the

---

[1]Material taken from class notes, Navy Chaplain School Basic Course Class 99010. Based upon Executive Order 10631 of August 17, 1955, as amended; and Department of Defense Directive 1300.7 of December 23, 1988.

[2]Reuters, Jon Herskovitz, Sept 23, 1997.

Devil is defeated. Our role as Christian soldiers is more of a mop up operation. We are to cast out areas of darkness where Satan, though defeated, still holds a strong grip. It is in this endeavor that we persevere. Even though our enemy is mortally wounded, and his final destination - the Lake of Fire - looms imminent, he seeks to destroy others. It is for this reason we continue to wage war. The Devil is still able to torment us and make our lives quite miserable (and God often allows this to happen to us, as He did to Job in the Old Testament), but to surrender is folly. Christ has secured victory for His people. As the Apostle reminds us: *"thanks be to God! He gives us the victory through our Lord Jesus Christ. Therefore ... stand firm. Let nothing move you. Always give yourselves fully to the work of the Lord, because your labor in the Lord is not in vain"* (1 Co. 15:57-58).

I will never give up in the face of those forces that seek to suppress the gospel. John Calvin, one of the finest minds in the history of the Church, gave the name "perseverance" to this quality of never giving up. The Christian perseveres for the cause of Christ in the face of all opposition. In Paul's letter to the Philippian church, the imprisoned Apostle poignantly writes of perseverance:

> *"Therefore, my dear friends ... continue to work out your salvation with fear and trembling, for it is God who works in you to will and to act according to his good purpose"* (Phil. 2:12-13).
>
> *"I press on to take hold of that for which Christ Jesus took hold of me. Brothers, I do not consider myself yet to have taken hold of it. But one thing I do: Forgetting what is behind and straining toward what is ahead, I press on toward the goal to win the prize for which God has called me heavenward in Christ Jesus"* (Phil. 3:12-14).

Perseverance is a gift; it comes from God, and is the hallmark of a true believer. As Shoichi Yokoi was so inspired by the fallible emperor of Japan that he never gave up, so we, as believers in Christ — the infallible Emperor of all heaven and earth — likewise never give up. His Spirit has sealed us until that day He calls us to be with Him. We will never give up because the work is Christ's, not our own, and we keep our eyes on Him rather than on ourselves. As the Apostle Paul declares, *"he who began a good work in you will carry it on to completion until the day of Christ Jesus"* (Phil. 1:6). Christians often slip. We may temporarily harden our hearts against the true and the living God. We may "hurt and scandalize others, and bring temporal judgments upon" [3] ourselves, but God will bring repentance, and we will continue to show our faith by our works (Jas. 2:18) until that day we hear the words *'Well done, good and faithful servant! You have been faithful with a few things; I will put you in charge of many things. Come and share your master's happiness!'* (Mt. 25:21). The anonymous work entitled "I Am a Disciple of Jesus Christ," summarizes beautifully this precious gift of perseverance:

---

[3]Westminster Confession of Faith, (Glasgow: Free Presbyterian Publications, 1985), Chap. XVII, III, p. 75.

"I Am a Disciple of Jesus Christ"

I am a part of the fellowship of the unashamed. The die has been cast. I have stepped over the line. The decision has been made. I am a disciple of Jesus Christ.

I will not look back, let up, slow down, back away or be still. My past is redeemed, my present directed, my future secure. I am finished and done with low living, sight walking, small planning, smooth knees, myopic vision, mundane talking, mediocre giving and dwarfed goals. I no longer need preeminence, prosperity, position, promotion or popularity. I don't have to be first, recognized, praised, regarded or rewarded.

I now live in His presence, learn by faith, love by practice, lift by prayer and labor in His power. My pace is set, my gait is fast, my goal is heaven. The road is narrow, the way is rough, my companions few, my guide reliable, my mission clear.

I cannot be bought, compromised, detoured, lured away, lured back, diluted or delayed. I will not flinch in the face of sacrifice, hesitate in the presence of adversity, negotiate at the table of the enemy, ponder at the pool of popularity or meander in the maze of mediocrity.

I won't give up, back up, let up or hush up, till I have preached up, prayed up, paid up, stood up and stayed up for the cause of Jesus Christ.

I am a disciple of Jesus Christ. I must go 'til He returns, give 'til it hurts, preach 'til I drop, tell 'til all know and work 'til He comes. And when He comes to get His own, He'll have no problem recognizing me; my colors will be clear.

I will never give up in the face of those *forces that seek to suppress the gospel.* There are three very deadly spiritual forces that seek to suppress our message: the world, the flesh, and the Devil. The first of these, the "world" consists of external pressures that tempt us to do wrong. Perhaps the best Scriptural definition is found in 1 John 2:16 (NKJV): *"the lust of the flesh, the lust of the eyes, and the pride of life."* Lusts of the flesh are sensual passions gone awry: overeating, drinking too much, drug abuse, or lives dominated by sexual pleasure. Lust of the eyes is material greed: when life is defined by the things we own, the type of clothing we wear, or by how much money we have in the bank. The pride of life is arrogance: everything revolves around me; I can do whatever I like; I can be whatever I want. When anyone gets in my way, I become angry and strike back.

Every human being faces a life-long struggle with at least one of these lusts, and some battle with two or more. The world and all of its accompanying pressures focus on these prurient interests with a prowess that tempts even the strongest among us: "if you drink this beer … you are a real man." "If you purchase this late-model automobile … you will be hanging with the right crowd." "If you buy her a ring with this many carats … she will never leave your side." "Demand what is rightfully yours … after all, you deserve it." When we succumb to these kinds of temptations, our lives find meaning based on the things of the world rather than on the things of God, and as John so eloquently puts it: *"the world is passing away, and the lust of it; but he who does the will of God abides forever"* (1 John 2:17, NKJV). Jesus makes this perfectly clear to His followers when he declares, *"In this world you will have trouble. But take heart! I have overcome the world"* (John 16:33; c.f. 1 John 4:4). As servants of the Most High, we place our faith in Jesus Christ, the One who has overcome the temptations of this world. Anyone who follows our Commander shall overcome as well. For this reason alone, it is inherently important that we do not give up the good fight.

My good friend, Captain Jerry McNabb, once persevered with great success in the face enormous worldly pressure. His struggles took place with the Executive Officer (XO) of naval ship who had serious pride of life issues. Jerry is a member of the Navy Chaplain Corps. I first met him in 1980, only months after I had become a believer in Jesus Christ. I was assigned as a Line Officer to a combat supply ship that had been in commission for ten years. Jerry reported on board only a few months before I did and was a tremendous inspiration to me as a young Christian. In our conversations together, he once told me that he was the very first chaplain ever assigned to that particular ship. When he reported aboard for duty, he was greeted on the quarterdeck by the Executive Officer. The "XO" immediately informed him that he did not like chaplains, that he did not want a chaplain on board his ship, and that within two weeks he would be gone. "Welcome aboard." Fortunately, McNabb was not flustered by such bluster. He persevered in ministry, and completed his two year tour of duty. Many on board that ship came to know Christ as their Lord and Savior as a result of his faithful work. Years later, Chaplain McNabb received a late night phone call from his former XO, who informed him that he had become a Christian, and who now wanted to thank him personally for his faithfulness and perseverance.

A second spiritual force that seeks to suppress the gospel message is our own fleshly nature – the "flesh." We struggle every day against dark powers that well up within us. In his letter to the churches of Galatia, the Apostle Paul gives us an excellent definition: *"the works of the flesh are evident ... adultery, fornication, uncleanness, lewdness, idolatry, sorcery, hatred, contentions, jealousies, outbursts of wrath, selfish ambitions, dis-*

sensions, heresies, envy, murders, drunkenness, revelries, and the like" (Gal. 5:19-21, NKJV). If we make an honest inventory of our own lives, most of us would be forced to admit that we face terrible struggles with many of the sins found on this list. Paul, himself, admits to weakness in this area:

> *"For I know that in me (that is, in my flesh) nothing good dwells; for to will is present with me, but how to perform what is good I do not find. For the good that I will to do, I do not do; but the evil I will not to do, that I practice ... O wretched man that I am! Who will deliver me from this body of death?"* (Ro. 7:18, 24, NKJV).

He goes on to answer his own question: the deliverance comes from Jesus Christ our Lord. When we follow Him, the sting of our sin is taken away. *"There is ... no condemnation to those who do not walk according to the flesh, but according to the Spirit"* (Ro. 8:1). Although still sinners, the servants of the Most High have reoriented their thinking. Our salvation does not come from keeping a moral law; our salvation comes from following Christ. We no longer need to torment ourselves with how bad we are; we have been given the gift of the Spirit. As a result, we have tremendous allegiance to this General, and follow Him into spiritual combat with all of our heart and soul. The focus is no longer on our inadequacies; it is on His sufficiency. He has won the victory, and our sinful nature pales in comparison to the glory that will be revealed in us. As Peter puts it, *"His divine power has given us everything we need for life and godliness ... so that ... you may participate in the divine nature and escape the corruption in the world cause by evil desires"* (i.e. the flesh) (2 Pe. 1:3-4).

The Apostle Paul did not give up in the face of his struggles with the flesh – he probably did more for spreading the gospel of the kingdom of God than anyone before or since – and we should not give up either. God has great plans for each of us, despite the weakness of our own flesh.

The third spiritual force that comes against the gospel is the most sinister. The Devil and a legion of demonic spirits are the actual powers behind the first two forces we have discussed: the world and the flesh. But the Devil is a defeated enemy! The Scriptures tell us that Jesus has disarmed the powers and the authorities of this world, and has *"made a public spectacle of them, triumphing over them by the cross"* (Col. 2:15). The Apostle Paul tells us, *"The God of peace will soon crush Satan under your feet"* (Ro. 16:20), while John writes that he *"saw an angel coming down out of heaven ... He seized the dragon, that ancient serpent, who is the devil, or Satan, and bound him for a thousand years* (Rev. 20:1-2). He goes on to tell us that at some future date, this enemy will be cast into *"the lake of burning sulfur ... and ... will be tormented day and night for ever and ever"* (Rev. 20:10).

When Peter speaks of the Devil as a roaring lion, prowling around, *"looking for someone to devour"* (1 Pe. 5:8), he urges us to resist him, and for good reason – we can! Christ defeated him on the cross. Although the Devil is defeated and is no longer able to deceive entire nations (n. Rev. 20:3), his influence is still enormous. From his cell in the bottomless pit he commands immense authority over a realm of fallen angels. These demons roam the earth, and bring great spiritual destruction, but they can be resisted.

Mark Statler is a second mate in the Merchant Marine. A number of years ago, Mark and I were roommates at the United States Naval Academy. We were thrown together in the same room on the very first day of plebe summer. He was from Kansas; I was from upstate New York. Over the years we got involved in a lot of activities together. We spent four years in ninth company within the close confines of

Bancroft Hall; we were both involved with sailing programs at the Academy; and both of us were assigned to the very same warship as Surface Warfare Officers for our first tour of duty. A closer bond was formed, however, when we decided to purchase a sailboat and live onboard during the time that our ship was in drydock at the Hunter's Point shipyard in San Francisco. For about ten months, we lived on a 27' sloop in the village of Sausalito. I had just become a believer and was very excited about my new-found faith in Christ. Mark, although baptized as a teenager, had turned his back on God. During many of those long evenings onboard that sailboat, I found myself reading the Bible out loud to him. (I am not even sure if he wanted me to do that, but he was gracious enough to tolerate it). When our tour of duty ended, we sold the sailboat, and went our separate ways. About two years later, we hooked up again. Mark had purchased another sailboat, and told me a very incredible story. He was working on board his new purchase when he slipped and fell, cutting his arm in the process. A few hours later, he heard a "voice" that asked him if he "would like to have the power to heal himself." The voice was so evil that Mark instantly responded with a firm "NO!" Later that evening he prayed fervently to the Lord Jesus Christ for help and forgiveness. In his pilgrimage since then, Mark tells me that his greatest milestone was receiving the Sacraments of Penance and Confirmation in the Catholic Church, and the privilege to receive Holy Eucharist at Easter, 1993 *Anno Domini*. Mark resisted a very powerful enemy, dedicated to the destruction of the gospel, and came out victorious. We, likewise, should never give up!

There are many idealistic persons in our world who spend a lot of time and energy seeking to eliminate the Armed Forces of the United States and those of other military powers. They have an earnest belief that through human effort an era of peace can be ushered in where there is no more war. The late John Lennon, for example, sings:

"Imagine there's no countries,
It isn't hard to do,
Nothing to kill or die for,
No religion too,
Imagine all the people
living life in peace"[4]

History proves this theory wrong, time and again. Following the Treaty of Versailles, when the nations of Western Europe disarmed, Nazi Germany built up a military machine that marched virtually unopposed through those nations that laid down their arms. Lennon himself was assassinated by a crazed man on a cold New York City night who did not share his vision of a peaceful world. While it is important to work for peace, and for our diplomats to pursue it with all their might, the reality is that there will be wars upon the earth until the Lord Jesus Christ returns in glorious splendor, setting up a new heaven and a new earth. Until then, as the great philosopher Plato once said: "Only the dead have seen the end of war."[5] In the interim, the nations of our world keep their swords sharpened and their powder dry to keep internal peace against would be aggressors. This is a concept clearly understood in the Scriptures as well. Peter, for example, declares: *"Submit yourselves for the Lord's sake to every authority instituted among men: whether to the king, as the supreme authority, or to governors, who are sent by him to punish those who do wrong and to commend those who do right"* (1 Pe. 2:13-14). Paul writes: *"Everyone must submit himself to the governing authorities, for there is no authority except that which God has established ... for he (the one in authority) does not bear the sword for nothing. He is God's servant, an agent of wrath to bring punishment on the wrongdoer"* (Ro. 13:1,4).

---

[4]John Lennon, *Imagine,* Capitol Records, September 9, 1971.
[5]*Parade, The Sunday Newspaper Magazine,* (New York: Parade Pubs., May 7, 2000), p. 7.

For the same reason that the nations of our world do not surrender their arms in the idealistic hope that world peace will come, we, as servants of the Most High, must keep our spiritual weaponry in a high state of readiness. The forces that come against the gospel – the world, the flesh and the Devil – remain relentless in their opposition. We must not slack off. Christians tend to be overly idealistic; we believe that we can win the entire world to Christ in our lifetimes, but when we fail despair sets in. As our days draw to a close, we begin to wonder if we can even save ourselves. The missionary zeal at the close of the 19th century was a classic example of this. The idealism was so great, that the 20th century was initially labeled "The Christian Century." Two world wars, and a holocaust of unbelievable proportions, quickly brought disillusionment and caused many to wonder if faith in Christ had any value at all. But to think that we can create a heaven on earth is to be guilty of the sin of pride. Let us not be naive! Let us recognize that evil forces will resist us all of our days. The tares will grow alongside the wheat until the reaper comes (Mt. 13:24-30). The seas will contain both clean and unclean fish until the Master Fisherman runs His net through the waters (Mt. 13:47-50). Rain will fall on the just and the unjust until Christ returns and separates the good from the evil, relegating the latter to eternal perdition. We are in a battle with those forces until that happens. Let us not give up the fight. Let us continue to resist while we still have the strength.

The enemies of the gospel are fierce, relentless in their pursuit of its destruction. It is easy to despair, but the battle is Christ's, not ours. He has overcome the world; He is transforming our sinful nature into a glorious new creation (2 Co. 5:17), and has crushed the serpent's head. We are on the winning side and never give up, because victory belongs to God. Personnel in the American military train continually in order to preserve the freedoms we enjoy. Christians persevere with the proclamation of the good news in order that people everywhere be set free from the powers of sin and death.

***As a leader, I will carry out my responsibilities* and never lose hope.** Nothing is more destructive in the military than when a leader gives up. Nothing is more destructive in the Church. No matter how dark the hour, no matter how bleak things may appear, the Church leader never gives up. How a Christian behaves when the chips are down influences the non-believer in a much more profound way than how one acts when things are going well. In a seminary class, Dr. Jay Adams,[6] a well-known Christian counselor, once summarized his counseling method in four short words: "Act right, Feel right!" Do not base your life on how you feel; base them on doing the right things. If in despair, continue to do the right things: pray, read the Word, worship, provide godly leadership, and treat others with dignity and respect. A time will come when the feelings reorient themselves and you will feel good, as well.

The Christmas hymn, written by the poet Henry Wadsworth Longfellow, summarizes what Dr. Adams teaches. Notice the contrast between stanzas three and four of *I Heard the Bells on Christmas Day:*

---

[6]Some of the many books written by Dr. Adams include *The Christian Counselor's Manual; Handbook of Church Discipline; Essays on Biblical Preaching; Marriage, Divorce, and Remarriage in the Bible; and Preaching with Purpose.*

And in despair I bowed my head:
"There is no peace on earth," I said,
"For hate is strong, and mocks the song
Of peace on earth, good will to men."

Yet pealed the bells more loud and deep:
"God is not dead, nor doth He sleep;
The wrong shall fail, the right prevail,
With peace on earth, good will to men."[7]

We carry out our responsibilities because God is in charge.

As a leader, I will carry out my responsibilities and *never lose hope.*

> Life's but a walking shadow, a poor player, that struts and frets his hour upon the stage and then is heard no more. It is a tale told by an idiot, full of sound and fury signifying nothing.[8]

As Christians, we need not walk around like Shakespeare's *Macbeth* when things take a turn for the worse. The Christian faith is not self-generated human optimism; it is hope: hope in a risen Savior, and hope in the battle against the world, the flesh, and the Devil. Our hope is in Christ, the greatest person who ever walked this earth, who promises to come again in order to restore our world to its original splendor. In light of this, Christian leaders never lose hope.

Winston Churchill filled the free world with words of hope at the beginning of World War II. The panzer divisions and aircraft of Nazi Germany had annexed Austria, invad-

---

[7]"I Heard the Bells on Christmas Day." Text: Henry W. Longfellow. Music: Jean Baptiste Calkin. *THE HYMNAL for Worship & Celebration.* WORD MUSIC, Waco, Texas, 1986, #152.

[8]*The Complete Works of William Shakespeare*, (New York, NY: Walter J. Black, Inc.) *Macbeth*, Act 5, scene 5, p. 1124.

ed Czechoslovakia, destroyed Poland, and had blizkrieged through Holland and Belgium. France was about to fall, and the island nation of England seemed doomed. When it would have been easy to surrender, Churchill persevered. He knew the cause that united the Allied Powers was just, while the fascism Nazi Germany promised to the world was wrong. His first speech to the House of Commons as Prime Minister (13 May 1940) included the following:

> We have before us an ordeal of the most grievous kind. We have before us many, many long months of struggle and of suffering. You ask, What is our policy? I will say: It is to wage war, by sea, land and air, with all our might and with all the strength that God can give us: to wage war against a monstrous tyranny, never surpassed in the dark, lamentable catalogue of human crime. That is our policy. You ask, what is our aim: I can answer in one word: Victory — victory at all costs, victory in spite of all terror, victory, however long and hard the road may be.[9]

Following the successful, but humiliating evacuation of British and Allied troops from the European continent, on June 4, 1940, Churchill again addressed the House of Commons with words that energized the free world:

> Even though large tracts of Europe and many old and famous States have fallen or may fall into the grip of ... Nazi rule, we shall not flag or fail. We shall go on to the end. We shall fight in France, we shall fight on the seas and oceans, we shall fight with growing confidence and growing strength in the air, we shall defend our island, whatever the cost may be. We shall fight on the beaches, we

[9]*Sacred and Secular,* (Grand Rapids: William B. Eerdmans Publishing Company, 1975), p. 18.

> shall fight on the landing grounds, we shall fight in the fields and in the streets, we shall fight in the hills; we shall never surrender ...[10]

Churchill filled the free world with words of hope, and the Allied Forces responded. Christians know that Christ, ultimately, will rule over heaven and earth. His final victory over the forces of evil will be complete and absolute. As such, the servants of the Most High never lose hope.

---

[10]Martin Gilbert, *Winston S. Churchill, Finest Hour, 1939-1941*, (Boston: Houghton Mifflin Company, 1983), p. 468

Article Three

"I Have Victory Over Sin"

"When in difficult country, do not encamp."

Sun Tzu[1]

When I sin against others or against God, I will confess it, I will repent, make restitution, and seek to have victory in that area of my life. I will not justify my sin or hold anger in my heart against another.

The commentary for Article III of the Code of Conduct For Members of the Armed Forces reads as follows: "The duty of a member of the Armed Forces to use all means available to resist the enemy is not lessened by the misfortune of captivity. A POW is still legally bound by the Uniform Code of Military Justice and ethically guided by the Code of Conduct ... as a matter of conscious determination, a POW must plan to escape, try to escape, and assist others to escape

[1]Sun Tzu, *The Art of War,* James Clavell, ed., (New York, NY: Delacorte Press, 1983), p. 37.

... enemies engaged by U.S. forces ... have used a variety of tactics and pressures, including physical and mental mistreatment, torture and medical neglect to exploit POWs ... Such enemies have attempted to lure American POWs into accepting special favors or privileges in exchange for statements, acts, or information ... a POW must neither seek nor accept special favors or privileges."[2]

For the man or woman who is a member of the Armed Forces, Article III describes the type of behavior expected if captured by the enemy. Many POWs from wars gone by have resisted valiantly; some of their stories are almost beyond the pale of imagination. There are several good books on the subject.[3] In *Honor Bound, American Prisoners of War in Southeast Asia,* 1961-1973, authors Stuart I. Rochester and Frederick Kiley describe how prisoners of war coped with daily living in solitary confinement. (And most POWs spent at least some of their time in solitary — sometimes in shackles, in total darkness, with only 3-4 square feet of floor space). Many drew strength to resist from "religious connections that had either lapsed or become too casual." Collectively, through creative tapping on the walls, prisoners were able to memorize well-known hymns or long sections of Scripture. In the book, *In the Presence of Mine Enemies,* author Howard Rutledge described how he and fellow prisoner, George McKnight — neither particularly reverent prior to captivity — discovered that without the belief that God was with them in the cell, they would not have made it through imprisonment.

---

[2]Material taken from class notes, Navy Chaplain School Basic Course Class 99010. Based upon Executive Order 10631 of August 17, 1955, as amended; and Dept. of Defense Directive 1300.7 of DEC 23, 1988.

[3]In addition to the books mentioned below, *Man's Search for Meaning* by Victor E. Frankl, and *Den of Lions* by Terry Anderson are excellent reads.

Some POWs resisted through physical exercise. Many paced off more than five miles a day in their tiny cells. Others participated in sit-up or push-up contests. One prisoner had to stop doing sit-ups because the bones on his backsides broke through the skin. By the time the POWs were released, one man estimated that "the push-up record peaked at 1500 and the sit-up challenge was over 10,000!"

Other prisoners resisted by supplying the names of fellow aviators to interrogators. It is rather amusing that John Wayne, Clark Kent, and Dick Tracy were all flying missions over Vietnam at the time. Mispronunciations of North Vietnamese names — not printable here — not only served as a means of resistance, but were also cathartic and diverting. Prisoners would steal anything they could, and would do such things as add sand to enemy gas tanks to keep their sanity.[4]

In Rutledge's book, the author (who spent nearly seven years in captivity, five of them in solitary) notes that he can still reel off more than four hundred names and serial numbers that he memorized while in prison. This was accomplished through a "tap code" developed by POWs. Messages were pounded out on "honey buckets," on leg irons and even through cuffed hands locked behind a prisoner's back for weeks at a time. This memorization was a powerful means of resistance. Any POW who was released would be able to give an accurate roll call of who was still alive in the enemy camps.[5]

At Navy Chaplain School, fourteen other chaplains and I were privileged to spend an afternoon with Professor Porter Halyburton, a retired Navy Commander who spent seven and one half years in Vietnamese POW camps. Halyburton

---

[4]*Shipmate,* (Annapolis, MD: United States Naval Academy Alumni Association, September 1999), pp. 14-16.

[5]In the Presence of Mine Enemies, Howard and Phyllis Rutledge, (Fleming H. Revell, 1975), pp. 41, 46, 58.

told us how an ancient tap code (used 2000 years ago by the Greeks, and over 300 years ago by French death row inmates) worked. A grid was devised as follows:

	1	2	3	4	5
1	A	B	C	D	E
2	F	G	H	I	J
3	L	M	N	O	P
4	Q	R	S	T	U
5	V	W	X	Y	Z

The letter "K" was left off of the grid, since the letter "C" has the same sound. Two taps were sounded. The first tap indicated the row number and the second tap indicated the column. One tap followed by three taps, for example, was the letter "C." In addition to serving as a building block for a word, "C" by itself meant that it was clear to talk. Two bits meant "yes;" one bit meant "no;" three bits meant "I don't know;" and a series of bits meant "I did not copy." To "make the phone ring," POWs would tap out the little ditty "shave and a haircut." When the corresponding "dot, dot" was sounded, the one who was calling knew that a fellow POW had answered, and that it was safe to communicate. A captured Air Force Pilot by the name of Smitty Harris introduced the code to his fellow prisoners. Harris had learned it informally from an instructor at an aviator training school. Halyburton learned it from the washroom wall at the "Hanoi Hilton." Initially, he learned it incorrectly, but after he mastered the code, it took him fifty days to teach it to the man in the next cell. To this day, Professor Halyburton knows how to communicate very rapidly using the tap code. Resistance of this type kept our men alive in an almost hopeless situation.

The Christian is to resist the enemy in all arenas. We are to resist the Devil. When he raises his sinister voice by ridiculing the local church, by mocking the message of Christ, or by steering us away from worship, we come against him. He is a liar, and there is no truth in him. We are to resist the flesh. When disrespect, gossip, or greed rear up their ugly heads within us, we make the conscious decision not to succumb to the temptation, choosing rather to do the things Christ would have us do. We are to resist the world. When our peers pressure us to behave contrary to the teachings of Scripture we gracefully decline. The resistance that the Christian shows in the face of spiritual evil is analogous to that demonstrated by the valiant POWs of the Vietnam era as they resisted the physical evils thrust upon them by their captors. Exercising the mind; exercising the body; reflecting upon the fiery destruction that Christ will one day send upon the world, the flesh, and the Devil; and frequent faithful communication with other believers are excellent ways to resist the wiles of our enemy.

***When I sin against others or against God*, I will confess it, I will repent, make restitution, and seek to have victory in that area of my life.** The Bible tells us that *"all have sinned, and come short of the glory of God" (Ro. 3:23, KJV)*, and that *"There is not a righteous man on earth who does what is right and never sins"* (Ecc. 7:20; c.f. 1 Ki. 8:46; 2 Chr. 6:36). As mentioned above, all humans struggle with at least one of three categories of sin: *"the lust of the flesh, and the lust of the eyes, and the pride of life"* (1 John 2:16, KJV). You may not be afflicted with the sins of gluttony, drunkenness or sexual immorality (lust of the flesh); but you may struggle with greed: always needing a new car, a new house, or lots of money (lust of the eyes). Perhaps material things do not tempt you, but the constant desire to be in the spotlight does: you sing in the best choir, are a member of the largest church, and are known everywhere as "pillar" in the local community (pride of life). At least one of these categories snares all.

Article III for the military code says, "*If* I am captured," while the corresponding article for the spiritual code declares, "*When* I sin." The distinction is important. Not every soldier is captured by the enemy; fortunately, only a small percentage of those who have gone into harm's way have had to endure that terrible ordeal. But unfortunately, every Christian sins against others and against God. To deny this is to be guilty of the sin of arrogance. "Holier than thou" attitudes, the belief that Christians can achieve perfection in this life, have probably driven more people away from the Church than anything else; and the teaching is completely contrary to Scripture. John writes: *"If we say that we have no sin, we deceive ourselves, and the truth is not in us"* (1 John 1:8, KJV). Paul declares: *"I know that nothing good lives in me ... I have the desire to do what is good, but I cannot carry it out. For what I do is not the good I want to do; no, the evil I do not want to do— this I keep on doing"* (Ro. 7:18,19). Christians, like everyone else, are terrible sinners. To deny this is simply dishonest. The difference is that we are forgiven.

No one should ever get the "creeps" when he enters a house of worship, feeling that he can never "measure up." Servants of the Most High should be humble enough to admit their shortcomings, and not act as if their lives are perfect. Self-righteousness, one of the greatest weapons in the arsenal of the enemy, renders us completely ineffective in sharing the love of God with others. It is the humble spirit who pleases God. The one able to confess his own sin is highly effective in touching the lives of others. Would it not be fascinating if churches opened their meetings in the same manner that Alcoholics Anonymous begins theirs? Might not these twelve steps set the tone for a powerful moving of God's Spirit?

1. We admitted that we were powerless over our addiction, that our lives had become unmanageable.
2. We came to believe that a Power greater than ourselves could restore us to sanity.
3. We made a decision to turn our will and our lives over to the care of God as we understood Him.
4. We made a searching and fearless moral inventory of ourselves.
5. We admitted to God, to ourselves, and to another human being the exact nature of our wrongs.
6. We were entirely ready to have God remove all these defects of character.
7. We humbly asked Him to remove our shortcomings.
8. We made a list of all persons we had harmed, and became willing to make amends to them all.
9. We made direct amends to such people wherever possible, except when to do so would injure them or others.
10. We continued to take personal inventory and when we were wrong promptly admitted it.
11. We sought through prayer and meditation to improve our conscious contact with God as we understood Him, praying only for knowledge of His will for us and the power to carry that out.
12. Having had a spiritual awakening as a result of these steps, we tried to carry this message to addicts, and to practice these principles in all our affairs.[6]

---

[6]*Narcotics Anonymous,* (VanNuys: World Service Office, Inc., Fifth Edition, 1988), p. 17.

As Christians, we know who God is. He has revealed Himself to us; but the principles of confession, faith, repentance, the seeking of forgiveness from others, and even the evangelism that we see in this 12-step program is refreshingly honest. It all begins with step number one: addressing the sins which we have committed.

When I sin against others or against God, *I will confess it*, I will repent, make restitution, and seek to have victory in that area of my life. Confession is good for the soul. The Bible says, *"If we confess our sins, he is faithful and just and will forgive us our sins and purify us from all unrighteousness"* (1 John 1:9). Confession has both a vertical and a horizontal element. We confess to God, but it is also important to confess our sins to others, especially to those we have harmed. Converts from Roman Catholicism to Protestantism often rejoice in the fact that they no longer have to "go to confession." While it is true that confession to a priest is not essential to salvation, Protestants often miss out on many of God's blessings because they are unable to admit areas of weakness to others. All people need to confess their sins, even priests! In confessing our sins to God and to others, we initiate the first step in the healing process. The Apostle Paul recognizes this when he writes, *"when I am weak, then am I strong"* (2 Co. 12:10). Efforts made by American POWs at the "Hanoi Hilton" to communicate with each other were, among other things, ways in which they could confess weakness to each other. Servants of the Most High can learn much from them.

When I sin against others or against God, I will confess it; *I will repent*, make restitution, and seek to have victory in that area of my life. During the Korean conflict, the forces of the United Nations found themselves overwhelmed by the huge Chinese army that had entered the war. General Douglas MacArthur ordered a retreat in order to prevent the total annihilation of his troops.[7]

That is exactly what is meant by repentance: acknowledge the error of your ways, turn around, and go in the opposite direction. MacArthur's repentance on the battlefield saved the lives of thousands of soldiers. Spiritual repentance brings salvation. If you do not have a personal relationship with Jesus Christ, or if you never think about God at all, you are going in the wrong direction. If you continue in that path, the enemy will destroy you. But if you acknowledge the error of your ways, ask Christ for the forgiveness of your sins, turn around and honor God with your life; you will find a salvation for your soul that no one can take away, and will gain entrance to the kingdom of heaven.

The Bible describes King David as "a man after God's own heart" (Acts 13:22), beloved by the Lord; but it does not suggest he was without flaw. Perhaps the most notorious series of events that occurred in his life was when he failed to deploy with his army in a war against the Ammonites. Staying behind in Jerusalem, David noticed a lovely lady by the name of Bathsheba who was bathing on an adjacent rooftop. Desiring her for himself, a servant was sent to request her presence in the palace. Succumbing to the advances of the king (and perhaps immensely enjoying the glamour of it all), Bathsheba slept with David and conceived.

King David knew that Bathsheba was a married woman. Her husband, Uriah, was one of the soldiers who served in his army. David conveniently arranged for Uriah's demise by having him placed on the front line and then removing all support. Uriah was killed, and for an entire year it seemed as if David had gotten away with his tryst. But God raised up

---

[7]*The American Caesar,* William Manchester

a prophet by the name of Nathan who tactfully confronted the king. When Nathan announced the nature of what was perpetrated and boldly stood before David and declared "you are the man," the king's heart melted from within. He repented. Above all else, he grieved over sinning against God. Some of the most beautiful expressions of God's forgiveness flowed out of this repentance (n. Psalms 32 and 51), and as a result, David was a new man, effective once again in bringing the Lord's battle against the forces of evil (2 Sa. 11:1-12:14).

Do you repent when confronted with the hideousness of your sin? Does your heart melt from within when the Spirit of the living God says "you are the man (or the woman)?" Turn away from the nature of your wrong doing, experience the forgiveness of God, and be restored to that place of honor where you belong in the armies of the Most High.

When I sin against others or against God, I will confess it, I will repent, *make restitution*, and seek to have victory in that area of my life. In order for your ministry with others to be effective, you must make restitution to those you have harmed along the way. If you have spoken ill of them or to them, you must apologize. If you have caused financial loss, you must repay (n. Lev. 6:4). If you have hurt someone publicly, you must apologize publicly. Only then will God begin to work in your life. You will not have victory if repentance and restitution are absent. Jesus made that abundantly clear in the Sermon on the Mount when He declared: *"if you are offering your gift at the altar and there remember that your brother has something against you, leave your gift there in front of the altar. First go and be reconciled to your brother; then come and offer your gift"* (Mt. 5:23-24).

When I sin against others or against God, I will confess it, I will repent, make restitution, and *seek to have victory in that area of my life.* Once repentance and restitution have taken place, pursue the right behavior with a holy zeal. This will bring victory. As Paul tells Timothy, *"Flee the evil desires of youth, and pursue righteousness, faith, love and peace, along with those who call on the Lord out of a pure heart"* (2 Ti. 2:22). The Devil knows where our weaknesses lie, and he seeks to exploit the chinks in our armor; but when we confess our sins, repent of them, and make restitution for what we have done; we begin to rely on God rather than upon ourselves. When that happens, we tap into a divine power that gives us *"everything we need for life and godliness"* (2 Pe. 1:3), and we begin to have victory in the weak areas of our lives.

I will not justify my sin or hold anger in my heart against another. For a soldier to admit that he has been captured by the enemy is quite easy; there is no possibility of denial. For the Christian, though, it is quite easy to deny the nature of the sin which ensnares us. Once denial takes place, the cover-up begins and healing will not occur. Rather than repent, it becomes easier to justify our behavior, and hold anger in our hearts toward anyone who suspects a problem. But the Bible warns us: *"you may be sure that your sin will find you out"* (Nu. 32:23), and again, *"God will bring every deed into judgment, including every hidden thing"* (Ecc. 12:14).

Professor Halyburton holds no anger in his heart toward his former captors. This is what kept him alive during his captivity and gives him peace to this day. As Servants of the Most High, we will not blame others for the consequences of our own sinful behavior. We choose, rather, to confess our sins, and seek the healing and forgiveness that God promises. This action will liberate us from the stronghold of the enemy. We do not assign blame or failure to anyone else. We desire to remove the log from our own eye before we take the speck of sawdust from our neighbor's.

I have victory over sin because of what Christ has done. I humbly cling to Him, and acknowledge my dependence upon Him. As the writer of the book of Hebrews puts it: *"let us lay aside every weight, and the sin which doth so easily beset us, and let us run with patience the race that is set before us, Looking unto Jesus the author and finisher of our faith"* (Heb. 12:1-2, KJV).

Article Four

"I am Faithful to my Church"

"Without harmony in the state, no military expedition can be undertaken; without harmony in the army, no battle array can be formed."

Sun Tzu[1]

In this warfare, I will be loyal to my church. I will be faithful to my brothers and sisters in Christ. I will support my church leaders and pastors. As a leader, I will take initiative and be faithful to the gospel of Jesus Christ.

The commentary for Article IV of the Code of Conduct For Members of the Armed Forces reads as follows: "Informing, or any other action to the detriment of a fellow prisoner, is despicable and is expressly forbidden ... Discipline is the key to camp organization, resistance, and even survival ... Officers and noncommissioned officers of the United States must continue to carry out their responsibilities and exercise their authority in captivity. The senior, re-

[1]Sun Tzu, *The Art of War*, James Clavell, ed., (New York, NY: Delacorte Press, 1983), p. 30.

gardless of Service must accept command. This responsibility, and accountability may not be evaded ... Camp leaders should make every effort to inform all POW's of the chain of command and try to represent them in dealing with enemy authorities. The responsibility of subordinates to obey the lawful orders of ranking American military personnel remains unchanged in captivity."[2]

As I have gotten older, I find it more difficult to do physical exercise; yet I am involved in a profession that requires me to be in top physical form. Long distance running, pull-ups, and sit-ups are the three most important exercises required to maintain that conditioning. I no longer run by myself. I find it much easier to run with others, and I find it easiest of all to run with a group of Marines in formation. Often, a very skilled Gunnery Sergeant will come alongside, calling a cadence such as: "I say dedicate, you say motivate," in order to elicit the best possible performance from his men. The enthusiasm for "PT" that can be generated by a man calling the cadence inspires nearly everyone to higher performance.

So it is with church. It may be the pastor or an influential lay leader calling the cadence, but when we are in step, going in the same direction, we are inspired to a higher level of Christian living. The local church is the single most important organization for the propagation of the gospel. If the church is not strong, the impact it will have on her community will be minimal; and the grace, forgiveness, and compassion so needed in human society will be absent. For the local church to be strong, the people of God must affiliate and be loyal to it. Loyalty involves submitting oneself to the godly leadership of the church, enthusiastically embracing

---

[2]Material taken from class notes, Navy Chaplain School Basic Course Class 99010. Based upon Executive Order 10631 of August 17, 1955, as amended; and Department of Defense Directive 1300.7 of December 23, 1988.

its mission, and using one's gifts and abilities to advance the kingdom of God in a corporate setting. For the Christian, there is no other social organization more important.

POWs understand the need for unit cohesion and loyalty. Often their very survival depends on it. Although Christians are not imprisoned, we do operate in enemy territory, and in order to survive we must be united. But we want to do more than survive; we want to bring a message of hope to the people of our time. We want to cast out the darkness of this world and let the light of Christ shine. For that to happen, loyalty to one's church is paramount. Church leaders must be bold in their proclamations and in their actions. Honesty, integrity, and love should be characteristic of their work. Church members should render unswerving support to those who faithfully lead. Paul's letter to the Thessalonians declares: *"respect those who work hard among you, who are over you in the Lord and who admonish you. Hold them in the highest regard in love because of their work."* Leaders are to *"warn those who are idle, encourage the timid, help the weak, be patient with everyone"* (1 Th. 5:12-14). If these elements are present in a local congregation, the community in which it ministers will be affected profoundly by the gospel of Jesus Christ.

Philip, one of the twelve Apostles, was nearly as skeptical in his faith as the Apostle Thomas (a.k.a. Doubting Thomas). On one occasion, Philip blurted out: *"Lord, show us the Father and that will be enough for us."* Jesus answered: *"Don't you know me, Philip, even after I have been among you such a long time? Anyone who has seen me has seen the Father. How can you say, 'Show us the Father'?"* (John 14:8-9). As Jesus continued, he told Philip that *"anyone who has faith in me will do what I have been doing. He will do even greater things than these, because I am going to the Father. And I will do whatever you ask in my name, so that the Son may bring glory to the Father. You may ask me for anything in my name, and I will do it"* (John 14:12-14).

The "you" in Christ's answer is plural. Whatever you, collectively as the people of God, ask in the name of Jesus Christ, He will do. As you reflect upon the history of the Church, think of the good things it has brought to the world: *Public education* — high schools and universities challenging and enlightening the minds of those who are made in God's image; *hospitals, nursing homes, and hospices*— bringing compassionate care to those who are suffering; *social welfare systems* — taking care of those afflicted with poverty; and *judicial systems* — tempering justice with mercy in a very violent world. In America, nearly every important human rights campaign ever launched had its origins in the Church. Believers in Jesus Christ brought about the abolition of slavery; the Church started the women's suffrage movement, and servants of the Most High brought leadership to the civil rights movement of the 1960's.

Nearly every charitable institution in today's world had its beginnings in the Church. When Christ spoke of His people accomplishing even greater things than He, it was as if our Lord was looking down the strands of time, reflecting upon the accomplishments of modern medicine, engineering, or physics. Today's high schooler has a deeper understanding of the sciences than either Aristotle or Newton in his prime. The miracles of modern medicine surpass those of Jesus when He walked the earth. Christ walked on water, but architects construct bridges capable of transporting millions of people across vast expanses of water. Jesus fed five thousand; farmers in the Midwest can feed the world. Jesus healed blind Bartimaeus; doctors around the world perform laser surgery, restoring sight to millions.

"Jesus saw productive possibilities in crooked tax collectors, women of the streets, palace servants, scholars, and even a man who ran naked through the cemetery screaming. Together they would someday accomplish greater things than He himself had even done."[3] The Church, when it is effective, also sees those productive possibilities, and is able to gather a wide diversity of people together for the common good, inspiring them to great accomplishment. The qualities of grace, mercy, respect, and dignity preached by the Church always elicits humanity's best. But if the Church fails to do this, very little will be accomplished in advancing the kingdom of God. Loyalty to the local church, to its leadership, and to her people is tantamount to loyalty to Christ Himself.

In this warfare, *I will be loyal to my church.* The local church is on the "cutting edge" of spiritual warfare; it is a fighting unit, similar to a ship of the line or to a battalion-size force of men. Those who serve in the local church work together in carrying out its mission. In the same way that good leadership, sound doctrine, and continual training are essential to the success of a military unit; leadership, doctrine and training are needed in the local church. And above all else, loyalty is paramount.

On May 12, 1962, General Douglas MacArthur, the great military leader who commanded the Southwest Pacific theater in World War II, administered postwar Japan and led the United Nations' forces during the first nine months of the Korean war, delivered one of the most memorable speeches of our era to cadets at the United States Military Academy at West Point. His message began simply: "Duty, Honor, and Country. Those three hallowed words reverently dictate what you ought to be, what you can be, what you will be. They are your rallying points: to build courage when courage seems to fail; to regain faith when there seems to be little cause for faith; to create hope when hope becomes forlorn."

---

[3] J. Daniel Lupton, *I Like Church, But...*, (Shippensburg, PA: Destiny Image Publishers, Inc., 1996), p. 84.

The message ended powerfully:

> "You are the leaven which binds together the entire fabric of our national system of defense. From your ranks come the great captains who hold the nation's destiny in their hands the moment the war tocsin sounds. The Long Gray Line has never failed us. Were you to do so, a million ghosts in olive drab, in brown khaki, in blue and gray, would rise from their white crosses thundering those magic words — Duty — Honor — Country."[4]

MacArthur's words might well have been delivered to the members of any local church; they are the words of loyalty. Effective Christians must be involved with the men, women and children of the community. We need to worship and pray with others. There may be times when courage seems to fail, when there is little cause for faith, and when hope becomes forlorn; but those are precisely the times when loyalty is most needed. God places His people in every community, but when loyalty is not shown during the difficult times, His Spirit may depart, abandoning a good work begun by members of an earlier era. Darkness will take over where there was once light, and victory can be chalked up for the enemy.

Marines cultivate loyalty for their organization from day one. When a young man or woman makes it through boot camp and is awarded the "eagle, globe, and anchor," great pride fills the heart. That individual has become a member of the world's most elite branch of the armed services. In like manner, when men or women choose to follow Jesus Christ, the great General of the heavenly armies, they have joined a vast body of believers that, from its inception, has brought

---

[4]*Parade, The Sunday Newspaper Magazine,* (New York: Parade Pubs., May 7, 2000), p. 7.

improvement and salvation to the human condition. Pride in what God and His people have accomplished should fill our hearts. As a Marine develops his or her skills and attains a certain time in rank, promotion to Corporal is inevitable. At that point in the Marine's career, words of the non-commissioned officer (NCO) creed are administered. It is obvious that the purpose of the creed is to instill loyalty to the organization.

NCO CREED

> I am an NCO dedicated to training new Marines and influencing the old. I am forever conscious of each Marine under my charge, and by example will inspire him to the highest standards possible. I will strive to be patient, understanding, just, and firm. I will commend the deserving and encourage the wayward.
>
> I will never forget that I am responsible to my Commanding Officer for the morale, discipline, and efficiency of my men and their performance will reflect an image of me.

When a new Christian affiliates with a local church, a creed or document meant to instill loyalty is highly appropriate. The New York congregation where I served as Pastor for seven years had a church covenant with which new members became acquainted. The covenant was read frequently at communion services to refresh longtime members with its contents. These words, like those of the NCO creed, are meant to instill loyalty:

> Having been led, as we believe, by the Spirit of God to receive the Lord Jesus as our Saviour, and having been baptized into the name of the Father and of the Son and of the Holy Spirit, we agree to live together as one body in Christ.

> Therefore, relying upon His gracious aid, we purpose to walk together in Christian love, to strive for the advancement of our church in knowledge, holiness, and comfort; to promote its prosperity and spiritual well-being; to support its worship, ordinances, discipline, and doctrines, not neglecting the assembling of ourselves together;
>
> And to give regularly and cheerfully to the support of the ministry, the expenses of the church, the relief of the poor, and the spread of the Gospel throughout the whole world.
>
> We also purpose, by divine aid, to make our homes centers of Christian influence, to educate our children in the nurture of the Lord, and by pure and winsome example, to lead our kindred and neighbors to the Saviour; To be just in our dealings, faithful in our engagements, slow to take offense, but, according to the rule of the Master, to seek reconciliation without delay, and by tenderness and sympathy to bear one another's burdens and sorrows.
>
> We moreover engage that if we remove from this place, we will if possible unite with a church where we can carry out the spirit of this Covenant
>
> We will in all things seek to live to the glory of him who has called us out of sin into service and out of darkness into His marvelous light.

If a Marine decides to stay in the Corps past his or her initial four-year tour, promotion to the rank of Staff Sergeant is likely. At this point, yet another creed is administered to instill further loyalty to the institution. The Staff Noncommissioned Officer Creed could be tailored easily for use in installing new deacons, elders or trustees in the local church.

STAFF NCO CREED

I am a Staff Noncommissioned Officer in the United States Marine Corps. As such, I am a member of the most unique group of professional military practitioners in the world. I am bound by duty to God, Country and my fellow Marines to execute the demands of my position to and beyond what I believe to be the limits of my capabilities. I realize I am the mainstay of Marine Corps discipline, and I carry myself with military grace, unbowed by the weight of command, unflinching in the execution of lawful orders, unswerving in my dedication to the most complete success of my assigned mission. Both my professional and personal demeanor shall be such that I may take pride if my juniors emulate me, and knowing perfection to lie beyond the grasp of any mortal hand, I shall yet strive to maintain perfection that I ever be aware of my needs and capabilities to improve myself. I shall be fair in my personal relations, just in the enforcement of discipline, true to myself and my fellow Marines and equitable in my dealings with every man.

I will be faithful to my brothers and sisters in Christ. One of the most treacherous spy scandals in the history of the United States revolved around a Chief Warrant Officer (CWO) in the Navy by the name of John Walker. In the late 1970's and in the early eighties, at the height of the Cold War, Navy Admirals were baffled. Every time a ship of the Seventh Fleet left port, the Navy of the Soviet Union was there to observe. For at least eighteen years, CWO Walker had been involved in an operation that sold millions of dollars worth of communications software and hardware to the Soviet Union. Although he retired from the Navy in 1976,

Walker was able to continue his treacherous work through family members and friends who were still on active duty. One of those "friends" was Senior Chief Radioman Jerry Whitworth. Whitworth was the officer in charge of communications security at the Alameda Naval Air Station in California, from 1979-1982.[5] In this position, he was entrusted to hand out daily, weekly, and monthly cryptographic materials to the confidential materials security (CMS) custodians on each of the ships in the fleet. In addition to doing his job, Whitworth also sold copies of the material to agents of the USSR. As the CMS custodian for a navy warship in the Bay area, I had gone to Senior Chief's office on numerous occasions in order to keep current. From outward appearances, everything seemed normal. The sailors who were responsible for the materials seemed efficient and professional, but underneath the outward appearance was a devastating activity which could, in wartime, have led to the destruction of the U.S. Seventh Fleet. Walker, Whitworth, and their cronies were neither faithful to the cause of the U.S. government nor to the men and women who served in uniform.

For someone to take a leadership role in the local church without the desire to serve God and to help others is a recipe for disaster. For men and women to "use" the church for the purpose of garnering votes in the next election or for establishing business contacts is treachery of the highest order. The effect upon the Body of Christ is no less devastating than what was accomplished by the Walker family. We are to be faithful to one another and to the Most High God.

One of the saddest comments outsiders often make of church people is that "Christians kill their wounded." In the military, if a man or woman is wounded in battle, ev-

---

[5]Jack Kneece, *Family Treason, The Walker Spy Case*, (Briarcliff Manor, NY: Stein and Day/Publishers, 1986), p. 176.

ery possible effort is made to get that person off of the front lines and into the rear, where medical and spiritual help can be received.[6] But if a brother or sister serving on the front lines of gospel ministry falls into sin, the individual is often shunned, judged or excommunicated. Outward pleasantries may be exchanged on Sunday mornings, but beneath the surface seethes a deadly unfaithfulness. At the precise moment when a fellow believer needs a kind word or a compassionate embrace, the evangelical troops march on, leaving him or her in the dust of the battlefield, never again fit to serve in the armies of the Most High. My own particular denomination has had tendencies in the past to "build a pure church." We were encouraged to "be separate" from everything that had the slightest leaning toward evil. Unfortunately, the only place where such purity will be found is in heaven. In every other place, you will find broken human beings who will need a break from "front line activities." The following anonymous poem summarizes quite well what to expect in any local church:

If you should find the PERFECT Church
without one fault or smear,
For goodness sake don't join that church,
You'd spoil the atmosphere.
But since no perfect church exists,
Where people never sin.
Let's cease in looking for that church.
And love the one we're in!

Pastors and church leaders should be faithful to their brothers and sisters in Christ by being compassionate when flaws in character appear. No one should be expected to

[6]See comments regarding the laws of war on pp. 38.

teach a Sunday School class "until Jesus comes." Give a break to your leaders and teachers, as well as to your pastors. On occasion, remove them from front-line activity in order that they might enjoy some well-deserved rest and recreation. If someone "falls into a sin" that is not becoming the name of Christ, provide godly counsel for the "sinner," offer help, seek to restore. Members of the church should be careful what they say about others. How much more noble are the encouraging words spoken directly to the one who is hurting rather than whispers of destructive gossip behind his or her back! I will be faithful to my brothers and sisters in Christ.

I will support my church leaders and pastors. My first day at the U.S. Naval Academy was shocking. I could hear the voices of newly-indoctrinated plebes running down the center of hallways, squaring corners, shouting "Beat Army, sir" at the top of their lungs. "Yes, sir;" "no, sir;" "aye, aye, sir;" "I'll find out, sir;" and "no excuse, sir" were the five most common expressions you would hear coming from the mouth of a plebe. I had come from a rural family in upstate New York. Prior to that first day at Annapolis, I had never been anywhere near a military base. To me, "sir" was the language of slavery; it was an anachronism from another era. I remember telling a friend that, unlike the plebes we could hear running up and down the halls of that venerable institution, I would never stoop to calling someone else "sir" — especially when that person was younger than me. And then I entered Bancroft Hall!

One of the most difficult things for young recruits to learn upon entering the military is submission to lawful authority. Often it can grate on a member of the Armed Forces throughout his or her career. By nature, human beings are stubborn, rebellious people. We do not like authority; we do not like submitting to authority; and above all peoples,

Americans are most notorious. Our founding document as a nation is the Declaration of Independence. We enjoy our freedoms. The famous poem Invictus summarizes the feelings of many.

Invictus

Out of the night that covers me,
Black as the Pit from pole to pole,
I thank whatever gods may be
For my unconquerable soul.

In the fell clutch of circumstance
I have not winced nor cried aloud.
Under the bludgeonings of chance
My head is bloody, but unbowed.

Beyond this place of wrath and tears
Looms but the Horror of the shade,
And yet the menace of the years
Find, and shall find, me unafraid
It matters not how strait the gate,
How charged with punishments the scroll,
I am the master of my fate:
I am the captain of my soul.[7]

Perhaps the greatest of all paradoxes, however, is the freedom that comes through submission to others and to God. When you have a humble spirit, you will be able to see beyond the flaws of the leaders who are above you, and notice the beautiful qualities with which God has endowed them. You will support that which is good, and your church

---

[7]William Ernest Henley, "Invictus," *It Can Be Done, Poems of Inspiration,* (New York: George Sully & Company, 1921), p.5.

will be strong. So many churches have destroyed themselves from within because of personality conflicts, because of egos that are not harnessed, and because of rebellious unforgiving spirits. Jesus said, *"a house divided against itself will fall"* (Luke 11:17). The most important of all leadership traits is humility, and the concept that "good followers make good leaders," is critical to the success of any organization.

As a leader, *I will take initiative* and be faithful to the gospel of Jesus Christ. Wars are won because great military leaders take the battle to the enemy. In the Second World War, "D-Day" was a major turning point in the European theater. General Eisenhower took the initiative to land troops on the beaches at Normandy. A decisive turning point in the Korean War was when General MacArthur landed troops at Inchon, a beachhead deemed untenable by North Korean forces. General Schwarzkopf took the initiative during the first Gulf war by feinting an amphibious landing on Kuwaiti beaches, only to envelop unsuspecting Iraqi troops with a massive tank movement hundreds of miles away.

Leaders in the local church take the initiative by bringing the gospel to people in need of a dose of good news. So often, one who is hurting finds himself alone and isolated at precisely the moment in life when God is needed the most. When a person loses a loved one, people tend to avoid the one grieving because they do not know what to say. But leaders take the initiative and speak about the deceased. They make mention of fun times enjoyed in the past. By being there, the leader becomes a physical manifestation of God's presence. Leaders also take the initiative and bring good news to those caught in embarrassing situations. They talk to young people who have been arrested for drug abuse, offering words of hope. They speak to the middle-aged man or woman who lost a job, or whose marriage just exploded.

They talk to the person who has been involved in a horrible accident and will be disfigured for life. They are bold with the man or a woman who is openly hostile to the gospel. Leaders always take the initiative; they speak to those others are avoiding. In so doing, they catch the enemy off guard, and win strategic battles for the kingdom of God.

As a leader, I will take initiative and *be faithful to the gospel of Jesus Christ.* United States Marines enjoy doing physical training, or "PT." They love to come together regularly for workouts at the gym or to run or swim. If you were to ask a Marine what would happen if they failed to "PT," the response, invariably, would be something like: "I would get fat and sluggish." When asked, 'is it easier to "PT" alone or with others,' most would admit that they find much it easier to train with others. The group brings the needed encouragement to persevere.

Christians need to do regular spiritual "PT." We need to gather together in the presence of God to worship. When we fail to do this, we become spiritually sluggish. Gossip, greed, and anger begin to dominate our lives. Worship – spiritual "PT" – strengthens our resolve against these enemies of the soul, and is essential to a victorious Christian life. As a Line Officer in the Navy, I frequently swapped watch standing responsibilities with other officers in order to attend Sunday morning worship services. If a fellow officer was slated for the midwatch (midnight - 4:00 a.m.) on Saturday night, I would offer to take his watch if he would stand my Sunday morning duty from 8:00 a.m. - noon. Often, members of the wardroom would look at me in amazement, and inquire as to why I would do such a thing. When I responded that it was my desire to attend Sunday morning chapel service, a clear message was sent about the importance of faithfulness in worship.

Being faithful to the gospel of Jesus Christ involves regular worship — joyous and heartfelt singing, fervent and sincere prayer, sermons filled with passion and truth, and sacraments celebrated with reverence. When we are not faithful in worship, problems develop – not only on a personal level – but also corporately. When we are faithful in worship, the entire community in which God has placed us is blessed. When Moses went to the top of the mountain in order to receive the Ten Commandments, he stood in the presence of God for all of the Israelites (Ex. 34:32). When we gather in our places of worship, we do so for the entire community. As Chaplain for the 1st Combat Engineer Battalion, I conducted weekly Bible studies for each of the companies. If ten percent of the Marines in that company actually showed up, it was considered a good turnout. But something else was happening as we worshipped together: Marines who were not physically present soon encountered those who had been in the Bible study. The entire community, miraculously and vicariously, somehow knew that God loved them. Morale and esprit de corps for the entire battalion improved. Harold MacMillan, a former Prime Minister of Great Britain, understood this principle very well. He once noted that the power of the great Empire began to wane when its citizens were no longer faithful in worship on Sunday mornings.[8]

Being faithful to the gospel of Jesus Christ involves caring for others. The Navy and Marine Corps Relief Society comes to the aid of thousands of military personnel. Each year, men and women, serving far from their homes, often receive grants or interest free loans in order to be with their families in times of great crisis. Personnel who have automobile problems, who are about to have children, who are

---

[8]Dr. John Gladstone, "Pastoral Care and Discipling." A message delivered at the Billy Graham School of Evangelism in Halifax, Nova Scotia, on Thursday, August 1, 1996.

having financial difficulty, who are attending college classes, or who have children about to matriculate, often find themselves in line for assistance from an institution that provides tangible care in time of need. Jesus operated the same way. When the imprisoned John the Baptist asked if Jesus was the expected Messiah, our Lord's answer was revealing: *"Go back and report to John what you hear and see: The blind receive sight, the lame walk, those who have leprosy are cured, the deaf hear, the dead are raised, and the good news is preached to the poor"* (Mt. 11:4-5). Each of the things Jesus mentioned met a tangible physical need. Because of Christ's answer, John the Baptist knew that the kingdom of God had come. The early Church understood this as well. As recorded in the book of Acts: *"There were no needy persons among them. For from time to time those who owned lands or houses sold them, brought the money from the sales and put it at the apostles' feet, and it was distributed to anyone as he had need"* (Acts 4:34-35).

Caring is the most tangible way of showing God's love. Caring is kindness; caring is dignity; caring means that pocket books open up to those who are in need. In the two communities where I was privileged to serve as a church pastor, we collected a monthly offering to be used specifically for those in need within our own church family. The "Deacons Fund" gave away thousands of dollars every year to those who were struggling to make ends meet. In addition, the congregations contributed generously to various local social service agencies. Church members took pride in what those agencies were accomplishing, and often personally escorted people in need to the appropriate place of assistance. We are fortunate to live in a nation whose constitutional preamble declares: "We the People of the United States, in order to form a more perfect Union ... promote the general welfare ... do ordain and establish this Constitution." Many of our tax dollars promote the general welfare of our citizens, serving as a safety net for those who "fall through the cracks." For these reasons and more, the servant of the Most High pays his taxes with a smile on his face. She gives cheerfully to the church and other charitable causes because she cares. What a great way to say to the people of our communities, "God loves you, and so do we!"

Finally, being faithful to the gospel of Jesus Christ means exactly that: we are a Christ-centered community. God sent His Son to die for our sins, and raised Him from the dead on the third day. The Scriptures declare: *"there is no other name under heaven given to men by which we must be saved"* (Acts 4:12). In the Gospel of John, Jesus says, *"I am the way and the truth and the life. No one comes to the Father except through me"* (John 14:6). Servants of the Most High should never compromise on this. It is the keystone of the Christian faith, the bridge that connects sinful humanity with a Holy God. God commands – He does not merely suggest — that people everywhere repent and believe the gospel. The Apostle Paul, for example, in debating with the Greek philosophers on Mars Hill declares: *"In the past God overlooked such ignorance, but now he commands all people everywhere to repent. For he has set a day when he will judge the world with justice by the man he has appointed. He has given proof of this to all men by raising him from the dead"* (Acts 17:30-31). Above all else, may we be faithful to the message of the gospel, proclaiming it with grace and dignity. This alone brings hope and life to a world filled with so much despair and death.

Article Five

"I am Faithful to the Broader Chrisitan Community"

I pray … that all of them may be one …
John 17:20-21

I will be a faithful witness to Christ in my dealings with those outside my church. I will support the Biblical witness of other churches in my community. I will not make disparaging remarks against my church or any other churches.

The commentary for Article V of the Code of Conduct For Members of the Armed Forces reads as follows: "When questioned, a prisoner of war is required by the Geneva Convention and this Code to give name, rank, service number (social security number), and date of birth. The prisoner should make every effort to avoid giving the captor any additional information ... Recent experiences of American prisoners of war have proved that, although enemy interrogation sessions may be harsh and cruel, one can resist brutal mistreatment when the will to resist remains intact. The best way for a prisoner to keep faith with country, fellow prisoners and self is to provide the enemy with a little information as possible."[1]

U.S. Navy Captain Sean Stackley is a good friend, classmate, and company-mate from the Naval Academy. During our time at Annapolis it was a joy to visit the Stackley home in Baltimore, Maryland. The rich Irish-Catholic faith exuded by the entire family made many of our peers feel welcome. (The fact that Sean had five very attractive sisters may have been an additional draw to the isolated midshipmen who enjoyed very little female companionship at the Academy). Sean lived his faith and inspired his classmates. On one occasion when we were walking to class together, I muttered out loud my doubt as to whether there even was a God. Sean immediately looked straight up at the sky. I asked him what he was doing, and he told me that he wanted to make sure he didn't get struck by lightning. Over the years, he has ministered to me greatly. We may differ in some of the finer points of theology, but we both love Christ in our hearts. The times of fellowship we have enjoyed are far more important than the hatred and division that often accompany acrimonious theological debate.

When in the presence of non-Christians, servants of the Most High should avoid speaking poorly about other Christians, churches, or denominations. Instead, we should focus upon the positive, Biblical things a particular group or individual does well. In so doing, we point others to Christ, the One in whom all churches and denominations find meaning and purpose. Let our disagreements with the theological positions of a brother or sister be handled behind closed

---

[1]Material taken from class notes, Navy Chaplain School Basic Course Class 99010. Based upon Executive Order 10631 of August 17, 1955, as amended; and Department of Defense Directive 1300.7 of December 23, 1988.

doors in the presence of other believers. Public destructive comments about other Christians point people away from Christ, often into new and dangerous spiritual innovations. The entire Church is thus weakened. POWs do not speak poorly about their own country, their country's allies, or about fellow prisoners to the enemy; they understand how destructive that would be to their cause. When POWs are faithful to each other, their chances of survival improve, and the position of the enemy is weakened. How much greater is this truth on a spiritual level!

I will be a faithful witness to Christ in my dealings with those outside my church. There were 47 nations involved in World War II. During that horrible war, 17 million soldiers and 30 million civilians were killed. Twenty million of these casualties were citizens of the Soviet Union, and six million were Jews. Ten million civilians were displaced from their homes.[2] A megalomaniac who sought to rule the world for a thousand years was at the head of the forces bringing about this devastation. His regime was racist. People of Aryan background were to be in charge; all others were to be enslaved. The United States was involved in a war against this regime for four years, but we never would have emerged victorious were it not for our allies. Had Chinese troops not resisted the Japanese in Burma, we would not have won the war. Had the underground French resistance movement not softened the will of German soldiers, D-Day never would have occurred. Had British aircraft and troops not defeated Rommel in North Africa, the invasion of Italy would have been out of the question. Had millions of Russian soldiers not swallowed up divisions of Hitler's men on the eastern front, the Axis Powers would not have been defeated, and the world would be an entirely different place today. We

---

[2]*Encyclopedia Americana*, (Danbury, Connecticut: Grolier Incorporated, vol. 29, 1996), pp. 364-531.

need allies on the battlefield. Although the tactics and war-fighting philosophies of America, China, and Russia all differ, these and other nations came together for the greater good of ending a tyranny that threatened to destroy the free world.

Faithfulness to Christ involves bringing one's faith into the public arena. This means working together with people of other faith traditions as well as with those of no faith at all. When Christians of different stripes agree to do this, amazing things happen. While serving as a pastor in up-state New York, two other ministers and I approached high school and college officials on behalf of the local council of churches. With the high school officials, we were able to reach an agreement, reinstituting a baccalaureate service that had been discontinued thirty years earlier on the grounds of "separation of Church and State." The high school officials agreed that the baccalaureate – a farewell sermon and worship service to honor graduating seniors – would be appropriate if it was voluntary and took place off campus. Scores of graduates attended the first one. As a result, young people throughout the community started several Bible study and prayer groups.

With the college officials, we lobbied to allow members of local churches to assist students during the annual "Move in Day" — that hectic time when thousands of students from all over the country bring their worldly possessions and move into a small room on campus. The administration agreed with the plan, and scores of volunteers from various faith traditions proved to be a great blessing to the campus, to the students, and to the community. As a result of this effort, college student attendance at local churches skyrocketed, and two new Christian groups were established on campus.

The first question that came out of the mouths of both high school and college officials was: "What churches are involved?" They were very concerned that these events would be sectarian in nature, but when they understood that almost all of the churches in the community were united behind the effort, approval was granted. This is what Jesus meant when He prayed that we would be one (John 17:21). This is what Paul meant, while addressing some of the divisions between churches of his day, when he asked the rhetorical question: *"Is Christ divided?* (1 Co. 1:13), or when he states: *"Make every effort to keep the unity of the Spirit through the bond of peace. There is one body and one Spirit— just as you were called to one hope when you were called — one Lord, one faith, one baptism; one God and Father of all, who is over all and through all and in all"* (Eph. 4:3-6).

Could you have imagined victory in WWII if the Allied nations had spent their time continually sniping at each other? Tragically, many Christians get so tangled up in their own denominational distinctives that they fail to unite behind issues that are really important. Every major Christian denomination, and nearly every large independent church, teaches that Jesus is the Son of God who came to this world to die for our sins in order that we might have life. This, surely, is a message behind which we can unite. The Apostles' Creed, recited in so many of our churches, is often used as a statement of unity. Let the disputes about baptism, charismatic gifts, the celebration of the Lord's Supper, how the world began and how it will end, be worked out in the local church. The greater community, served by numerous local churches, needs to witness the unity we enjoy in the midst of diversity. Only then do we have an impact for good and begin to experience victory in the struggle against the world, the flesh, and the Devil.

The Apostles' Creed

I believe in God the Father Almighty, Maker of heaven and earth:

And in Jesus Christ, his only Son, our Lord, Who was conceived by the Holy Ghost, Born of the Virgin Mary, Suffered under Pontius Pilate, Was crucified, dead and buried: He descended into hell; The third day he rose again from the dead; He ascended into Heaven, And sitteth on the right hand of God the Father Almighty; From thence he shall come to judge the quick and the dead.

I believe in the Holy Ghost; The Holy catholic Church; The Communion of Saints; the Forgiveness of sins; the Resurrection of the body, and the Life everlasting. Amen.[3]

I will support the Biblical witness of other churches in my community. God wants His people to work together. The gospel writer Mark records a conversation that took place between Jesus and the Apostle John: "*"Teacher ... we saw a man driving out demons in your name and we told him to stop, because he was not one of us." "Do not stop him," Jesus said. "No one who does a miracle in my name can in the next moment say anything bad about me, for whoever is not against us is for us"*" (Mark 9:38-40).

Christians need allies in the battle for human souls, and although the Presbyterian Christian will never completely agree with the Lutheran, and the "non-denominational" Christian will find many areas in which she disagrees with the Roman Catholic; there are certain ministries that each of these groups do better than others. And when these minis-

---

[3]*Service Book and Hymnal,* and Hymnal, (United States of America: Authorized by the Lutheran Churches cooperating in The Commission on the Liturgy, 11th Printing, 1968), p.5.

tries are Biblically based, servants of the Most High are compelled to embrace them enthusiastically. Perhaps the megachurch has more power in its worship and a greater variety of staffed programs than the Presbyterian church, but the Presbyterian church may offer a more profound theological teaching than the megachurch. Perhaps the ministries of First Baptist result in more conversions every year than those of First Methodist, but First Methodist is doing a much better job at jail and nursing home visitation. The local Roman Catholic church may capture the majesty and transcendence of Almighty God far better than the Pentecostal church, but the Pentecostal church may excel in meeting the emotional needs of people who otherwise feel quite powerless. We need each other. The kingdom of God is far bigger than any one church or theological understanding. The myriad of Christian denominations need not always be seen in a bad light. Sometimes one denomination can offer a very special glimpse of the kingdom that others cannot. When we rally together and celebrate the biblical witness that can be found in such diversity, the kingdom of God will expand.

This is not a call for blind ecumenism. There are certain "houses of worship" which are, in actuality, "synagogues of Satan." With the latter we do not wish to ally ourselves. There are four characteristics that mark a legitimate church: first and foremost is the centrality of Jesus Christ. A true church acknowledges that Jesus is the Son of God, who came to this world to die for our sins, rising from the dead on the third day. In Paul's letter to the Christians at Ephesus we read: *"you are no longer foreigners and aliens, but fellow citizens with God's people and members of God's household, built on the foundation of the apostles and prophets, with Christ Jesus himself as the chief cornerstone. In him the whole building is joined together and rises to become a holy temple in the Lord"* (Eph. 2:19-20). Any church that does not place Christ at the center of worship is not an ally; flee from it.

Secondly, the true church will emphasize the preaching and teaching of the Scriptures. Some churches prefer an exegetical style of delivery where every point of the text is carefully explained. Other churches prefer topical studies, where themes coursing through the Bible are "unpacked" during the sermon time. Still other churches choose story-telling to drive home a Biblical truth. (This, incidentally, was the style of our Lord). Styles may vary, but the Scriptures cannot be ignored. In Paul's letter to Timothy we read that, "*All Scripture is God-breathed and is useful for teaching, rebuking, correcting and training in righteousness, so that the man of God may be thoroughly equipped for every good work* (2 Ti. 3:16-17). We ignore this truth to our detriment.

Thirdly, the true church celebrates the sacraments (ordinances) of baptism and communion. This is something Jesus Himself commanded (n. Mt. 28:19; 1 Co. 11:23-25). Although there are significant variations in practice (yet another explanation for the rise of so many different denominations), the issue is one of obedience. Some churches practice believer's baptism; others baptize infants. Some churches baptize by total immersion, others by affusion (pouring) or aspersion (sprinkling). There are churches which baptize in the name of the Father, Son and Holy Spirit; others in the name of Jesus only. Within these broader categories, there are numerous variant interpretations.

There are also significant variations in the practice and understanding of the Lord's Supper (communion). Churches that hold to transubstantiation believe that the elements of bread and wine become the body and blood of Christ when consecrated by a priest. Churches that hold to consubstantiation believe that once the elements of communion are ingested, they become the body and blood of Christ. And then there are churches which do not believe either; they view the bread and cup as powerful symbols, participating in and pointing us to the life-giving event that took place two thousand years ago on a cross outside of the city of Jerusalem. The elements used during communion services vary as well: some churches use wine and unleavened bread, others grape juice and leavened bread. Some churches say that it doesn't matter what elements are used. There are even great differences as to when communion is to be celebrated: some churches believe the Lord's Supper should be part of every worship service; others celebrate monthly, quarterly or annually.

It is likely that these kinds of differences will never be reconciled. The Scriptures do not tell us *how* to celebrate the sacraments; we are merely commanded to observe them. (Perhaps God is more concerned about how we handle our differences on issues such as these than He is in the precise way we worship). The bigger picture, to be sure, is to acknowledge that both of these sacraments proclaim the death and resurrection of Jesus Christ. Regardless of interpretation, may that be the message we proclaim!

Finally, the true church is concerned for the lost. Evangelism and missions must be a high priority. Jesus took a lot of heat for associating with "sinners" (n. Luke 19:7). Servants of the Most High should likewise seek out those who are desperate to find meaning in life, and introduce them to the One who offers it. The local church is the instrument which makes it happen. Missions work can take place on a large scale through donated resources to denominational headquarters (funds that pay for the salaries of career missionaries), or it can occur at a local level in the immediate community by creatively introducing others to Christ. Ideally, it happens at both places. If the local church does not faithfully engage in missions/evangelism work, within fifty years it may cease to exist. Most of the time, the best form of evangelism is living your life with integrity, not being ashamed of what you believe. Sometimes evangelism might mean going door-to-door, introducing yourself, and telling others about the church you attend. On other occasions, it might mean sponsoring a missionary who has dedicated his or her life to working in a different culture. Some churches are involved in soup kitchens, prison ministry, or hospital visitation. Others are highly involved in community affairs, ensuring that people of faith sit on influential boards and committees, shining the light of Christ in the highest levels of society. No one church can do it all, but each should do something.

We need faithful allies – churches that embody the four characteristics listed above – in order to bring the message of God's kingdom to the kingdoms of this world. In WWII, each of our Allies had unique warfighting strategies, different kinds of military hardware, and various procedures for deploying it, but all were committed to ending the fascist reign of terror that threatened the free world. Recognizing their differences and finding strength in diversity, the Allies worked together, defeated the enemy and ended the war. Had the British refused American help because we flew a different kind of airplane, or had the Russians rejected Canadian assistance because their tankers did not follow Soviet military procedure, the Allies would have been defeated. In like manner, there are times when local churches and larger denominations need to set aside minor disagreements in theology and focus on the bigger picture of sharing the gospel with a needy world. We may have different strategies for sharing our faith, but if we can find strength in diversity in the same way as the Allied nations of WWII, our message would be unstoppable, and the world a better place.

I will not make disparaging remarks against my church or any other churches. "Divide and Conquer" has been a military strategy for millennia. If the enemy is able to cause division between the churches of a community, the corporate impact for Christ will be weakened.

During my pastorate in upstate New York, a minister moved into town with a group of followers and, almost overnight, established a vibrant church fellowship. The worship was exciting, the music was of the highest quality, and the preaching was exceptionally dynamic. Crowds of young people flocked to the sanctuary, and the ministry soon began to have a significant impact in the local community. The church established a lovely bookstore in a historic downtown building. It started an adoption agency to care for women with unwanted pregnancies, and it espoused numerous other worthy causes. But there was one major problem: the pastor and other church leaders had "cult-like" control over the congregation. Church elders decided where members were to live, whom they were to marry, and how much money they were obligated to give towards the Lord's work. Church-wide workdays were held on Saturdays in order to make major renovations to the pastor's personal home. Although the shepherd of the flock already lived in one of the finest homes in the city, church leaders informed the men of the congregation that "out of respect" for the "man of God," they should volunteer their time. The elders likewise required that the women of the church work *pro bono* for the newly established bookstore. Worst of all, church financial records were not open to public scrutiny. No one except the "inner circle" knew how much money was being made and how it was spent.

After seven years of ministry, the pastor abruptly left town, taking a considerable amount of the church's wealth with him; and the once vibrant fellowship collapsed. The city newspaper ran a week-long exposé on the church, the departed pastor, and the ensuing corruption. Local clergy discovered the man had moved to Florida in order to establish another "ministry." Enraged that this "wolf in sheep's clothing" had wrought so much havoc in their community, the clergymen wanted to prevent this kind of situation from ever happening again. They decided to send a signed letter, accompanied by the newspaper articles, to leadership in the Florida community. And then something totally unexpected happened: pastors who were part of the local evangelical ministers' association refused to place their signatures on the same document with pastors who were part of the local council of churches. The sentiment of those serving on the council of churches was identical: they wanted nothing to do with ministers who were part of the evangelical organization.[4] Even though both groups recognized the need to address a sinful situation, and both acknowledged the importance of unified, corporate action; neither would cooperate with the other, and the desired result was not achieved. The errant pastor was able to conduct new ministry in a different locale, no doubt wreaking similar destruction. How sad! Had ministers and churches been able to put aside their differences and ally themselves in the cause of truth, they would have preempted the ministrations of a shady character who cast aspersion and doubt upon a message that is supposed to bring life and hope.

Article IV in the Christian Code of Conduct speaks of the importance of involvement in the local church, and of the need for loyalty; but so often we cultivate unhealthy loyalties that bring harm to the broader Christian community. When we make destructive comments against other churches (or when our evangelism efforts target their members), we drive non-believers away. Life is difficult enough! Who wants to be involved in something that leads to unnecessary strife? Christ came to bring life, and when local churches cooperate in proclaiming His message, they bring blessing to entire communities.

POWs resist making propaganda-laden oral or written statements to the enemy because they are detrimental to the mission of the United States and its allies. Destructive comments that churches bring against other congregations or that individual Christians make against fellow believers have the same effect. When we speak poorly of other churches, our words harm their ministries, our own efforts, and ulti-

[4]Tragically, this is standard procedure for the two major Protestant organizations in our country. Members of the National Association of Evangelicals are not allowed to join the National Council of Churches and vice versa. What a statement that makes to those who might be considering the claims of Christ!

mately the message of Christ. How much better would it be to focus upon the redeeming qualities of other churches and get our own house of worship in order before we begin to criticize the work of others? May we never grant the enemy of our soul a single opportunity to divide and conquer the work of God's people.[5]

[5]Some recommended readings to encourage Christian unity include: *Mere Christianity,* C.S. Lewis and *Evangelicals & Catholics Toward a Common Mission Together,* Charles Colson and Richard John Neuhaus, editors, Word Publishing, 1995.

Article Six

"I am a Child of the King"

"Had I but served my God with half the zeal I served my King ..."

William Shakespeare, Henry VIII

I will never forget that I am a child of God, redeemed by the blood of Jesus Christ, responsible for my actions, dedicated to the cause of the gospel which has set me free. I will trust in God and in the person and work of His Son, Jesus Christ.

The American POW remembers who he is: he is the soldier of a nation that stands for freedom — freedom of religion, freedom of the press, freedom to assemble and the freedom to express one's ideas. He represents a country whose founding document speaks of "life, liberty, and the pursuit of happiness," whose Statue of Liberty beckons from New York Harbor:

> Give me your tired, your poor, your huddled masses yearning to breathe free, the wretched refuse of your teeming shore. Send these, the homeless, tempest-tost, to me, I lift my lamp beside the golden door.

In the midst of torture or harsh interrogation, the American POW remembers the principles for which she is fighting: fundamental issues of human dignity and respect. The good soldier does not forget this. In face of darkest tyranny, the American GI serves a greater good; she holds her head high, serving a nation that cares for her and looks out for her welfare. If members of the Armed Forces are detained by the enemy, the United States Government will ensure that pay and allowances, eligibility and procedures for promotion, and benefits for dependents will continue.

Christians, likewise, need to remember who they are, especially in the face of great opposition. We are children of the King, cared for and loved by God. As the Scripture says, *"For God so loved the world that he gave his one and only Son, that whoever believes in him shall not perish but have eternal life"* (John 3:16). Because of what God through Christ has done, I will remain faithful to Him. I will dedicate my life to Him, even in the darkest of circumstances.

I will never forget **that I am a child of God, redeemed by the blood of Jesus Christ, responsible for my actions, dedicated to the cause of the gospel which has set me free.** Memory is a powerful force able to inspire human beings to superlative performance. Think of the wars that have been won by the United States through the use of memory-invoking slogans.

Texans fighting for independence from Mexico rallied around the motto, "Remember the Alamo." Soldiers serving under the command of General Sam Houston recalled the famous resistance effort in 1836, when 184 of their comrades held off 6000 Mexican soldiers for thirteen days at the Franciscan mission in San Antonio before being overwhelmed and annihilated. Their efforts enabled the Texas Army to regroup and ultimately defeat the armies of the Mexican General, Santa Anna.[1]

"Remember the *Maine*" was the slogan that inspired the young nation of the United States to stand up to Spain in 1898. Cuba was struggling for independence from the European power when the U.S. Battleship Maine was sunk in Havana harbor (purportedly by Spanish loyalists), killing 260 seamen on board. An enraged nation involved itself in the conflict, ultimately removing Spanish influence from the Western Hemisphere.[2]

"Remember the *Lusitania*" was the battle cry of American GIs as they enlisted to serve their country in World War I. On May 7, 1915, the British ocean liner was enroute Liverpool, England, from New York City, when a German submarine sank it. This incident, which occurred with the full blessing of the German government, led to the deaths of 1198 people, including 128 U.S. citizens.[3]

And most famous of all: "Remember Pearl Harbor." Early on Sunday morning, December 7, 1941, 360 aircraft launched from the six-carrier Japanese fleet screamed in from the north and destroyed five battleships, three cruisers, three destroyers, and 180 U.S. aircraft. 2300 American military personnel lost their lives in that attack with fewer than 100 Japanese losing theirs. The heart of the U.S. Pacific Fleet

---

[1]*The Encyclopaedia Britannica,* (USA: 15th ed., vol. 1), 1997, p. 200.
[2]*The Encyclopaedia Britannica,* (USA: 15th ed., vol. 7), 1997, p. 709.
[3]*ibid.,* (USA: 15th ed., vol. 7), 1997, p. 570.

was destroyed, but the memory of what took place inspired the United States troops to victory in both European and Pacific theaters.[4]

In each of these examples a major defeat in battle ultimately turned the tables of human resolve and led to victory in war. As Christians, we remember the cross and the horrible death Christ suffered on it, a death that brings victory and life to all who believe. We must not forget the hell from which He delivered us, and how His death ripped us from the clutches of the enemy, giving us the right to be called the children of God. At the cross, Jesus destroyed evil's stronghold over humanity, swallowing up death in victory, leading His people out of the kingdom of darkness into the kingdom of light. We will never forget.

I will never forget that *I am a child of God*, redeemed by the blood of Jesus Christ, responsible for my actions, dedicated to the cause of the gospel which has set me free. The Scriptures tell us that those who receive Christ, "*to those who believed in his name, he gave the right to become children of God*" (John 1:12). All human beings are made in the image of God (Gen. 1:27), but that image, like the shards of a great mirror, has been shattered. When we place our faith in Christ, we are adopted into God's family – we become the children of God – and the shattered image of broken humanity is restored to its full splendor.

There are many people who admire the Armed Forces of our nation and have great respect for the generals and the admirals who lead our young men and women into combat. But these admirers are not part of the Armed Forces until they sign enlistment papers, swear allegiance to the Constitution, and complete boot camp. Only then, are they con-

[4] *The Encyclopaedia Britannica*, (USA: 15th ed., vol. 9), 1997, p. 227.

sidered members of the military family. In like manner, no one becomes a member of God's family until he repents of his sins and believes in Christ. This, the only requirement for salvation, is the equivalent of completing boot camp. Once a man has placed his faith in Christ he is a child of God. To be sure, significant spiritual growth has yet to take place, but the new private in God's army is well on his way, following the greatest of all Generals – the One who has overcome sin, death, and hell.

I am assuming that you, the reader, are already a child of God, that you are a believer in Jesus Christ, a Christian. If you do not believe in Christ, you are not a child of God. In fact, you are under the control of the powers and principalities of this world. Jesus said, *"Except a man be born again, he cannot see the kingdom of God"* (John 3:3, KJV). Peter declared *"there is no other name under heaven given to men by which* we *must be saved"* (Acts 4:12). If you are not sure of your spiritual status, close your eyes, go to God in prayer, and con-

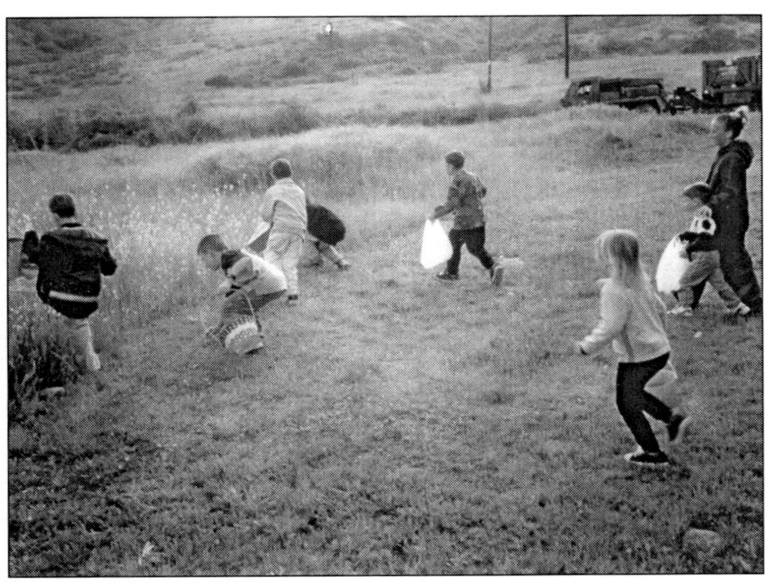

fess to Him that you are a sinner needing help. Believe that Christ died for your sins and rose again from the dead. Ask Him to be Lord of your life. If you are genuine in your confession, and truly trust in the leadership of Jesus Christ, you are now a child of God. Walk with assurance. Rejoice! Hold your head up high. As John declares, *"I write these things to you who believe in the name of the Son of God so that you may know that you have eternal life"* (1 John 5:13).

I will never forget that I am a child of God, *redeemed by the blood of Jesus Christ*, responsible for my actions, dedicated to the cause of the gospel which has set me free. To redeem means to "buy back." In many states, when a person buys beer or soda from a merchant, an additional five cents per container is added to the total cost. When the customer finishes drinking the beverage and returns the container to the merchant, he gets his five cents back. For one nickel, the merchant redeems the can or bottle he owned in the first place.

God has redeemed us. In the beginning, human beings were flawless, without sin. God's ownership was stamped all over us. Adam's sin, however, plunged humanity into darkness. We transferred our allegiance to the tempting serpent and were cast out of the Garden. But God, in His great love, redeemed us; and as Peter declares, *"It was not with perishable things such as silver or gold that you were redeemed from the empty way of life handed down to you from your forefathers, but with the precious blood of Christ, a lamb without blemish or defect"* (1 Pe. 1:18-19). What an incredible purchase price! What a great God! We dare not forget the cost of our redemption.

I will never forget that I am a child of God, redeemed by the blood of Jesus Christ, *responsible for my actions,* dedicated to the cause of the gospel which has set me free. With great freedom comes great responsibility and, hallelujah, Christ has set me free. I do not fear what others can do to me.

One of the very first things midshipmen at the United States Naval Academy learn is RHIP – Rank Has Its Privileges. It is far better to be a First Class Midshipman than a Plebe, and this a lesson that holds true throughout the military establishment. Senior ranking personnel always have greater privileges — more pay and benefits, nicer quarters, more liberty opportunities, less accountability, and various other perks not available to their subordinates. Newcomers to the military often bristle at such inequalities, but the purpose of RHIP is to inspire others, through good performance, to seek higher rank. But there is another teaching at the Academy of equal importance: RHIR — Rank Has Its Responsibilities. A senior officer or enlisted man will quickly lose privileges if he acts irresponsibly. More than a few Commanding Officers have been relieved of command for irresponsible behavior: most often involving inappropriate relationships with members of the opposite sex, abuse of alcohol, or financial improprieties.

As a Christian, I want to act in a way that honors God. I want to follow the Ten Commandments as an ethical guide for responsible living. I want to love my neighbor as I love myself, honest in my dealings with others. I stand for dignity and respect. I do not want to do anything that disparages the name of my Savior. Although the poor behavior of a Christian will not bar the gates to the Kingdom, on the Day of Judgment the rewards will be slim and the embarrassment great to those who irresponsibly abuse the freedoms Christ has given. As the Scripture declares: *"From everyone who has been given much, much will be demanded"* (Luke 12:48).

In addition to their professional responsibilities, Naval Officers are expected to participate in the social functions of the wardroom. In fact, it is a fairly serious infraction to absent oneself from such gatherings without valid reason. On one occasion, I decided not to attend a wardroom function because it was being held at Hugh Hefner's Playboy mansion in Los Angeles. The following day, I was called into the stateroom of the Executive Officer (XO) and told to "get off of this religious crusade." Apparently several other officers had elected not to attend the function, and the XO believed that I was responsible for the poor turnout. (All of the men who failed to appear at the Playboy mansion had been attending a Bible study that I was leading, but I had not told them to skip the officer function). I told the XO that I was not responsible for the choices that the other officers had made. He vented for a few minutes and then dismissed me. A few weeks later, the Commanding Officer told me that it was wrong to have held the officers' function at such a place, and that my decision not to attend was appropriate. I felt relieved and glad that I had not compromised on an issue extremely important to my Christian witness.

I will never forget that I am a child of God, redeemed by the blood of Jesus Christ, responsible for my actions, *dedicated to the cause of the gospel which has set me free.* As discussed above, the word "gospel" means "good news," and the servants of the Most High God dedicate themselves to it. [5]

American GIs dedicate their lives to the service of their country, and the military is an institution that has near total control over those who serve in it. Personnel often change residences every two to three years (sometimes even more

---

[5]pp. 64-69.

frequently) and move all around the globe. Families are separated for months on end. The amount of pay is determined. The clothing one wears is decided ahead of time. The military monitors length of hair and the activities in which the soldier is involved, even while off duty. In a moment's notice — any time, anywhere — the soldier can be called into combat, risking his life for the republic he serves. There is no other job like it in the world. To survive, one must be dedicated; nothing else is tolerated.

Ought not the servants of the Most High have a similar attitude? Paul's words to the church in Corinth clearly address the dedication expected of the follower of Jesus:

> *"We are fools for Christ ... We are weak ... we are dishonored! To this very hour we go hungry and thirsty, we are in rags, we are brutally treated, we are homeless. We work hard with our own hands. When we are cursed, we bless; when we are persecuted, we endure it; when we are slandered, we answer kindly. Up to this moment we have become the scum of the earth, the refuse of the world"* (1 Co. 4:10-13; 2 Co. 11:23-33).

Most of us have difficulty getting out of bed on Sunday morning in order to meet for worship, and we pride ourselves when we do! What would happen if Christian people truly dedicated themselves to the gospel message?

People who came of age during World War II have a great respect for the United States of America. Europeans, Asians, and various African nations remember being liberated by American soldiers. There were great celebrations. There was dancing in the streets. Honors were extended to those who served valiantly, and excitement was in the air. Where tyranny once ruled, freedom had moved in, and oppression fled. After a time, the initial euphoria disappeared, but the respect remained, especially among those who were set free.

So too with the Christian faith. When Christ set me free from the tyranny of the enemy, He energized my soul. When the King of Glory conquered the dark areas of my heart and drove out the oppressor, I was excited: I wanted to sing; I wanted to dance; I wanted to tell the world "Jesus is Lord." I was passionate about prayer, zealous to read the Scriptures and faithful in attending church. God had triggered an adrenaline rush. With time, the initial euphoria disappeared; but faith has become stronger, and it carries me through the hard times of life. I remember what Christ has done, and I want to honor Him with my life. I dedicate myself to the cause of the gospel, the only power in this world capable of liberating the human soul.

I will trust in God and in the person and work of His Son, Jesus Christ. Twenty-nine Palms is a huge Marine Corps base in the middle of California's Mohave Desert. Nearly 1000 square miles of rugged terrain allow ample room for Marines to use every weapon in their arsenal. The First Combat Engineer Battalion, where I served as Chaplain, rarely deploys as a unit. One of the five companies, for example, provides engineer services for the Fifth Marine Regiment (Fifth Marines), while another assists the Seventh Marines. During major training exercises at Twenty-nine Palms, the Marines of my battalion were thus scattered over the entire base. In order to conduct worship services during those times, a "High Mobility Multipurpose Wheeled Vehicle" (Humvee) and a driver were assigned to me. It was essential that the driver be qualified in land navigation and in radio procedure, because it was quite easy to become disoriented in the massive

California desert. One night, during a tactical portion of the "Steel Knight" exercise, my driver Sergeant Sweet was tasked with returning me to the base camp at Gypsum Ridge. We traveled for over an hour in sheer darkness. (Going tactical means that headlights and other navigational aids are turned off). Sgt. Sweet skillfully maneuvered the Humvee along a very perilous desert route, and safely delivered me to the base camp. I could not drive the Humvee because I was unable to see, but Sgt. Sweet was equipped with NVGs (Night Vision Goggles); he could see through the darkness. I placed my complete trust in him and in his abilities to navigate our vehicle safely home.

In the same way, Christians trust in the person and in the work of Jesus Christ to bring us through the darkness of this world to our heavenly home. As the famous hymn declares:

> "I dare not trust the sweetest frame, but wholly lean on Jesus' name. On Christ the solid rock I stand, all other ground is sinking sand."[6]

I can do nothing on my own strength. It is God who causes me mount up with wings like an eagle ... It is God who arms me for battle ... It is in God that I live and move and have my being. The very moment that I take my spiritual eyes off of Him, like Peter, I will sink into the waters of despair (n. Mt. 14:30).

I trust in the one God who exists in three Persons: the Father, the Son, and the Holy Spirit. The Father created me from the dust of the earth, and unlike other creatures that share this world with me, my Father made me in His image, unique among the animal kingdom. The Son, Jesus Christ,

---

[6]"The Solid Rock," Text: Edward Mote. Music: John B. Dykes. *THE HYMNAL for Worship & Celebration*, (Waco, Texas: WORD MUSIC, 1986), #402.

is my Redeemer. Fully God, yet fully man, He came to die for my sins, redeeming me by shedding His own blood. I am now a child of God. The Holy Spirit is my Sanctifier; He makes me holy. The Spirit reminds me of God's will; He points me to Christ, and brings humility and repentance. I cannot forget this great God who has set me free. Regardless of the external circumstance — even if imprisoned like the valiant POWs mentioned above — I will not forget what God has done. May we, the servants of the Most High, respond in the same way as Peter, who, when asked by Jesus if he wanted to desert him responded: *"Lord, to whom shall we go? You have the words of eternal life"* (John 6:68).

Part Two / Eleven Leadership Principles

Introduction

"These recruits are entrusted to my care. I will train them to the best of my ability. I will develop them into smartly disciplined, physically fit, basically trained Marines, thoroughly indoctrinated in love of Corps and country. I will demand of them and demonstrate by my own example, the highest standards of personal conduct, morality and professional skill."

— Drill Instructor's Creed[1]

An effective leader has to create an atmosphere where obtaining the objective is possible. He or she has to function in such a way as to:

1. Establish and maintain direction of an organization (bring vision)
2. Align people
3. Motivate and inspire people
4. Institutionalize a leadership-centered culture[2]

---

[1]In correspondence with Eugene Alvarez, PH.D., "Parris Island: The Cradle Of The Corps," General (later Commandant) Wallace M. Greene, Jr., attributed "The D.I. Creed" to Colonel Richard ("Dick") Huizenga, written in 1956.

[2]*Student Guide for Basic Officer Leadership Course,* (Pensacola, FL: Chief of Naval Education and Training, May 1997), p. 1-2-15.

Jesus was a master at all four. He *established the Church,*[3] an organization that brings hope and joy to people, which has profoundly changed our world forever. Through this invisible institution, made manifest in a myriad of denominations, God brings victory and life. Jesus *aligned people for the cause*. His original followers were very diverse: a tax collector who compromised with Rome, a zealot who wanted to overthrow the empire, men with violent tempers, and women with shady pasts. All of them served valiantly in the causes Jesus espoused. He *motivated and inspired people*. Those living in the most remote corner of the Roman Empire were the "salt of the earth," and "the light of the world." He told His followers that they would do even greater things than He, while empowering them with the gifts required to make it happen. Jesus *institutionalized a leadership culture*. The Church He established would exist until the end of the age; even the gates of hell cannot prevail against it. Christ delegated authority to the men and women who followed Him. To the very first Church leaders Jesus said, "Whatever you bind on earth will be bound in heaven." To Simon, the first of the Apostles to confess that Jesus is the Messiah, our Lord said, "You are Peter, and on this Rock I will build my Church." Later, following the resurrection, Jesus charged Peter to "Feed my Sheep."

One writer declares: "He never wrote a book; yet the libraries of the world are filled with volumes that have been written about Him. He never penned a musical note; yet He is the theme of more songs than any other subject in the world." Napoleon Bonaparte, looking back over his years of conquest, reportedly once said, "Alexander, Caesar, Charlemagne and I have built great empires. But upon what did

---

[3]Here, as before, I am using the word "Church," with a capital "C," in a universal sense, transcending time and denomination.

they depend? They depended on force. But centuries ago Jesus started an empire that was built on love, and even to this day millions will die for him."[4] The leadership of Jesus Christ changed our world forever.

Good leadership is essential to the health of every local church. If any of the four elements listed above is missing, ministry will be ineffective. If the church has no direction or vision, the ministry will have no focus. If its leaders are unable to align people from various backgrounds, the scope of ministry will be very limited. If members of the church are not continually motivated and inspired to serve God, they will soon drift away from fellowship; and if a leadership culture is not established, the local church will go through great agony every time a charismatic pastor leaves.

Good leadership can be learned. Baseball great Yogi Berra's comment on America's pastime, "You can see a lot just by observing,"[5] is easily applied to leadership. If a local church has it, its ministries will prosper and the kingdom of God will expand. If a local church does not have it, its impact for Christ on the outside world will be minimal, regardless of how well the pastor preaches or how piously its people are living. Since most of local church leadership is voluntary, it is essential for those in leadership positions to learn as much as they can and apply what they have learned to the ministry of the board/committee/small group to which God has entrusted them. Pastors should be well acquainted with good leadership principles. They should be perpetual students of the subject, prepared to teach leadership to lay leaders within their congregations. Far too many churches disintegrate

---

[4]Martin Luther King, Jr., *Strength to Love*, (New York: Harper & Row, Pub., Inc., 1963), p. 41.

[5]Yogi Berra with Tom Horton, *Yogi, It Ain't Over ...*, (New York: McGraw-Hill Publishing Company, 1989), p. 7.

when paid staff is not present. Good leadership, however, will ensure that the local church will continue to advance the kingdom of God even in the absence of "professionals."

Leadership can be learned from two different books: the Holy Bible, a divinely inspired collection of writings passed down from the Prophets of the Old Testament and the Apostles of the New; and the book of human experience, precious texts handed down to us by various teachers in the "school of hard knocks." The purpose of this section of *Code of Conduct for Servants of the Most High God* is to look at the leadership techniques taught by the United States Marine Corps and note how these time-tested values, so pivotal to the success of the finest fighting force in the world, are truths that resonate not only with human experience, but also find their origins in the Scripture. Christians can learn much from the Marine Corps. If we are able to tailor the techniques taught to young Marines, and apply them to the spiritual warfare in which we are involved, our efforts in bringing the gospel message to a needy world will bear considerable fruit.

The Marine Corps is a leadership-oriented culture. Every Marine who goes through boot camp memorizes a list of eleven leadership principles and fourteen leadership traits that are found in a series of books entitled *Marine Battle Skills Training Handbooks*. I am convinced that these principles and traits can be tailored to provide excellent training for Christians who serve in the army of the Most High. One of the reasons for this is that Marines have been very successful in keeping their standards high while coexisting in a culture where much of the moral foundation has eroded away. The eleven principles of Marine Corps leadership are time tested. They have proven successful in peacetime as well as in war. Principles do not change, regardless of external circumstances; they are never compromised.

In the section that follows, we will look at each of the eleven leadership principles in depth, weaving into the discussion the fourteen leadership traits. The leadership traits are qualities one expects to find in a principled person; they describe what an effective leader looks like. We, as Christian leaders, should strive with all of our might to live exemplary lives in a culture where Biblical morality is rapidly becoming a distant memory. We do this for two reasons: first, we are a special people called to be light and salt in a dark and unsavory world, called to offer praise to Him who has given everlasting life. Secondly, we strive to live exemplary lives because judgment begins first at the house of God (1 Pe. 4:17). A listing of the eleven leadership principles and the fourteen leadership traits of the United States Marine Corps follows:

Principles of Leadership

1. Know yourself and seek improvement.
2. Be technically and tactically proficient.
3. Develop a sense of responsibility among your subordinates.
4. Make sound and timely decisions.
5. Set the example.
6. Know your Marines and look out for their welfare.
7. Keep your Marines informed.
8. Seek responsibility and take responsibility for your actions.
9. Ensure assigned tasks are understood, supervised, and accomplished.
10. Train your Marines as a team.
11. Employ your command in accordance with its capabilities.[6]

---

[6]*Marine Battle Skills Training Handbook, Book 1, PVT-GYSGT, General Military Subjects,* (Arlington, VA: Marine Corps Institute, November 1994), p. 1-5-14.

Traits of Leadership

1. Dependability - The certainty of proper performance of duty.
2. Bearing - Creating a favorable impression in carriage, appearance, and personal conduct at all times.
3. Courage - The mental quality that recognizes fear of danger or criticism, but enables a man to proceed in the face of it with calmness and firmness.
4. Decisiveness - Ability to make decisions promptly and to announce them in a clear, forceful manner.
5. Endurance - The mental and physical stamina measured by the ability to withstand pain, fatigue, stress, and hardship.
6. Enthusiasm - The display of sincere interest and exuberance in the performance of duty.
7. Initiative - Taking action in the absence of orders.
8. Integrity - Uprightness of character and soundness of moral principles; includes the qualities of truthfulness and honesty.
9. Judgment - The ability to weigh facts and possible solutions on which to base sound decisions.
10. Justice - Giving reward and punishment according to merits of the case in question. The ability to administer a system of rewards and punishments impartially and consistently.
11. Knowledge - Understanding of a science or an art. The range of one's information, including professional knowledge, and an understanding of your Marines.
12. Tact - The ability to deal with others without creating offense.
13. Unselfishness - Avoidance of providing for one's own comfort and personal advancement at the expense of others.
14. Loyalty - The quality of faithfulness to country, the Corps, the unit, to one's seniors, subordinates, and peers.[7]

[7]*ibid.*, pp. 1-5-14, 1-5-15.

Principle One

Know yourself and seek improvement

"My memory is nearly gone, but I remember two things: That I am a great sinner, and Christ is a great Savior."

John Newton[1]

Major Hal Angus is an inspirational Marine leader as well as a man who trusts Jesus Christ and seeks to spread the good news of His kingdom. One of the things that impressed me about Major Angus when he served as the Executive Officer of my battalion was his ability to admit when he made a mistake. On one occasion, the Commanding Officer of the First Combat Engineer Battalion was conducting a "school circle" prior to a long liberty weekend. (A school circle is when all of the men of the unit circle around the CO in order that he might speak to them directly). The topic of the day was the danger of drinking and driving. Several Marines throughout the Corps had been killed in alcohol related accidents, and

[1]*Christian History*, (Carol Stream, IL: Christianity Today, Inc., vol. X, no 3, Issue 31), p. 21.

the CO wanted to communicate with his men in such a way as to avert further tragedies. He asked the "XO" to speak. Rather than "preach" to the Marines, Major Angus simply related a story of what had happened to him when he was a young college student. He told of an incident when he had stayed up far too late, had partied too hard, and had decided to drive hundreds of miles with three friends through the night in order to continue the "fun" in Las Vegas. The exhaustion and the alcohol factor resulted in the driver falling asleep, and the car spinning out of control off of the highway and rolling over onto its roof. Fortunately no one was killed or seriously injured. Major Angus' willingness to share his story with younger Marines was far more effective than simply telling them "don't drink and drive." It showed them he, too, was human, had made errors of judgment in his past, and had learned from them.

So often, Christians come off as "holier than thou." We act as if we have never done anything wrong, as if our thoughts are always pure and holy. Newcomers investigating the claims of Christ are frequently repelled by such attitudes and never again set foot within the church. The first leadership principle of the Marine Corps, "Know yourself and seek improvement," is the most important of the eleven, and undergirds the remaining ten. If servants of the Most High take principle number one seriously, it requires an honest assessment of one's life, and the ability to acknowledge human frailty. Improvement in the human condition begins with confession: something is broken! Once we acknowledge our sinfulness, God begins to work in our lives. Confessions of sin and of the need for improvement are hallmarks of the believer, regardless of age or Christian maturity. It is an attitude that follows us until the day of death. When we know ourselves and understand our need for improvement, we become much more compassionate to others, effectively eliminating the haughty spiritual attitudes often found in houses of worship. Many, who have turned away from Christ because of overly pious attitudes, often find solace in the teachings of eastern religions, particularly those of Confucius, teachings that emphasize the importance of showing humanity toward others and respect for oneself.[2] But Christ offers so much more than Confucius, and there is no better way to communicate His message than to be honest about ourselves and our own need for improvement.

The Bible teaches two very important concepts about knowing ourselves: 1) all human beings are made in the image of God, and 2) we are all sinners.

---

[2]This is the first of five "Deliberate traditions" taught by Confucius. Listed in order, the five traditions include:

1) Jen — feeling of humanity toward others and respect for oneself
2) Chun-tzu — the gentleman.
   Righteousness in heart leads to beauty in character
   Beauty in character leads to harmony in the home
   Harmony in the home leads to order in the nation
   Order in the nation leads to peace in the world
3) Li — Propriety (the way things should be done) i.e.: five key relationships
   The loving father, the reverential son
   The gentle older brother, the respectful younger brother
   The good husband, the "listening" wife
   The considerate older friend, the deferential younger friend
   The benevolent ruler, the loyal subject
   — Ritual (a pattern for every act)
4) Te— power
   Government is to provide for economic sufficiency
   Government is to provide for military sufficiency
   Government is to win the confidence of the people
   (According to Confucious, the confidence of the people was the most important concept of Te, and everything depends upon the moral character of the man at the top).
5) Wen — arts of peace. Music, art, poetry, etc.

Huston Smith, *The Religions of Man.* (Chicago, Illinois: Mentor Books, 1958), pp. 167-174.

Human Beings as the image of God

In the book of Genesis we read: *'Then God said, "Let us make man in our image, in our likeness, and let them rule over the fish of the sea and the birds of the air, over the livestock, over all the earth, and over all the creatures that move along the ground." So God created man in his own image, in the image of God he created him; male and female he created them'* (Gen. 1:26-27). The Psalmist likewise spoke of humans being created in the image of God: *"O LORD, our Lord, how majestic is your name in all the earth ... what is man that you are mindful of him, the son of man that you care for him? You made him a little lower than the heavenly beings and crowned him with glory and honor. You made him ruler over the works of your hands; you put everything under his feet: all flocks and herds, and the beasts of the field, the birds of the air, and the fish of the sea, all that swim the paths of the seas. O LORD, our Lord, how majestic is your name in all the earth!"* (Ps. 8:1, 4-9).

Being made in the image of God should inspire us. As the saying goes, "God don't make no junk." The Psalmist recognizes this when he writes: *"you created my inmost being; you knit me together in my mother's womb. I praise you because I am fearfully and wonderfully made; your works are wonderful, I know that full well"* (Ps. 139:13-14). Being made in the image of God speaks of nobility, dignity, and grace.

The theologian speaks of humans being made in the image of God by suggesting that we are prophets, priests, and kings. Prophets speak the truth; and of all of God's creatures, humans are the most eloquent, able to communicate effectively with one another and pass knowledge from one generation to the next. Priests worship; and humans are the most spiritual of all creation, able to sense the presence of the divine, capable of worshipping with song, prayer and heart-felt reverence. Kings rule; and humans have dominion over all of creation, able to rule over the fish that swim through the seas, over animals which roam the earth, and over the birds which course their way through the skies. And Jesus, our role model, is the ideal man. He is the perfect image of the invisible God: He is the perfect Prophet, aptly named the Word of God (John 1:1, 14); the perfect Priest who laid down His life to take away the sins of the world; and the perfect King to whom all dominion has been given. Servants of the Most High strive to be like Him.

The philosopher speaks of humans being made in the image of God by addressing the matter of virtue. Aristotle, for example, singles out four cardinal virtues: prudence, fortitude, temperance and justice.[3] Jesus adds three more: faith, hope, and charity.[4] The Christian leader seeks to live a virtuous life, marked by all seven of these virtues. As the reader studies the eleven leadership principles of the Marine Corps, he will note that they include the four cardinal virtues. *Prudence* means to make sound and timely decisions (principle #4). *Fortitude* is the mental strength required to ensure assigned tasks are understood, supervised, and accomplished (principle #9). *Temperance*, in the military certainly, is the ability to employ your command in accordance with its capabilities (principle #10), while *justice* clearly undergirds the concept of knowing your Marines and looking out for their welfare (principle #6).[5] As we discuss each of the leadership principles in the chapters that follow, we will look at all four of these virtues in depth. Although the Christian virtues are not mentioned directly in any of the leadership principles, I would suggest they form a bedrock foundation for principle #6 and permeate the remaining ten. Effective leaders must

---

[3]*The New Encyclopaedia Britannica*, (Chicago: Encyclopaedia Britannica, Inc., 15th edition, vol. 12, 1985), p. 392.

[4]*Catechism of the Catholic Church*, (New York: Catholic Book Publishing Co., 1994), p. 446.

[5]Justice is also mentioned by name as leadership trait #10.

have faith in the people that work for them. They have hope that the cause is for the common good, and they must be able to show care for people, having compassion for them in their failings.

The fact that you are made in the image of God should keep you from despairing over the difficult moments of life. The fact that every man, woman, or child you will ever meet is also made in the image of God should inspire you to treat him/her with dignity, respect and grace. Provisions made in the Geneva standards concerning the treatment of enemy prisoners of war are derived from this concept: our worst enemy is also a human being made in God's image; he is not some sort of sub-human to be eliminated from the earth.

Human beings who do not follow Christ as Lord and Savior are beautiful people as well. Christians can always learn from them and find truth in them, even if their belief system does not allow for a relationship with God. What kinds of gifts, what kinds of abilities, what kinds of virtue can you see in other people that help you think of God — even among those you do not like? The Apostle Paul writes: *"whatever is true, whatever is noble, whatever is right, whatever is pure, whatever is lovely, whatever is admirable — if anything is excellent or praiseworthy — think about such things"* (Phil. 4:8). If you look for these things in others, and admittedly, you may have to look quite hard in some cases; you will find them and be blessed by what you see. When you treat others as being made in the image of God, as persons of dignity and worth, there will be far more opportunities for you to share your faith in Christ than if you continually refer to those outside of your circle as "heathen," "lost," or "pagan."

Human Beings as sinners[6]

Jeremiah the prophet writes, *"The heart is deceitful above all things and beyond cure. Who can understand it?"* (Jer. 17:9). Paul the Apostle writes, *"There is no one righteous, not even one; there is no one who understands, no one who seeks God. All have turned away, they have together become worthless; there is no one who does good, not even one"* (Ro. 3:10-12). And again, *"for all have sinned and fall short of the glory of God"* (Ro. 3:23). Jesus certainly understood this. The Scripture declares, *"he knew what was in a man"* (John 2:25). A major thrust of His teaching was to show us that there is no one who is good, except God (Luke 18:19). The very purpose of the Sermon on the Mount (Mt. 5-7) is to point out the sinfulness of humanity, and of our need for a Savior. When He says, *"It is not the healthy who need a doctor, but the sick"* (Mt. 9:12), the implication is that all are in need of healing.

Buddha recognized the sinfulness of human nature and proposed the "Noble 8-fold path" to eliminate it.[7] The Roman Catholic Church lists seven "deadly" sins: pride, ava-

---

[6]Some excellent literature on this topic includes: Augustine's *Confessions;* C.S. Lewis' *The Abolition of Man* and *The Screwtape Letters;* M. Scott Peck's *People of the Lie;* Dostoevsky's *Crime and Punishment;* Mark Twain's *The Innocents Abroad;* and Shakespeare's *Macbeth.*

[7]Buddha taught four truths about life: 1) Suffering is universal; 2) The cause of suffering is craving; evil desire; 3) The cure for suffering: eliminate craving; and 4) Eliminate craving by following the middle way: the Noble 8-fold path.

The Noble 8-fold path includes: 1) Right Viewpoint - i.e. knowledge of the 4 noble truths; 2) Right intentions; 3) Right Speech - i.e. speak the truth; 4) Right Behavior - selflessness and charity. Do not kill, steal, lie, be unchaste, or drink intoxicating beverages; 5) Right Occupation - occupations which promote life rather than destroy it. A career as a butcher or in the military would be inappropriate; 6) Right Effort - the will; 7) Right Mindfulness; and 8) Right Meditation.

Fritz Ridenour, *So What's the Difference,* (Glendale, CA: Regal Books, 1980), pp. 85-86. Smith, pp. 107-119.

rice, envy, wrath, lust, gluttony, and sloth.[8] If we think about any of these "deadlies" for very long, an honest self-assessment incriminates all. We quickly notice these flaws in others, and we should be equally quick to recognize them in ourselves. Isaiah, often called the "prince of the prophets," declares: *"Woe is me! for I am undone; because I am a man of unclean lips, and I dwell in the midst of a people of unclean lips: for mine eyes have seen the King, the LORD of hosts"* (Is. 6:5, KJV).

A few years ago the Navy was driven by a philosophy known as "Zero Defect Mentality." The concept actually resulted in very low morale, because no one was able to keep the ridiculously high standards. In speaking with Marine leaders about Zero Defect Mentality, the consensus was nearly unanimous: the philosophy was a hangman's noose waiting to string up the first poor unfortunate who made a mistake. Zero Defect Mentality led to a lack of initiative (Marines were afraid to attempt something innovative out of fear of making a mistake); it led to micro management (Generals and Colonels would bypass mid-level leadership in order to ensure that Lance Corporals and Privates perfectly understood their orders); and ultimately it led to hypocrisy. People would act as if there were no defects to be found within their commands. Fortunately Zero Defect Mentality is no longer part of our vocabulary. There is now an attitude in the military which promotes initiative, encourages responsibility, and allows people the opportunity to learn from their mistakes.

As we think about leadership, we must always take the sinful side of human nature into consideration. Even though all of us are made in the image of God, the image was shattered when Adam and Eve rebelled and were thrown out of the garden. What remains are shards. We can still see reflec-

[8]*Catechism of the Catholic Church*, (New York: Catholic Book Publishing Co., 1994), p. 457.

tions of the Divine One, and the virtues of which Aristotle spoke, but there are sharp edges and broken pieces that did not come with the original. Our minds are broken (Socrates surely recognized this when he declared that "I know nothing except the fact of my ignorance");[9] our bodies are limited in their abilities; and our will power is weak. In working with the broken pieces of what was once an original masterpiece, we often find ourselves cut and bleeding.

Those who lead must see themselves as sinners, touched by the grace of God, always ready to learn and improve. This should inspire humility among all who find themselves in positions of authority. A Lieutenant Colonel in the Marines once informed me that his most important guiding principle was that "he must be his own worst critic." Effective military leaders are likewise able to accept criticism from seniors, peers and subordinates. Although humility is not one of the fourteen traits or eleven principles of Marine Corps leadership, it certainly forms the foundation of everything that is said or done.

Humility should be characteristic of the Christian leader as well. If we are not humble, we will be very ineffective in communicating the gospel message to our needy world. Jesus declares, *"If anyone wants to be first, he must be the very last, and the servant of all"* (Mark 9:35). This should be the attitude of anyone who aspires to the position of deacon, elder, or trustee in the local church. We seek these positions not because of the authority that is inherent in them. We do not do it for glory, but out of a desire to serve God and human beings who are made in His image. As we see the sins of others in the parish, our reaction should be compassion and love rather than judgment and condemnation. The greatest in God's kingdom are the servants of all.

---

[9]John Bartlett, *Bartlett's Familiar Quotations,* (Boston: Little, Brown and Company, Fourteenth Edition, Fourth Printing, 1968), p. 87.

In leading others, we look for the best in them, but we should not become overly disappointed when the sinful nature becomes evident. This concept was well understood by the founders of our nation. In framing the Constitution, the fathers empowered the citizens of our land with the freedom to rule themselves, but the system of government they established divided that power into three separate branches, each able to curb any abuses with which the other two might be tempted. The system of checks and balances was put in place because of the inherent sinfulness found in any human organization. The wisdom of our forefathers has kept the Union strong through more than two centuries of challenges. Many believe the concept of the division of powers found in our Constitution originates from the biblical injunction found in Isaiah 33:22: *"For the LORD is our judge, the LORD is our lawgiver, the LORD is our king; it is he who will save us."*

It is dangerous to set people on pedestals, places where church pastors, in particular, often find themselves. The fall from such lofty heights is always devastating. Pastors, like anyone else, have their flaws. One of the purposes of a church board is to keep pastors from being placed on pedestals, and to help them in their weaknesses – a system of checks and balances as it were. The powerful wizard in Frank Baum's *Wizard of Oz* told Dorothy and her three friends to "never mind the man behind the curtain," but as leaders in the Kingdom, we need to pay attention to that little man. If not, the illusion of the flawless pastor will soon come crashing down. Real ministry begins when we recognize that all human beings, including pastors and other church leaders, are an admixture: part image of God and part broken-down sinner, in need of God's love and forgiveness.

The numbers of people who leave churches because of various transgressions are staggering. "Zero Defect Mentality" - type attitudes in our houses of worship often prevent repentance and spiritual growth. Individuals caught in embarrassing situations often feel so judged and humiliated that they are no longer able to muster up the courage to gather for worship. How this must grate against the purposes of the Most High! The local church is the very place where spiritual healing is to occur, the place where sinners should be able to go in order to hear words of grace, forgiveness and love. Wise leaders recognize this.

The need to seek improvement

The first principle of leadership is to know oneself and to seek improvement. In knowing ourselves, we recognize that we are made in the image of God, but we also acknowledge our sinful estate. We are capable of improvement precisely because of the Divine imprint stamped upon us, but we are in need of improvement because of our brokenness.

Improvement involves change: change on both individual and institutional levels. Good leaders recognize that change is always needed in order for improvement to occur, but the process is painful. Tragically, of all institutions, the local church is often one of the most resistant to innovative thought. We get set in our ways; we become comfortable in our worship; and then, we refuse to make changes. Those who are on the outside view this as arrogance, indicative of a "we have arrived" attitude, in need no input from others. A Navy, so mired in tradition that it refuses to change will soon become irrelevant. Can you imagine the sailing ships of John Paul Jones' era engaging the nuclear-powered vessels of our own? It is simply preposterous. While building on tradition, the U.S. Navy continues to improve its sailors and its ships, and in so doing, remains the number one sea power in the world. The changes that have taken place over the years have always been painful. Transitions from sail power to steam power to nuclear power were met with resistance every step of the way, but they were the right decisions.

In the same way, while building on the traditions of those who have gone before us, the Church needs to embrace change in order to remain on the cutting edge of discipleship. Songs that were sung in the 18th century may not be as relevant today. Clothing styles change, language changes, and social mores change. The church that does not recognize this soon becomes irrelevant. Thomas Jefferson's famous quote: "In matters of style, swim with the current; in matters of principle, stand like a rock"[10] certainly applies to church ministry. Only God is changeless. Sinners, made in His image, must constantly seek improvement in order to become the men and women He wants us to be. Church leadership must always recognize this and make the hard changes needed to improve worship and ministry for the people of God.

The great men and women of the Bible had a hunger for God; they were *"subjected to frustration ... in hope that the creation itself will be liberated from its bondage to decay and brought into the glorious freedom of the children of God"* (Ro. 8:20-21). We, like them, should never stop learning, never stop improving, and never cease striving after the perfection that will one day come. Even Jesus Himself, who told His followers to *"take my yoke upon you and learn from me"* (Mt. 11:29), *"grew in wisdom and stature, and in favor with God and men"* (Luke 2:52). Needless to say, leaders in His Church should always have an attitude humble enough to learn and willing enough to teach.

---

[10]http://www.brainyquote.com/quotes/quotes/t/thomasjeff121032.html.

PRINCIPLE TWO

BE TECHNICALLY AND TACTICALLY PROFICIENT

"The world is sleeping in the dark, that the church can't fight, cause it's asleep in the light"

KEITH GREEN[1]

This leadership principle involves the trait of knowledge. *Knowledge* is the understanding of a science or an art. It is the range of one's information, including professional knowledge, and an understanding of people.

The United States has the finest military force in the world, because the men and women who serve in the Armed Forces of our nation are led by men and women who are technically and tactically proficient. "They know their stuff." As a Surface Warfare Officer, I experienced first hand the proficiency of our men at sea. (There were only men serving on warships during my time of service as a Line Officer). We practiced engineering casualty control drills — what would happen if this pump or that engine failed. We practiced firefighting techniques — how to fight a fire that would occur if a helicopter were to crash on a flight deck, or if propulsion fuels ignited

[1]Keith Green, "Asleep in the Light," *No Compromise*, Sparrow Records, November 9, 1978.

in the engineering spaces. We practiced emergency breakaway procedures during underway replenishment operations — what to do if the ship refueling alongside suddenly lost steering control or had an engineering casualty. We learned how to navigate the ship if navigational satellites or other aids were rendered useless. We communicated by semaphore or Morse code if radio communications were lost. We maneuvered our ships in formation against simulated enemy forces. We practiced shore bombardment and missile launches; we evaded simulated torpedoes and practiced man overboard drills. All of this we did in order to be technically and tactically proficient, ready for any possible contingency the enemy, forces of nature, or even errors friendly forces might cause.

U.S. Marines continually hone their technical and tactical skills. Every Marine is a rifleman; most can disassemble and reassemble their M-16 in the dark. They adhere to strict safety rules, condition codes and commands to ensure professionalism[2]. Marines shoot with deadly accuracy because of continual training. (Each year they must qualify on the rifle, or their career as a Marine is severely threatened). In addition to the rifle, most Marines are experts in the use of various machine guns (240G, 50 caliber, and the 40 mm), squad automatic weapons, grenade launchers, anti-armor weapons (AT-4 missile), and the 9mm pistol (staff non-commissioned officers and above). The engineers with whom I worked are also ex-

---

[2]Safety Rules

These safety rules apply to all weapons at all times, and must never be violated

Rule #1 Treat every weapon as if it were loaded.

Rule #2 Never point a weapon at anything you do not intend to shoot.

Rule #3 Keep finger straight and off the trigger until you are ready to fire.

Rule #4 Keep weapon on safe until you intend to fire.

Condition Codes

A weapon's readiness/safety status is described by one of four conditions. The steps in the loading and unloading process take the weapon through four specific conditions which indicate the weapon's readiness for live fire.

Condition 1: To place a weapon in condition 1, a round must be in position to be fired and the safety must be on.

Condition 2: To place a weapon in condition 2, a round must be in position to be fired, the weapon's action must be closed, and the hammer must be forward. (This condition only applies to weapons that have external hammers.)

Condition 3: To place a weapon in condition 3, ammunition is in position to be chambered, the chamber is empty, the action is closed, and the safety is on.

Condition 4: To place a weapon in condition 4, all ammunition is removed, the chamber is empty, the action is closed, and the safety is on

Commands

"UNLOAD" is the command used to take a weapon from any condition to condition 4. "LOAD" is the command used to take a weapon from condition 4 to condition 3. "MAKE READY" is the command used to take a weapon from condition 2 or 3 to condition 1. "MAKE SAFE" is the command used to take a weapon from condition 1 to condition 3.

Marine Battle Skills Training Handbook, Book 2, PVT-LCPL, Individual Combat Basic Tasks, (Arlington, Virginia: Marine Corps Institute, January 1993), p.1..

perts in mine warfare and plastic explosives. Marines navigate by land, with and without the use of satellites; they perform first aid; they communicate by radio; they understand how to survive in a nuclear, biological or chemical war; they know how to maneuver for a long time with little food or rest; they are in wonderful physical condition; they can perform hand to hand combat; they can be rapidly inserted and extracted by helicopter; they can repel off mountains and can undergo all sorts of rigid swim qualifications. These are all technical skills.

Marines take these technical skills and use them tactically. They undergo rigid training in snowy mountainous areas, moving on snowshoes, skis, or tracked vehicles. They train for jungle warfare. They practice patrolling in an urban setting or in the desert. They are able to make amphibious landings on hostile beaches in the middle of the night. They understand the capabilities of the enemy, and train for every contingency. (One of the most interesting trips I made with one of the companies in my battalion was to the National Training Center in Fort Irwin, California. At that huge army base, Marines and Army personnel train against fully operational machinery and weapons that had been produced in the former Soviet Union. These weapons — tanks, personnel carriers, field guns, and various hand-held arms, captured in sundry military engagements over the years — are still in use today by many of the nations hostile to the U.S.). They learn the value of patience (one of the most common expressions you will hear in the military is "hurry up and wait"). There is an opportune time to strike. If you are impatient, you may lose tactical advantage. Marines are ready for any possible attack, in any environment, that enemy forces might throw at them. Tactical and technical proficiency proficient saves lives.

There is a very excellent example of soldiers in the Bible who were both technically and tactically proficient. In the Old Testament book of Joshua, the Scripture records a stunning victory the Israelites had over the inhabitants of Jericho. Following this spectacular victory, Joshua made a serious tactical error in underestimating the strength of the Amorites who were occupying the neighboring city of Ai. Spies were sent out to do reconnaissance of the region, and upon their return, they informed their leader that, *"Not all the people will have to go up against Ai. Send two or three thousand men to take it and do not weary all the people for only a few men are there."* Joshua followed the advice of the spies, and as a result, the Israelites were routed. They were chased from the city, and struck down on the slopes. As a result, *"the hearts of the people melted and became like water."* Joshua was devastated, and in his grief questioned God as to why such a thing could happen. The LORD's answer was pretty clear. *"Israel has sinned; they have violated my covenant ... they have taken some of the devoted things; they have lied, they have put them with their own possessions. That is why the Israelites cannot stand against their enemies.... Go, consecrate the people. Tell them, 'Consecrate yourselves in preparation for tomorrow'"* (Josh. 7:3-13). The nation of Israel presumed upon God. They neither prepared themselves for battle nor practiced the skills that would be needed to defeat a cunning enemy. As a result of the sobering defeat, Joshua and his armies regrouped, reevaluated, and aligned themselves closer to the will of God.

Following a time of corporate repentance, the LORD again spoke to His people and offered a strategic plan that resulted in the utter destruction of the city of Ai. First of all, Joshua was to take his whole army. The Israelites were to be at full strength. Thirty thousand of their best fighting men were given orders and sent out at night. These were to sit and wait in ambush behind the city. The balance of Joshua's army would then march on Ai, and when the men of the city came out against them, the Israelites were to flee. After the Amorites were lured out, those waiting in ambush were to rise up, take the city, and set it on fire. As the plan worked out, *"All the men of Ai were called to pursue them ... and were lured away from the city."* Joshua then held up the javelin that was in his hand and *"As soon as he did this, the men in the ambush rose quickly from their position and rushed forward. They entered the city and captured it and quickly set it on fire."* When the men of Ai looked back, it was too late; *"they had no chance to escape in any direction ... they were caught in the middle, with Israelites on both sides. Israel cut them down, leaving neither survivors nor fugitives."* As a result of technical and tactical proficiency, the young nation had achieved a stunning victory over the inhabitants of the land (Josh. 8:1-29).

American Christians often lack the technical and tactical skills required for spiritual warfare. In fact, our lack of basic Bible knowledge is frightening. Very few of our young people even know the story. As a pastor in a college town in the 1990's, I enjoyed the large influx of college students who attended our church services. For most, it was an entirely new experience. When I had the opportunity to meet with them individually, it was almost always necessary to explain the basic makeup of the Bible to them. I had to explain the reason for the division between the Old and New Testaments, and how to distinguish a chapter from a verse. Most had never read the Bible. Years later, as a Navy chaplain, I found this trend even more evident. I created a check-in sheet for the new Marines joining the battalion to which I had been assigned. The men ranged in age from 18-30. Most were under 25. Included on the check-in sheet were four questions.

Question 1: What is the meaning of Easter?
Question 2: What is the meaning of Passover?
Question 3: What is the meaning of Christmas?
Question 4: What is the meaning of Good Friday?

Out of the 218 Marines and Sailors who responded, 186 indicated that they had some sort of church background; but only 96 of them understood the significance of Easter Sunday, the most important holiday of the Christian faith. 7 individuals thought that Good Friday was the day Christ rose from the dead, and 9 indicated that Easter was the day of the crucifixion. Only 8 out of the 218 individuals got all four questions correct. I suspect that this is an accurate indicator of American culture as a whole.[3]

This is a sad commentary on the effectiveness of our churches, but it is also an exciting evangelistic opportunity. Most young people are looking for answers. The materialism and the pursuit of pleasure taught by our culture do not satisfy the deepest yearnings of the soul. Only the gospel of Jesus Christ is able to fill that void.

The Old Testament prophet Hosea writes: "*my people are destroyed from lack of knowledge. Because you have rejected knowledge, I also reject you as my priests; because you have ignored the law of your God, I also will ignore your children*" (4:6). If the Church begins to develop the technical and tactical skills needed to engage our culture, we will start to win some of the fierce spiritual battles that face us, and revival will sweep the

---

[3]Survey ran from Nov. 1999 – June 2001. Correct responses by faith group follow:

Faith group	# in group	Quest. 1	Quest. 2	Quest. 3	Quest. 4
Roman Catholic	*70*	*36*	6	57	13
Baptist	49	24	3	30	5
No Preference	32	11	2	28	4
Christian	25	13	3	20	4
Methodist	*11*	6	1	10	2
Lutheran	*11*	7	2	9	3
Misc. *	*20*	10	4	15	5
Total	**218**	**107**	**21**	**169**	**36**

*Includes: Pentecostal (4); Church of God (1); Jewish (2); Child of God (1); Armenian Orthodox (1); 7th Day Adventist (1); Church of Christ (1); Episcopalian (1); Wiccan (2); Latter Day Saint (3); Presbyterian (3)

land. If the Church does not rise up, the Christian faith in the United States will soon be a distant memory. We need to be technically and tactically proficient in order to advance God's Kingdom upon the earth. Needed technical skills include a good knowledge of Scripture, and a good understanding of theology. There are many Christians who have a good theological background as a result of catechism training experienced earlier in their lives, but have a very poor knowledge of the Bible. Conversely, there are Christians who have many passages of Scripture memorized, who have actually read through the Bible on numerous occasions, but have a poor understanding as to how it fits together. Good technical skills for the Christian include both Bible knowledge and theology. A leader should know the difference between a concordance, a catechism, and a commentary, and how to use each. Additionally, servants of the Most High should be students of history. What insights did the great men and women of God of an earlier era have? What mistakes did they make? How were they effective technically and tactically in engaging their culture?

Tactically, we need to understand those forces that oppose the gospel message and learn how to engage them. The military concept of knowing one's enemy is very important. We need to understand the belief systems of other religions, how they differ from traditional Christian teaching, and how to reach those who do not believe in Christ on terms to which they can relate. Training should take place in our churches on how to reach out to groups who have expressed hostility toward the things of God. And like the men and women in the military, we should be patient. As the Marine knows how to control his weapon, the Christian should know when to speak and when to remain silent. God's word *"is ... sharper than any double-edged sword"* (Heb. 4:12), and through its effective use will accomplish that which He desires (Is. 55:11). When Jesus commissioned the seventy, He told them that they should be "*wise as serpents, and harmless as doves*" (Mt. 10:16, KJV). His words apply to us as we grow in our technical abilities, and learn how to use them tactically for the glory of God.

It is especially important for leaders in the Church to be technically and tactically proficient. A deacon should know the things for which he is responsible. He should know how to talk to people, how to run a meeting, and how to get work accomplished. The elder, the usher, the trustee, the treasurer, the member of church council – anyone who takes a position of leadership — should know what her job entails, and hone her technical and tactical skills accordingly, in order that the church she serves will be effective in ministering to the local community.

Principle Three

Develop a Sense of Responsibility Among Your Subordinates

You and these people who come to you will only wear yourselves out. The work is too heavy for you; you cannot handle it alone

Exodus 18:18

This leadership principle involves the trait of loyalty. *Loyalty* is defined as the quality of faithfulness to country, the Corps, the unit, to one's seniors, subordinates, and peers.

The military is very good at practicing this principle. Men or women who are in leadership positions can easily become combat casualties at the beginning of a conflict. If others are not trained to take their places, the battle will be lost. At the United States Naval Academy, first class midshipmen (the Senior Class) – and not the commissioned officers stationed at Annapolis – are the ones who exercise authority in running the day-to-day operations of the Brigade. In the Marine Corps, the lowest ranking members of a platoon are often singled out to call cadence for the entire unit. One of the most impressive ceremonies I observed while serving with the Marines was when a Master Sergeant with over twenty years of service requested that his retirement ceremony be conducted entirely by lower-ranking enlisted men. This was a challenging request, because normally Staff Sergeants and Gunnery Sergeants conduct these types of ceremonies. Marines are very precise on military drill and on the proper wearing of their uniforms. Hours are spent in preparation for such significant events as these, and they need to be conducted properly. But for this particular ceremony, Corporals and Sergeants would be giving the orders. The young Marines drilled hard and presented one of the most beautiful celebrations I had seen in a long time. But a far more important thing happened that day. The experience had trained a new generation of Marines, confident in their abilities to lead others. The old Marine had inculcated a sense of responsibility in his subordinates by allowing them to take the lead roles in a highly visible command event. This sets an excellent example for our churches.

I remember a conversation with a dentist who was a faithful believer in Christ, active in a local congregation. I met him on my day off, while visiting my dad. He seemed utterly astonished that I was able to take a day off. The pastor of his church (which was quite a bit smaller than my own congregation) apparently never did. I asked the dentist what would happen to his morale if he worked seven days a week and never rested. My question caused him to pause, and I assured him that my state of mind would be quite similar to his if I spent every day at the office.

One of the biggest mistakes made by pastors and by local churches is the failure to develop leaders. In some churches, everyone in the congregation looks to the pastor or to a few significant lay leaders for all decision making. This can be heady stuff for any one individual, and the person who is charismatic by nature can flourish in such an environment.

But if the leader fails to delegate authority to others, much of the ministry he puts together over the years will collapse upon his departure.

Jethro, father-in-law to Moses, taught the principle of delegation to his famous son-in-law, who was arguably Israel's best leader ever. And Jethro was not even an Israelite; he was a priest of Midian. The following story from the book of Exodus illustrates how servants of the Most High have much to learn, even from those who do not follow the God of Scripture. Moses was the wisest of the Israelites, and the people came day and night for the adjudication of their affairs. But Moses was getting burned out. Jethro's advice was needed and timely:

> *"What you are doing is not good. You and these people who come to you will only wear yourselves out. The work is too heavy for you; you cannot handle it alone. You must be the people's representative before God and bring their disputes to him. Teach them the decrees and laws, and show them the way to live and the duties they are to perform. But select capable men from all the people – men who fear God, trustworthy men who hate dishonest gain – and appoint them as officials over thousands, hundreds, fifties and tens. Have them serve as judges for the people at all times, but have them bring every difficult case to you; the simple cases they can decide themselves. That will make your load lighter, because they will share it with you. If you do this and God so commands, you will be able to stand the strain, and all these people will go home satisfied"*
>
> (Ex. 18:17-23).

In addition to freeing up Moses' precious time, Jethro's advice produced a new generation of leaders. Those to whom Moses had delegated authority now understood what God expected, and were able to assist their leader in carrying out the expectations of the Most High. Moses was able to focus on the big picture of leading the nation, while a sense of responsibility had been developed among hundreds of his subordinates. The people of God were much stronger as a result.

Jesus certainly understood this principle. He began with twelve men (Mt. 10:1-16) and invested them with great power. Later, the number was increased to seventy-two, each of whom was sent to proclaim the good news of the Kingdom of God (Luke 10:1-20). As Jesus' ministry developed, He ultimately empowered all who place their faith in Him (Mt. 28:16-18). During His earthly ministry, our Lord told his followers that they would do greater things than Him (John 14:12), and with the coming of the Holy Spirit (Acts 2), He empowered the entire Church. 2000 years of history back up His claim. Knowledge has been passed on to future generations through Church-established schools and universities. Great improvement in the quality of peoples' lives has arisen as a result of Church-driven social welfare systems, hospitals and nursing homes. Theological understanding has improved exponentially, a direct result of the labor of godly theologians and philosophers. The people to whom Christ delegated authority have accomplished far more than what Jesus did in His lifetime.

We have been given the awesome task of spreading the message of God's Kingdom. If we fail to develop a sense of responsibility among those who fill our pews, and rely only upon pastoral leadership, our congregations will die; but if we understand what it means to develop a sense of responsibility in others, our churches will influence their surrounding communities long into the future.

It can be rather daunting to delegate to others, especially if you want to ensure that things are done correctly. But the talented leader will learn to delegate. He/she will allow mistakes to be made in order for people to learn from them. An investment of time is required to train subordinates, but it will reap dividends. Followers will cultivate their own sense of mission. Leaders will know their jobs even better as a result of having taught it to others, and they will be freed up to focus on the visionary things so essential to success. Subordinates, knowing that they are trusted, will work very hard in making the organization successful.

Good military officers with whom I have spoken tell me that their role is to work themselves out of a job. If the leader is so able to train his people that his own job becomes unnecessary, he has succeeded. Who wants to rise up in rank if that means being chained to a desk for twenty hours a day, never seeing your family? Many talented individuals, with promising military careers before them, decided to leave the service after reflecting upon the massive workloads senior officers took upon themselves. The long hours were simply not worth it. Many pastors have resigned their ministries because they refused to delegate to others. Years of grinding labor, without rest, burns out even the strongest among us. If a leader is too busy to take vacation, to take a day off, or to go out and play some golf, something is wrong. Part of being a Christian involves enjoying the life God has given.

Successful leaders always develop a sense of responsibility among their subordinates. Leadership training at the Naval Academy provides us with two maxims very helpful in putting this principle into practice:

1) *Delegate authority but not responsibility*. The Captain of a ship cannot possibly be on the bridge all of the time. When he is not present, he delegates the authority to navigate his vessel to the Officer of the Deck. However, the Captain does not abdicate responsibility for the ship's safety. If the vessel runs aground when the Captain is in his quarters, the Officer of the Deck will be relieved from his post, but

so will the Captain. This delegation of authority develops a sense of responsibility in younger officers who will one day command ships of their own. In the local church, if authority is delegated to boards, committees, and lay leaders — empowering them to act as needed — ministry will continue to press on, even in the absence of a pastor.

There are great pressures to "do" ministry, and not train leaders. Our parishioners expect a quality product, and we feel called to deliver. It is so easy to get into the mindset of doing it yourself and neglect the enormous responsibility of training new generations of leaders. We may be able to do it better and quicker than those with whom we serve (a rather arrogant attitude!), but the long-term effects of such practice will be devastating. It is our divine responsibility to delegate. Let others make a few mistakes in ministry, just as we do, in order that they, too, might learn from them. In the same way as the Captain of a ship cannot always be on deck, neither can the pastor of a church always be on call. Others must be trained, and authority must be delegated, or the local church will collapse every time a charismatic pastor departs.

2) Praise in public; rebuke in private. The biggest mistake I ever made as a Surface Warfare Officer occurred in the South China Sea. Several months prior to the incident, our ship had been operating off the coast of Southern California. While standing night watches in friendly U.S. waters, flash message traffic (radio messages that require immediate action) regarding Soviet Bear aircraft flying from Vladivostok to North Vietnam was routinely delivered to the Officer of the Deck. (Bear aircraft are intelligence-gathering planes). These messages were typically ignored, because the intelligence involved events transpiring halfway around the world. I took leave while the ship made a transit from San Francisco to Guam, and later rejoined ship's company just as preparations were being made to get underway for a patrol in the South China Sea. Now, we were much closer to action!

One night, while standing the midwatch (midnight to 4:00 a.m.), a flash message arrived regarding a Soviet Bear aircraft flying from Vladivostok to North Vietnam. As was routine, I ignored the message, completed my watch, and went to bed. At about 4:30 a.m., the messenger of the watch abruptly wakened me from a sound sleep, banging loudly on my stateroom door. The Captain requested my immediate presence in his cabin. A Bear aircraft had just flown over the ship, and he was livid. Something routinely ignored in Southern California was of paramount importance in the South China Sea, and the Captain pointed that out in no uncertain terms. But he did it privately. I was not embarrassed in front of my peers or in the presence of those who served under me, and I learned a very valuable lesson. Everything the Commanding Officer ever had to say about me in public was praiseworthy, but his strongest rebukes took place behind closed doors.

So often in church meetings, people are skewered publicly, and nothing could be more harmful to the Body of Christ. There are skeletons in everyone's closet, and no one enjoys hearing about them in public. The Church preaches grace. When rebuke is necessary, it should be done privately and without public embarrassment.

In developing a sense of responsibility among subordinates, Marines cultivate loyalty to their country, to the institution in which they serve, and to the to individuals in it. One Marine often greets another with the expression, "Semper Fi," short for "*Semper Fidelis*," the motto of the Corps. The Latin expression means "always faithful," and its verbalization is a reminder: I will always be faithful to my country, my Corps, and my fellow Marine. How much more should the Christian leader be concerned about cultivating loyalty to Christ, to the Church, and to brothers and sisters in the faith!

The Old Testament book of Ruth records the great loyalty of the Moabite heroine towards her Jewish mother-in-law, Naomi. Ruth's husband, her brother-in-law, and her father-in-law had all died. Naomi, in her grief, urged Ruth to return to Moab to find another husband; but Ruth refused, resolving rather to remain loyal to her mother-in-law in the midst of terrible circumstances. Her immortal words, "*Don't urge me to leave you or to turn back from you. Where you go I will go, and where you stay I will stay. Your people will be my people and your God my God*" (Ruth 1:16) are often read during wedding ceremonies. They are words of loyalty, a quality we want to develop in ourselves and in others.

No one is indispensable in the military or in the Church. A sense of responsibility must be developed in others, because the day is coming when we will no longer be around. When we invite young people to participate in the meetings of the church, to lead worship, and to coordinate major ministry events, we train others to take our place, while touching the future with the most life-transforming message our world has ever heard.

Principle Four

Make sound and timely decisions

Choose you this day whom ye will serve ... but as for me and my house, we will serve the LORD.
Joshua 24:15, KJV

This leadership principle involves the traits of decisiveness and judgment. *Decisiveness* means that the leader has the ability to make decisions promptly and to announce them in a clear, forceful manner. *Judgment* means that a leader will have the ability to weigh facts and possible solutions on which to base sound decisions.

How often have you heard the Biblical expression *"Do not judge, or you too will be judged"* (Mt. 7:1)? More than likely, the words were used out of context. The teaching Jesus offered on the subject of judging also included the words *"For in the same way you judge others, you will be judged"* (Mt. 7:2). In other words, Jesus was not saying that it is wrong to judge. He was saying, "be careful how you judge, for you will be judged by the very same standards you use on others." To make a sound and timely decision is to make a judgment. Failing to make a sound and timely decision often can be paralyzing. At issue, then, is the importance of being consistent and fair in the judgments we do make. The sixth amendment to the U.S. Constitution says almost the same thing. A man accused of a crime has the right to a speedy trial, a right to a sound and timely decision concerning his case.

Decision-making is part of life. We make decisions continually, some of them are good and some are bad. The key to good leadership is to make the right decision at the right time. Aristotle calls this prudence. In one of my better moments as a Surface Warfare Officer, I made a sound and timely decision that saved thousands of dollars of structural damage to the ship to which I was assigned. Human life may have been spared as well.

Underway replenishment at sea (UNREP) is a way of life for the Surface Warfare Officer. Ships need to refuel, to replenish food supplies, and to take on such items as potable water, aircraft parts, mail and ammunition. (A ship at sea cannot pull into port every time such items are needed). The supply ship sets a course and speed for the UNREP operation, and ships needing replenishment take position to its stern. At the appropriate time, the receiving ship will make its approach alongside, and begin to receive fuel oil or potable water through large six-inch hoses. Food, ammunition and other supplies are delivered via a trolley system attached to a thick steel cable connecting the two ships. Often there are four or more refueling/ replenishment stations, and it is not infrequent for two ships to be receiving supplies from one supply vessel at the same time. Ships are often alongside each other for many hours. Needless to say, the operation is extremely dangerous. The receiving ship needs to travel at the exact same speed as the supply ship, and a separation of 120-160 feet must be maintained between the two vessels. To accomplish such precision, the Officer of the Deck on the receiving ship adjusts the speed of his vessel by asking for an increase or decrease of one RPM on the ship's propeller(s). Course changes are made in one-degree increments on the ship's compass.

Imagine the shock on the face of my Commanding Officer when he overheard me give a right full rudder order while alongside a large oiler! He rushed over to my side of the bridge and noticed that we were exactly where we were supposed to be in relation to the supply ship. The oiler supplying us with fuel oil had lost steering control, and in order for our ship to maintain the proper distance from her, large rudder angles and engine order telegraph commands were required. The Captain allowed me to keep the conn, emergency breakaway procedures were initiated, and we survived the ordeal without incident. A situation had developed where a sound and timely decision was needed, and I was proud to have done the right thing.

The Bible is filled with examples of sound and timely decisions. Moses made one at the Red Sea. The Israelites, encamped near Pi Hahiroth, were trapped by mountains on one side, the desert on the other, and the sea in front of them. Pharaoh's armies were close behind, and the Israelites were terrified. Moses was very decisive:

> *'"Do not be afraid. Stand firm and you will see the deliverance the LORD will bring you today. The Egyptians you see today you will never see again. The LORD will fight for you; you need only to be still" ... Then Moses stretched out his hand over the sea, and all that night the LORD drove the sea back with a strong east wind and turned it into dry land. The waters were divided, and the Israelites went through the sea on dry ground, with a wall of water on their right and on their left'*
>
> (Ex. 14:13-14, 21-22).

His decision on that day saved the nation of Israel and resulted in the destruction of the armies of Pharaoh.

Esther, likewise, made a sound and timely decision that saved her people. Haman, the wicked advisor to the Persian king Xerxes, hated Jews, and was successful in persuading the king to sign a decree ordering their extermination. When Mordecai, Esther's uncle heard of the matter, he urged his niece to speak to the king and have the decree rescinded. But Esther hesitated. It was a very serious matter to enter into the king's presence uninvited. Even the Scripture records: *"All the king's officials and the people of the royal provinces know that for any man or woman who approaches the king in the inner court without being summoned the king has but one law: that he be put to death. The only exception to this is for the king to extend the gold scepter to him and spare his life"* (Esth. 4:11). Mordecai then spoke these immortal words:

> *"Do not think that because you are in the king's house you alone of all the Jews will escape. For if you remain silent at this time, relief and deliverance for the Jews will arise from another place, but you and your father's family will perish. And who knows but that you have come to royal position for such a time as this"*
>
> (ESTH. 4:13-14).

Esther made the decision to appeal for her people. Fortunately, Xerxes extended the gold scepter, Haman's wicked plot was exposed, and the Jewish people were saved. A sound and timely decision had been made.

Ultimately, our Lord made the sound and timely decision to go to the cross. Jesus was painfully aware of His destiny; He knew the exact day He was going to die. Throughout His earthly ministry, Jesus reminded His disciples that "His time was not yet," or that "His hour was not yet come" (John 2:4). In fulfillment of the Scriptures, the Lamb of God, who came to take away the sins of the world (John 1:29), lay down His life during the feast of Passover. His sound and timely decision brings salvation to all who believe.

The Bible is also replete with stories of men and women who failed to make a sound and timely decision. Adam failed to drive the serpent out of the garden. His inaction led to the fall of the human race (Gen. 3). Samson made a wrongheaded decision in succumbing to Delilah's temptations, resulting in his own physical harm and imprisonment (Ju. 16). Jephthah made a foolish and rash vow, placing the life of his own daughter at risk (Ju. 11:31-40). Judas decided to take the money, resulting in his own eternal perdition (Mt. 26:14-24).

So often in our churches we become paralyzed and are unable to make decisions. We worry so much about offending others that we do nothing, or we make wrongheaded decisions counterproductive to ministry. *Robert's Rules of Order* is a wonderful tool often utilized in church business meetings, but frequently it is used to "table" issues that require immediate action. Decision-making involves change; it involves pain, and it is often uncomfortable. It is easier to resist change than to be an instrument of it; but if needed changes are not made, institutions perish. The people murmured against Moses, Esther feared for her life, and Jesus was called a madman. Nearly all of the signers of the Declaration of Independence paid a dear price for their decision to break away from the rule of Great Britain. Nine of the 56 signers were killed in action in the ensuing war. Five died as prisoners of war, twelve had their homes burned, several lost sons, one man's wife died in prison, and sixteen were bankrupted.[1]

Would history have been any different if these leaders had not come against the popular opinions of their day and made prudent and timely choices? Leadership certainly involves "calling the shots," but it also means, "taking a few

---

[1]*Parade, The Sunday Newspaper Magazine,* (New York: Parade Pubs., July 2, 2000), p. 4.

shots," as well. To paraphrase Abraham Lincoln: "You can please all of the people some of the time; and you can even please some of the people all of the time; but you can't please all of the people all the time."[2]

At the Navy Chaplain School, new chaplains are given a course entitled "Basic Officer Leadership Training." Part of the curriculum involves a discussion concerning four decision-making styles:

1. authoritative — I'll decide
2. consultative — let's talk, then I'll decide
3. facilitative — let's talk, then we'll decide
4. delegative — you decide[3]

Church leaders need to understand the type of leadership required for any given situation. If a body of believers is planning long-range strategy on how to impact a particular community with the gospel message, either consultative or facilitative decision making is best. Some decisions need to be made quickly; there may be little time for discussion. In such situations, an authoritative decision by the pastor or by an appropriate board/official would be the most effective. Failing to act at the appropriate time can be disastrous for the health of a local congregation.

The most important decision an individual will ever make is to follow Jesus Christ. There comes a time in everyone's life, when God's revelation is so clear, that a decision must be made. Will I choose to follow the true and the living God, and find a peace that surpasses all human understanding (Phil. 4:7) or will I be like Cain of the Old Testament

---

[2]What Lincoln actually said was, "you may fool all the people some of the time; you can even fool some of the people all the time; but you can't fool all of the people all the time."
John Bartlett, *Bartlett's Familiar Quotations,* (Boston: Little, Brown and Company, Fourteenth Edition, Fourth Printing, 1968), p. 641.
[3]*Student Guide for Basic Officer Leadership Course,* (Pensacola, FL: Chief of Naval Education and Training, May 1997), p. 1-4-5.

(Gen. 4:14) and choose to harden my heart against the One who made me in His image, restlessly wandering the face of the earth all of my life? Like Joshua of old, I want to make a sound and timely decision: "*as for me and my household, we will serve the LORD*" (Josh. 24:15).

Principle Five

Set the Example

"We make men without chests and expect of them virtue and enterprise. We laugh at honour and are shocked to find traitors in our midst. We castrate and bid the geldings be fruitful."

C.S. Lewis[1]

This leadership principle involves the traits of bearing, enthusiasm, and integrity. *Bearing* means that a leader will create a favorable impression in carriage, appearance, and personal conduct at all times. *Enthusiasm* is defined as the display of sincere interest and exuberance in the performance of duty. *Integrity* means that the leader is upright in character, sound in moral principles and is truthful and honest.

One of the most grueling training events for the United States Marine is the conditioning hike. Informally, the Marine calls it a "hump." The hump is a fast-paced hike, gener-

[1]C.S. Lewis, *The Abolition of Man,* (New York: Macmillan Publishing Co., Inc., Seventeeth Printing, 1978), p. 35.

ally over hilly or mountainous terrain that can be anywhere from 10-25 miles in length. On the Marine's back is a fully loaded pack that includes such items as a tent shelter, stakes, spare uniforms, a spade, canteens of water, a first aid kit, a sleeping bag and a mat. The Marine wears a helmet and a flak jacket and carries either a 16mm rifle or a 9mm pistol. The total ensemble weighs approximately 75 pounds. By the time the hump is over, the Marine is exhausted and totally dehydrated. His camouflage uniform is thoroughly drenched with perspiration.

The most impressive part about the hump is its leadership. The commanding officer of the unit is up front, setting the pace for the entire battalion or regiment. The CO is generally a Lieutenant Colonel or a Colonel, and is often the oldest man present. He sets the example for hundreds of younger Marines who are less than half his age. As the young men in the rear of a battalion struggle to keep up, a very determined man who keeps the standards high for all inspires them.

Jesus set a perfect example for all of us. His bearing was flawless, his enthusiasm for the things of the Kingdom unfailing, and His integrity unquestioned. One of the most poignant stories of the New Testament occurred at the Last Supper. For three years, the followers of our Lord had seen miracles beyond their wildest imaginations: they had seen Jesus restore sight to those who were blind, they had seen Him cause the lame to walk, and dead men to rise. He turned water into wine at a wedding feast; He took a few loaves and fishes and fed thousands; He quieted storms at the sound of His voice, and walked on water. With no formal schooling, He baffled the most brilliant scholars, and after living in very close quarters with a devoted band of followers, no one ever saw Him do anything morally wrong. Who knows what other miraculous things He accomplished that were never recorded in the annals of the New Testament? Yet, at the Last Supper, this powerful man knelt down and washed the feet of His disciples — performing the most menial of tasks, normally assigned to household slaves. Peter vehemently protested this act of servitude, but Jesus persisted. When He finished washing all of the disciples' feet, Jesus then declared: *"I have set you an example that you should do as I have done for you"* (John 13:15). The example was one of service to others. Of all of Jesus' teachings, one of His most important was to the twelve men who ultimately brought the gospel message to the entire world: service to others is critical to good leadership.

Nearly all the world's religions recognize the importance of setting a good example. Confucius left his followers with "Chun tzu" — the concept of being a gentleman. When there is righteousness in the heart, there will be beauty in character. When there is beauty in character, there will be harmony in the home. When there is harmony in the home, there will be order in the nation. When there is order in the nation, there will be peace in the world.[2] The example set at each level inspires a greater good.

In Buddhism, the fourth step of the noble 8-fold path involves "right behavior." To eliminate the desires that control our lives, we seek change in the direction of selflessness and charity. Buddha suggests we cultivate lives that do not kill, that are not unchaste, that do not steal, lie, or drink intoxicating beverages.[3] Such behavior, unfortunately, does not eliminate desire from the human condition, but the Buddhist ethic often serves as an example to the follower of Christ. If Christians do not set a godly example for others,

---

[2]see footnote 2, p. 161.
[3]see footnote 7, p. 165.

seekers may choose to follow Buddha rather than the One who is able to present us sinless before the throne of the Most High.

Setting a good example means that one's *bearing* is praiseworthy. The leader presents himself/herself in such a way as to create a favorable impression. The physical descriptions of the lover and the beloved in the Song of Solomon are not mere words (n. 4:1-7; 5:10-16). Although it is very true that God judges the heart, outward appearances are of utmost importance; humans make all sorts of judgments based upon them. Christian leaders who do not take care of their own temple — who eat too much, drink too much, or fail to exercise do not bear good witness to their faith. The Navy and the Marine Corps, especially in the officer community, place much emphasis on outward appearance. Uniforms are striking when worn properly. They are made of expensive material and great care is taken to maintain them in top condition. The old saying, "you only have one chance at a first impression," is very true in our relationships with others, and often our first impressions are based solely on one's outward appearance.

The Christian, of course, has a message that goes much deeper than such externals, but it is so counterproductive to our cause when, because of a poor personal example, we drive others away long before the opportunity arises to speak. Like it or not, Christians are closely watched, especially when the chips are down. Others want to know if we have a message able to withstand the trials and rigors of this life. Often, the only witness we may have in this regard is through the personal example we set: the language we use, and the manner in which we treat others. In the military, it is impossible to escape the close observation of others. We live together in such confined quarters, that the motives of one's heart are quickly revealed. The same is true for the believer in Jesus Christ. Our personal deportment may be the only Bible some will ever read. A poor personal example may cause those outside of the Kingdom to close the book, never again willing to investigate the claims of Christ.

Setting a good example means that *one's enthusiasm* for the mission is high. (The word is of Greek origin, meaning, "to put God in"). Marines often greet each other with an enthusiastic "Ooh-rah," an expression that means, "I'm motivated and ready to go." As a chaplain, serving with the Marines, I often ask, "how's it going?" More often than not they respond with a one-word answer: "outstanding." Ask about some aspect of a task in which they are involved, and you will learn a wealth of information, more than you ever expected. Granted, for some, the expressions may be parrot-like responses; but for many they are genuine. Regardless, servants of the Most High can learn much from an institution characterized by enthusiasm for mission.

The Bible speaks much of enthusiasm. Caleb was enthusiastic about going into the Promised Land (Nu. 13:30). King David was enthusiastic as his priests brought the Ark of the Covenant into Jerusalem (1 Chr. 15:16-28). The author of Ecclesiastes writes: *"Whatever your hand finds to do, do it with all your might"* (Ecc. 9:10). Paul writes to the Romans: *"Never be lacking in zeal, but keep your spiritual fervor, serving the Lord"* (Ro. 12:11). We are to be enthusiastic in remembering the poor (Gal. 2:10), in keeping unity in the Church (Eph. 4:3), in studying the Scriptures (2 Ti. 2:15), and in living a virtuous life (2 Pe. 3:14). Ralph Waldo Emerson once said:

> "Enthusiasm is one of the most powerful engines of success. When you do a thing, do it with your might. Put your whole soul into it. Stamp it with

> your own personality. Be active, be energetic, be enthusiastic and faithful, and you will accomplish your object. Nothing great was ever achieved without enthusiasm."[4]

I am enthusiastic about the work I do as a leader in the Church of Jesus Christ. I am excited when others embrace the gospel message. I am energized when our houses of worship are filled people who zealously want to attend, where strangers feel comfortable congregating in order to investigate the claims of Christ. We have the greatest message in the world, and we serve the great God who created us in His image. For the Christian leader to act without passion or enthusiasm is as destructive as teaching false doctrine. Charles Swindoll declares,

> 'I get weary of believers who live their entire lives with such long faces and nothing but woe-is-me words pouring from their mouths ... I look at some who claim to be "happy within," and wonder if maybe they were baptized in freshly squeezed lemon juice ... Each time I look up and see Dr. Dryasdust and his wife Grimly making their way toward me, I find myself wanting to run and hide or, better, be raptured out!'[5]

Setting a good example means that one's *integrity* is intact. The honor code at West Point, the oldest military institution in our country, reads as follows: "A cadet will not

---

[4]John Bartlett, *Bartlett's Familiar Quotations,* (Boston: Little, Brown and Company, Fourteenth Edition, Fourth Printing, 1968), p. 607.

[5]Charles R. Swindoll, *Maybe it's time to ... Laugh Again, Experience Outrageous Joy,* (NewYork: Walker and Company, First Large Print Edition, 1993), p. 283.

lie,steal, cheat or tolerate those who do."[6] This time-honored code summarizes clearly what it means to be a person of integrity. "Integrity" means "oneness, completeness, wholeness." In mathematics, integers are whole numbers, which cannot be divided into fractions. Likewise, our lives are not to be marked by divided loyalties. We are persons of honor; our actions must be consistent with our words; and we must always do the right thing, even when no one is watching. As our Leader declares, *"A good tree cannot bear bad fruit"* (Mt. 7:18).

While attending seminary in Philadelphia, I made a living by painting houses and by doing odd repair jobs. On one occasion I contracted for work to do interior painting. I received the job because others knew that I was going to be a minister and had passed on my name. The bid was for $1500. I asked the homeowner for $500 down, $500 when halfway through the job, and the balance upon successful completion. The homeowner pulled out a roll of $100 bills, quickly peeled off several, and gave them to me. In counting them, I discovered that he gave me $600 rather than the agreed upon $500. I pointed out his error, and gave back $100. A few weeks later, this man (who was involved in the Mafia) was arrested for firebombing the home of someone who had double-crossed him in a business deal. Looking back on the incident, I am certain he was "checking me out," when he gave me too much. I was very thankful that I had not compromised my integrity!

One of the most spectacular events in the military is the change of command ceremony. All of the stops are pulled out. The troops enter the parade field, unit-by-unit, dressed in their finest uniforms, carrying the national ensign and appropriate battle colors. The parade field itself is decorated

---

[6]*Parade, The Sunday Newspaper Magazine,* (New York: Parade Pubs., May 7, 2000), p.7.

with the flags of every state in the Union. VIPs sit under a colorful canopy, enjoying the patriotic music of a military band, observing the sharp precision of manual of arms displays, and listening to the eloquent speeches of powerful military leaders. Sharply dressed escorts deliver bouquets of roses to the spouses of the incoming and outgoing commanders, and cannons sound the appropriate number of rounds to honor those present. The ceremony culminates with the command "Pass in Review," and all of the units, with great military precision, march past incoming and outgoing commanders. The power and beauty of such ceremonies are breathtaking. Many people have made the decision to join the military based solely on the pageantry of such events. But how well do the units involved behave when the spotlight is turned off? Do they possess the prerequisite skills needed to defend their country? Is morale high within each? Are people treated with dignity and respect? It may quite easy to fool the general public with occasional displays of military prowess, but integrity demands that the inner workings of a military unit line up with outward displays.

The same principle holds true for the local church. Even if the worship music is of Nashville-grade quality and the oratory emanating from the pulpit is top-notch, if the Spirit of God is absent, the whole program lacks integrity. How well do those who worship there honor God? Do they love the stranger who comes into their midst? Is the behavior on Wednesday afternoons consistent with what is professed on Sunday mornings? Integrity demands that we live consistent lives, both in and out of the spotlight of the worship hour.

Military service is a public trust. Members of the Armed Forces are not to participate in unethical or illegal behavior. In addition, we are to "refrain from any appearance of impropriety."[7] To guide its sailors in this regard, the Department of the Navy lists standards of conduct to which all personnel must adhere. Some of these standards include:

1. Do nothing that conflicts with your Navy duties and responsibilities.
2. Don't sell things to subordinates.
3. Don't give gifts to superiors or solicit from subordinates.
4. Don't accept gifts from defense contractors.
5. No gambling on government property.
6. Pay your debts on time.
7. Do not use government property for personal use.

The Bible tells us to *"abstain from all appearance of evil"* (1 Th. 5:22, KJV). In tailoring the Navy's standards of conduct to a Church context, we might suggest:

1. Do nothing that conflicts with your Christian duties and responsibilities. (i.e. What Would Jesus Do?)
2. Don't take advantage of the poor.
3. Don't try to manipulate church policies with your money. Don't use threats against people to "bring them into the fold."
4. Don't seek to become a power broker in the political world.
5. Do not tempt the Lord your God.
6. Be a forgiving person.
7. Do not use the name "Christian" for financial gain.

---

[7]Secretary of the Navy Instruction 5370.2J.

The man Job serves as an excellent Biblical example of one who did not compromise his integrity. Messenger after messenger came to recount a string of bad news: A band of thugs stole his oxen and donkeys. A firestorm from heaven killed his sheep and his servants. A raiding party stole his camels; and finally, a windstorm demolished the home of his oldest son, killing all of his children. Rather stoically, Job declared, *"Naked I came from my mother's womb, and naked I will depart. The LORD gave and the LORD has taken away; may the name of the LORD be praised"* (Job 1:21). Later, when Satan took even his health from him, Job's wife suggested that he *"curse God and die."* Job's response? *You are talking like a foolish woman. Shall we accept good from God, and not trouble?"* (Job 2:9-10). Through all of these terrible calamities, Job never lost integrity.

Polycarp (c. 69 – c. 155 AD), an early bishop in the ancient church of Smyrna (a city located in present day Turkey), is a man whose faithful testimony has coursed through the strands of time. In the midst of an ongoing empire-wide persecution, Polycarp was asked to renounce his faith in Christ or lose his life. The elderly man chose the latter, leaving his final words recorded for posterity: "For eighty-six years I have been his servant, and he has done me no wrong. How can I blaspheme my King who saved me?"[8] Polycarp's life and death serve as a sterling example of integrity.

Military commanders expect high standards of behavior from the personnel who serve in their commands, and a good leader enforces those standards. But woe to the man or woman who exercises strong discipline yet does not personally adhere to it. The troops immediately recognize such hypocrisy, and the consequences are devastating. Command

---

[8]J.B. Lightfoot and J.R. Harmer, translators; Michael W. Holmes, editor, *The Apostolic Fathers, Second Edition,* "The Martyrdom of Polycarp," (Grand Rapids, Michigan: Baker Book House, 1989), p. 139.

morale is destroyed, respect for authority shattered, and unit cohesion weakened. Scandals such as cheating on exams at military academies, affairs between senior officers and the spouses of their subordinates, and paranoid behavior of high ranking officers are all examples of how a lack of integrity crushes the spirit of close knit communities. The integrity of the leader always has a reverberating impact throughout a military command. In like manner, it is essential for Church leaders to live their lives with integrity. High ethical standards will result in healthy congregations; poor personal integrity will bring shame upon the name of our Lord and upon the message of His Kingdom.

It is expected that the Chaplain serve as a moral compass for the unit in which he or she serves. To assist in this, instructors at the Navy Chaplain School teach three different ethical theories to Chaplain Candidates. The first, *cognitive moral reasoning*, is a school of thought that emphasizes doing one's duty. Cognitive moral reasoning involves thinking things through. Adherents are not to do anything based upon feelings or emotions. They are to reflect upon what duty requires in any given situation, and then make the appropriate moral decision to do the right thing. The second ethical theory, *non-cognitive moral reasoning*, is based on feelings. In this school of thought, the end justifies the means. Non-cognitive moral reasoning is utilitarian; it is authentic. A certain way of behaving has always been successful in the past, and it would be silly to deviate from it in the future. The third school of ethical theory, *the divine command theory*, is based on the revelation of God. The Most High has spoken; He has revealed Himself to His people, and to be successful in life, one hears and obeys. Revelation from God always takes precedence over human reason.

Military commanders may not care which ethical school has the most influence upon the people in their commands, but they do expect certain high standards of behavior. God also expects a high standard of behavior from those who serve Him, but He is also very concerned about our motives. He loves us, and has given us commands in order that we might have life. It is important to know God's commands and to live by them. Can you, for example, cite from memory the Ten Commandments? Do you know where to find them in the Bible? What did Jesus call the greatest commandment? The moral teachings of the Bible are essential for effective Christian living and leadership; we must know and put into practice that which God has commanded. Cognitive and non-cognitive moral reasoning may play significant roles in our decision-making processes, but the primary source of our ethic is divine, and the Christian who seeks to set a good example must obey the One who commands.

One of the greatest Biblical commands is to love our neighbor as much as we love ourselves (n. Lev. 19:18; Mt. 5:43), but I cannot begin to count the people I have met who have been wounded by the Church. In seeking to bring problem-laden Marines, sailors, and/or family members into a closer relationship with God, I find that many have been harmed spiritually almost beyond healing. Some were forced against their will to attend church services three and four nights a week. Others, sporting tattoos, were told by Bible-believing Christians that it was impossible for them to get into heaven. Those who went through divorces or struggled with addictions to nicotine or alcohol were viewed as second-class citizens. Young adults who, as youths, had difficulties adjusting to the mores of society were declared demon-possessed. Those who did not dress or speak in certain ways did not belong. Horrible scars resulting from hurtful comments have kept throngs of people from evaluating the claims of Jesus Christ. And we wonder why our churches are devoid of young people. The Bible tells us that our attitude should be *"the same as that of Christ Jesus: Who, being in very nature God, did not consider equality with God something to be grasped, but made himself nothing, taking the very nature of a servant, being made in human likeness. And being found in appearance as a man, he humbled himself and became obedient to death — even death on a cross!"* (Phil. 2:5-8).

Christ set a perfect example for us, humbling Himself and embracing us with all of our flaws. It is essential, that we who profess to know Him, respond in same way to others who may not be like us. As servants of the Most High, we must set the example for the children of this world. It is by our winsome example, by our love for humanity, that others will see the kingdom of God.

Principle Six

Know your Marines (people) and look out for their welfare

"There is no limit to what a man can do or where he can go if he doesn't mind who gets the credit."
Ronald Reagan[1]

This principle involves the traits of justice, tact, and unselfishness. *Justice* is defined as giving reward and punishment according to merits of the case in question. It is the ability to administer a system of rewards and punishment impartially and consistently. *Tact* is the ability to deal with others without creating offense. *Unselfishness* is the avoidance of providing for one's own comfort and personal advancement at the expense of others.

Marines come from every arena of life. Some come from urban ghettos, others from large remote ranches. I met one 19 year-old private who already held a bachelor's degree from a major U.S. University. His father was on the Board of

[1]H.W. Crocker III, *Robert E. Lee On Leadership*, (Rocklin, CA: Prima Publishing, 1999), p. 17.

Directors for SONY Corp., and his mother was an executive vice-president for Bank of America. I met another who came from the U.S. Protectorate of the Tongan islands, and still another from the Choctaw Indian Reservation in Mississippi. Many are immigrants from other nations, not even U.S. citizens. I have met U.S. Marines who are citizens of Mexico, Azerbaijan, Russia, and the Ukraine. Some are white, some are black, others Native American, Hispanic or Asian. Good leadership plays no favorites; it treats each individual fairly and with dignity, and is able to bring together this kind of diversity, molding it into an effective squad or platoon, capable of accomplishing great things. But in order for this to happen, the leader must know his people and look out for their welfare.

In 1999, a man who had served in the First Combat Engineer Battalion thirty years earlier walked into my office, reminiscing. He related to me that, after he had finished his four-year tour of duty, he left the Marines and landed a lucrative position in the computer industry. He secured his new job, on the very first interview, based on his answer to the question, "What is the most important leadership quality?" His answer? "Take care of your people." The principle he had learned during his time in the Marine Corps was precisely that for which the employer was looking. Successful Marine leaders know their people: they know who can carry more weight up a hill when it comes time to take it; they know the best shooters in their units, and who is better at steadying the arms of the one taking aim. They know who is married, who is single, and who is engaged. The good Marine leader is sensitive to the religious practices and family backgrounds of his people. He knows that each man in his unit has a very different personality, and understands how to elicit the very best performance out of each. Such knowledge wins battles.

For the Christian, it is important to know the people with whom we serve and to love them in the name of God. For the Christian leader it is essential. We need to know the names of those who attend our churches, and have a genuine interest in their lives and in their families. We who represent Christ must be sensitive to the strengths and weaknesses of those who worship with us, and we need to pray for them. During Plebe Summer at the United States Naval Academy, one of the very first exercises for the newly-inducted midshipman is to learn the names and hometowns of company mates. In 1975, there were about 30 of us in our company. We were in the same boat together (no pun intended), and it was essential to look out for each other in order to survive the brutal regimen. To this day, I still know the names and hometowns of almost everyone who survived that summer with me. What we learned during the first days of our exposure to the military was an important concept we carried with us throughout our careers in the Armed Forces and beyond.

As a congregation ascertains its role in the community, good church leaders will cultivate the gifts found in each of their congregants. I have been in some churches where everyone took a turn at leading worship – an utterly disastrous situation, to be sure! Some people should never be up front leading, while others do not desire the role. To place people in positions who lack either the competence or the desire brings great harm to all involved. Healthy churches take time to discover the spiritual gifts of their members and then place them in positions where they will be successful. The Apostle Paul writes, in a very rhetorical way, "*Are all apostles? Are all prophets? Are all teachers? Do all work miracles? Do all have gifts of healing? Do all speak in tongues? Do all interpret?*" (1 Co. 12:29-30). The implication is, "no!" We are all wired very differently.

There are several ways of psychologically profiling an individual, but none have improved much upon the work of the ancient Greek physicians. These men suggested four basic personality types.[2] The *choleric* man or woman is a driven individual, determined and strong-willed. He or she prefers to be in charge. The Apostle Paul is an excellent Biblical example, in that he almost single-handedly established churches throughout most of the Roman Empire, writing more than half of the New Testament in the process. A choleric person often makes a good board chairmen, preacher or choir director. The phlegmatic personality is peaceful, amiable, and likes to avoid conflict. In the Scripture, Barnabas is such a person. His ability to bring together peoples of radically different backgrounds stands out (Acts 9:27). A phlegmatic person makes an excellent usher or greeter. The *melancholic* personality is analytical, conscientious and reserved. The Apostle Thomas fits the bill. He needed visible proof before he would believe anything, doubting that which could not be verified (John 11:16; 14:5; 20:25). The melancholic person tends toward perfectionism. Such a one would make a good secretary or treasurer. The *sanguine* personality likes bright clothing, is expressive, popular, energetic, and enthusiastic. The Apostle Peter was the first to jump out of the boat (Mt. 14:29; John 21:7), the first to draw his sword (John 18:10), and the first to declare that Jesus was the Messiah (Mt. 16:16). A person with a sanguine personality makes a good youth group leader or worship leader.

It is dangerous to oversimplify, but the point being made is that everyone is different; each offers various gifts and abilities beneficial to the larger community. The Apostle Paul's metaphor of the Church as the Body of Christ is especially helpful in illustrating this concept (n. Ro. 12:3-8; 1 Co. 12).

---

[2]*The New Encyclopaedia Britannica*, (Chicago: Encyclopaedia Britannica, Inc., vol. 25, 15th edition, 1985), p. 497.

In looking out for the welfare of the people in our congregations, it is important that the leader show justice to all. There are many churches, and even entire denominations, where strong stances are made that forbid divorced persons from holding leadership positions. Yet churches sometimes compromise on this when a very successful pastor suffers a tragic divorce. They often overlook the incident, carrying on as if nothing was amiss. Although I struggle with such rules anyway, the spiritual fallout resulting from inconsistent enforcement is far more devastating than the rule. How many talented young men and women are turned away from leadership opportunities because they do not meet a particular church's high standards? How do they feel when that same church reverses its policy in order to accommodate a pastor who has done the very same thing? If the Commanding Officer of a U.S. warship were to act in such a way — forgiving the offense of one sailor while harshly punishing several others who did the very same thing — it would not be long before the entire ship heard about it, and morale would plummet. The Uniform Code of Military Justice helps military commanders determine the appropriate punishment for any given transgression. In the Church, there are not always such clear-cut standards as the UCMJ, but the leader, nonetheless, must be consistent in his or her judgments.

In seeking to be just in our dealings with others, we must remind ourselves that, in this world, there is no such thing as perfect justice. Perfect justice took place on the Cross. It was there that Christ paid for the sins of the world. Those who trust Him are forgiven; those who do not will have Divine justice poured out upon them on the Day of Judgment, and will be held accountable for every sin they have ever committed. The just desserts for our behavior is eternal damnation, but God, in His mercy, poured out His wrath upon His Son in order that we would not have to stand before Him in our own strength. As humans, we want justice, especially when we have been wronged; but when we have wronged others, we look for mercy. In our struggles to be just, may we remind ourselves that the very best justice is always tempered with mercy.

In looking out for the welfare of the people in our congregations, it is important that the leader exercise tact. In *The American Caesar*, William Manchester describes an incident where a little bit of tact would have gone a long way. General Douglas MacArthur was the Supreme Commander of the Allied Forces in the Pacific Theater during World War II. He brought about the surrender of Imperial Japan following a brilliant island hopping campaign through Indonesia, the South Pacific islands and the Philippines. Following Japan's unconditional surrender, MacArthur became the leader of the occupying forces. He ruled with grace and dignity, rewriting the constitution of the defeated nation, creating a new post-war state. Later MacArthur was asked to lead UN forces in the Korean conflict. He accepted the position, but later openly, flagrantly and wrongly opposed Truman administration policies. Tact would have requested the resignation of the great leader, but as Manchester records the event, President Truman purportedly said, "The son of a bitch isn't going to resign on me! I want him fired!"[3] Later, when diplomats from fifty-one nations were invited to San Francisco to attend the signing of the Japanese peace treaty, the very man who wrote the new nation's constitution was not even invited to attend.[4] Tragically, this is how things often transpire in the world of politics. Men and women spend more time tearing each other apart in the campaign than they do focusing on the issues or working for the common good.

[3]*The American Caesar*, p. 770
[4]*ibid.*, p. 824

Politics in the local church are just as intense as anything that takes place in the world. Some people are better suited to hold church office than others, and occasionally there are individuals who need to be removed from leadership positions. As a church sorts through difficult personnel issues, those making the decisions to hire and fire must always show tact. Grace and dignity (along with decent separation packages) must always be extended to those asked to step aside. Servants of the Most High always treat others in a spirit of prayer and in a manner that brings honor to Christ, especially in conflicted situations.

The story of David and Bathsheba (2 Sam. 11-12) offers a great example of tactful leadership. David, as required of kings, was supposed to lead his troops into battle. But this story begins with Israel's finest choosing to stay at home, enjoying the comforts of the palace, while his generals conducted the war. While at home, the king noticed Bathsheba, wife of Uriah the Hittite, bathing on the rooftop of an adjacent residence. David's resulting misdeeds, previously mentioned in Article III (pp. 101-102), relegate some of the political shenanigans in our own day to the status of mere child's play. His advisor Nathan, however, an anointed prophet, provides an excellent example of tactful leadership in the midst of the ongoing drama. In confronting the king, he tells a story:

> *"There were two men in a certain town, one rich and the other poor. The rich man had a very large number of sheep and cattle, but the poor man had nothing except one little ewe lamb he had bought. He raised it, and it grew up with him and his children. It shared his food, drank from his cup and even slept in his arms. It was like a daughter to him. Now a traveler came to the rich man, but the rich man refrained from taking*

> *one of his own sheep or cattle to prepare a meal for the traveler who had come to him. Instead, he took the ewe lamb that belonged to the poor man and prepared it for the one who had come to him"*
>
> (2 Sa. 12:1-4).

When King David heard this story, he was furious and declared that the offender must die. With great fear and trembling, to be sure, Nathan responded: *"You are the man!"* (2 Sa. 12:7). In a very tactful way, God's prophet brought to the king's attention the gravity of his misdeeds and their ramifications to the nation. David repented of his behavior, and Nathan kept his head – all because of brilliant, tactful leadership.

What an example this is for us! In most unchristian ways, we often relish in the public humiliation of our elected officials. We enjoy expressing righteous indignation, but consistently fail to show tact toward those who have erred. All of us are sinners, yet none of us would wish to be on the receiving end of what we often heap upon others. The Apostle Paul writes, *"If it is possible, as far as it depends on you, live at peace with everyone"* (Ro. 12:18). Tactful leadership demands as much.

In looking out for the welfare of the people in our congregations, we must be unselfish. The leader must take into consideration the needs of others before she demands her own rights. The classic virtue of temperance, keeping the ego under control, plays a huge role. We often volunteer for leadership positions for all the wrong reasons, believing that high visibility will lead to career advancement or will serve as an insurance policy to protect selfish interests. More than a few Navy chaplains have used their authority to write up prestigious awards for themselves, hoping to secure their own promotions, while ignoring the men and women who work for them. Nothing could be more destructive to the cause of Christ. During field operations, Marine officers eat last. They ensure that all of their men eat before they do. The chow line begins with the most junior Marine eating first, progressing eventually to those more senior in rank. On more than one occasion I watched the food supply run out, long before senior personnel were served. What an example this is for those who would be leaders in our churches! Every church leader should aspire to his/her position of authority for the purpose of serving others, and of seeing them come to know Christ. Others should come first. Leaders are to serve the flock of God, not lord over them. It is often said that to find joy in your own life, place Jesus first, Others second and Yourself last.

The Old Testament story of Abraham and Lot offers a great example of unselfishness. As the two men looked out over the lush plains of the Jordan River, both wanted the fertile valley as a place for their herdsmen and cattle. Knowing that the area could not support both his and Lot's herds, Abraham allowed his younger nephew to choose first (Gen. 13:9). In so doing, he modeled unselfishness, an area about which Lot had much to learn.

One of the ways in which Christian leaders model unselfishness is through giving. My family and I were on the receiving end of financial unselfishness on numerous occasions. Shortly after we were married, I announced to my wife that I would be resigning my active duty commission as a Line Officer in the U.S. Navy to pursue a theological education. Instead of earning a good salary, I began spending large sums of money with very little income. In addition, we decided to have a family. All three of our children were born during the time I spent at seminary. Needless to say, funds were short. It is very difficult to put into words the encouragement I felt when I when an old friend from the

Navy called one night and told me, "The Lord has led me to give you one half of my tithe while you are still in seminary." For the next two years, this brother personally mailed a $200 check every month. His spirit of unselfishness encouraged me beyond measure.

We give unselfishly to the kingdom of God out of appreciation for what God has done. Jesus said, "*It is more blessed to give than to receive*" (Acts 20:35). Many religious traditions in the world emphasize the importance of giving. The Jew practices great acts of charity on Yom Kippur. The Muslim gives 1/40th of his income to help alleviate poverty.[5] Taking care of those who are less fortunate is an area that separates the human race from the rest of the animal kingdom. The servants of the Most High should give cheerfully and unselfishly, exceeding all others in this endeavor.

---

[5]Almsgiving: one of the five pillars of Islam. (Ridenour, *op. cit.*, pp. 68-69).

1) Statement of Belief: the Shahadah – "There is no God but Allah, and Muhammad is His Messenger."
2) Prayer: five times daily, facing Mecca.
3) Almsgiving: 1/40th of one's income given to orphans, widows, and the sick.
4) Fasting: daylight hours during the month of Ramadan.
5) Haj: Pilgrimage to Mecca once in one's lifetime.

Principle Seven

Keep your Marines (people) INFORMED

"An army without its baggage train is lost"

Sun Tzu[1]

One of the first lessons midshipmen receive during their training at the US Naval Academy are the commands that an Officer of the Deck (OOD) would give on the bridge of a naval vessel. For example, the commands given to the helmsman are very important. An example of good communication follows:

OOD: "Helmsman, right full rudder."

Helm: "Right full rudder aye, sir (or ma'am)."

Helm: "Sir, my rudder is right full."

OOD: "Very Well."

---

[1]Sun Tzu, *The Art of War,* James Clavell, ed., (New York, NY: Delacorte Press, 1983), p. 32.

In this simple communication, the Officer of the Deck tells the helmsman what he wants done. The helmsman repeats the command, and acknowledges that he will comply. This ensures that the information has been passed on correctly. Once the helmsman has obeyed the order, and the rudder is in its proper position, he communicates this fact to the OOD, who, in turn, indicates his understanding of the situation by declaring, "Very Well." Effective communication always follows this format. The leader expresses his or her intent. Those who receive the message acknowledge it, by stating they understand that which has been communicated. They will later provide feedback, informing the leader what they have accomplished in regards to the matter. A good leader will then express thanks for a job well-done, or offer constructive criticism, as appropriate.

A chief strategy in warfare is to destroy the enemy's ability to communicate. If entrenched soldiers are not able to speak with their generals, they will quickly lose hope and surrender, rendering the war effort unsuccessful. The thousands of Iraqi soldiers who came out of their bunkers and surrendered to American troops during Operation Desert Storm bear witness to this. Their lines of communication had been severed by nearly forty days of relentless air bombardment. The soldiers had no hope. They were filled with despair and gave up.

A military commander must communicate with his troops. He must ensure they have enough food, potable water, ammunition, and a clear understanding of overall strategy. If communication in any of these areas is severed, the war will be lost. It is paramount that reliable supply lines be established; that commanders communicate their intentions; and that troops listen, obey, and respond. On occasion, human commanders fail to keep their troops informed. Sometimes they are delinquent in passing on essential information. Sometimes the breakdown occurs in the chain of command. On other occasions, enemy commanders sever all lines of communication. Each of these scenarios can result in disaster.

In spiritual warfare, the Most High has perfectly communicated His intentions; He has not failed in keeping His creation informed. *"His divine power has given us everything we need for life and godliness"* (2 Peter 1:3). *"In the past God spoke to our forefathers through the prophets at many times and in various ways, but in these last days he has spoken to us by his Son"* (Heb. 1:1-2). The Devil, however, seeks to interrupt this flow of information by attacking those on the receiving end. He succeeds when we fail to listen to and obey God's Word. If we do not heed the still small voice of the Spirit, if we do not gather for public worship of the Most High, if we do not take the opportunity to read the Scriptures so graciously supplied by our heavenly Commander; we cut ourselves off from the source of all spiritual power.

Communication is two-way: 1) God speaks. His people listen and obey; and 2) we speak, and God listens and responds. The Bible says, *"if my people, who are called by my name, will humble themselves and pray and seek my face and turn from their wicked ways, then will I hear from heaven and will forgive their sin and will heal their land"* (2 Chronicles 7:14). It is essential that the Christian leader quiet himself on a daily basis in order to hear God's Word. It is critical that the servant of the Most High pray in order that her heart is centered in His will!

Church leaders need to keep their people informed and be good listeners. What are the needs of your congregants? What are your pastors or staff members actually saying? For a church board or a committee to be effective, leaders must have an understanding of the issues at hand, agree to work together, and be good communicators. Church members should have access to essential information. Bulletins, church newsletters, annual reports, business meetings, and e-mails are all good sources; leaders should emphasis their use. The worship service, generally, is not the place to communicate business information; the practice distracts from the nature of worship and has great potential for consuming time that should be allocated to communion with God. Business meetings should be open and above board, with all invited to attend. Board members should have agendas in their hands, well-in-advance of any meetings, and the minutes of such gatherings should be published as soon as possible afterwards. All church-related information should flow through the office in order to resolve potential conflicts and clear up misunderstandings. Leaders should not make excessive use of acronyms or of scholarly theological language unless these are clearly explained to the intended audience. Good leaders create an atmosphere where church members feel free to ask questions. Keeping people informed is paramount to the success of a church, a board, a committee, or any other organization. Servants of the Most High need to do it well.

Principle Eight

Seek Responsibility and Take Responsibility for Your Actions

"It is not the critic who counts: not the man who points out how the strong man stumbles or where the doer of deeds could have done better. The credit belongs to the man who is actually in the arena, who face is marred by dust and sweat and blood ..."

Teddy Roosevelt[1]

This leadership principle involves the traits of initiative and dependability. *Initiative* is the ability to take action in the absence of orders. *Dependability* is the certainty of proper performance of duties.

The young Surface Warfare Officer on a Navy ship is in training to become a Commanding Officer. This involves gaining competency in each of five major shipboard departments: Operations, Engineering, Deck, Weapons, and Navigation. With sufficient experience in each of these areas, the officer should know enough about shipboard life and

[1] "Citizenship in a Republic," Speech at the Sorbonne, Paris, April 23, 1910.

operations to take command. My own personal experience involved Division Officer tours as a Communications Officer (Operations Department) and as a Main Propulsion Assistant (Engineering Department), but during that time it became very clear that God had other plans. My calling was not to become the Commanding Officer of a ship; it was to preach the gospel of Jesus Christ.

To be sure, the calling to preach was very clear, but there were other indicators that command at sea was "not in the cards." One of them was a lack of interest in the position of Communications Officer. I do not enjoy electronics or sound wave propagation, and did only what was necessary to complete my work. Without a doubt, the Commanding Officer picked up on my lack of initiative, and recorded his observations in subsequent performance evaluations. Fortunately, I had a much greater interest in ship handling and in engineering. Follow-on tours of duty were much more successful because I took an avid interest in solving problems as they arose, without waiting around for orders.

The leader of anything must take charge. He must hunger for better and more effective ways of accomplishing the task at hand. A good preacher will seek to improve communication skills. How can he share the gospel more effectively? How can she better understand her audience? What makes people tick? How can we reach the hearts of others with the greatest message in the world? All of this involves initiative, going the extra mile in order to be more effective.

In addition to taking the initiative, preachers and church leaders must be dependable, faithful to their callings. In a constantly changing world, the members of our congregations need stability. *"Simply let your 'Yes' be 'Yes,' and your 'No,' 'No'; anything beyond this comes from the evil one"* (Mt. 5:37). It is inexcusable for a church leader to say, "yes, I will serve as a deacon or as an elder," and then never show up to any of the meetings. If a helicopter fails to arrive at the appointed rendezvous place at the proper time, and does not radio ahead to give warning, an entire platoon of soldiers could find themselves mercilessly slaughtered by the enemy. The ramifications for unreliable spiritual leadership are equally grave. God is faithful all the time; we who represent Him should likewise be dependable.

The story of Adam and Eve illustrates what happens when humans fail to seek responsibility or to take responsibility for their actions. Adam was tasked with taking care of the garden (Gen. 2:15). When the snake entered, he should have immediately destroyed it. Instead, he succumbed to its temptations and ate the forbidden fruit. His disobedience plunged the entire human race into spiritual darkness. When confronted by God for his misdeeds, Adam blamed his wife (Gen. 3:12). The story of Cain and Abel likewise illustrates failure to take responsibility. Cain murdered his brother. When confronted by God for his horrendous act, he retorted, *"Am I my brother's keeper?"* (Gen. 4:9; c.f. Ex. 32: 21-24). We often do the same kinds of things. Rather than take responsibility for our actions, we tend to justify our behavior, and pass along blame to others. When spiritual leaders do this, it destroys all credibility.

Jesus challenges us to seek responsibility and to take responsibility for our actions. He commissions us to *"go and make disciples of all nations"* (Mt. 28:19). These are not passive words; they are not "sit around in the church office and let people come to me words." They are words of action. The servant of God must seek responsibility. He must be faithful, and take the initiative, proactive in ministry. The best defense is a good offense. Take it to the streets! Look around! What needs to be done? Make it happen!

Each of us has very special calling from God. Your calling, or vocation,[2] should be something in which you have a passionate interest. If you are in the process of choosing a career, follow the desire of your heart; do not follow the easy money. Pursue those things in which you are truly interested, and God will meet your financial needs. Ralph Waldo Emerson once said, "If a man can write a better book, preach a better sermon, or make a better mousetrap than his neighbour, tho' he build his house in the woods, the world will make a beaten path to his door."[3] When you sense a calling from God, follow it with all your might. Learn it with all of your strength. Take full responsibility for what you are doing, and take the initiative in finding newer, better, and more efficient ways of mastering your calling.

Every Christian has a special gift he or she can share with the Body of Christ. You may have a great interest in spiritual matters. Perhaps God is calling you to teach or to serve on a board of elders. You may enjoy working with your hands. Perhaps you can serve God on the property committee. You may enjoy working with finances. Maybe service on a fund-raising committee or as a trustee is your niche. You may enjoy working with small children, with teenagers, or with college students. A great ministry awaits your talents and interests; you are an important cog in the Church of Jesus Christ. Use your gifts in an area that brings joy. To be sure, there will be setbacks and frustrations, but remember who has called you into service. Take responsibility for a ministry; take the initiative, and in your own special way, help advance God's Kingdom. A church that conducts ministry only through its

---

[2]The word "vocation" comes from the Latin "vocatio," which means "calling."

[3]Martin Luther King, Jr., *Strength to Love,* (New York: Harper & Row, Publishers, Incorporated, 1963), p. 70.

pastors or paid staff will not be very effective. The Church functions best when all give of their time and talents, striving towards a common goal. A wise man once said, "The church is what's left when the building burns down, and the preacher leaves town."

PRINCIPLE NINE

ENSURE ASSIGNED TASKS ARE UNDERSTOOD, SUPERVISED, AND ACCOMPLISHED

"The devil is in the details, and everything we do is a detail."

ADMIRAL HYMAN G. RICKOVER

This leadership principle involves the traits of courage and endurance. *Courage* is that mental quality which recognizes fear of danger or criticism, but enables a man to proceed in the face of it with calmness and firmness. The ancient Greeks called this quality fortitude. *Endurance* is the mental and physical stamina measured by the ability to withstand pain, fatigue, stress, and hardship.

The late Admiral Hymen G. Rickover epitomized this principle. Up until the time of his retirement in 1982, every naval officer who ever served in the nuclear power program was personally interviewed by this "father of the nuclear Navy." He knew everyone of his commanders by name, and many of the details of their lives. The men who worked for Rickover clearly understood what was required of them, and knew that the admiral would ensure the tasks were completed exactly as he spelled out. The accounts of some of Rickover's interviews are legendary, and were widely circulated at the U.S. Naval Academy. On one occasion, a midshipman who desired to go to nuclear power school appeared somewhat nervous as he sat before the admiral's desk. Rickover called him a "wimp." "I bet you couldn't even make me angry if you tried," the famous admiral declared. Seizing the opportunity, the midshipman balled his fist and smashed the plastic model of the U.S.S. *Nautilus*, the very first nuclear powered submarine that proudly adorned Rickover's desk. The admiral was furious, but the midshipman also got the job. He was the type of man Rickover wanted in his program.

On another occasion, a midshipman who was engaged to be married sought matriculation into nuclear power school. Upon finding out that the young man was engaged, Rickover suggested that he call off the wedding because there would "be no time for a wife in today's modern nuclear navy." He motioned to the telephone on his desk, implying that nuclear power school was his simply by calling off the marriage. Nonplused, the young midshipman picked up the phone, dialed his fiancee, and said, "Honey, I guess we're going Navy Air." Rickover saw a quality for which was looking, and immediately hired him.

My interview was less dramatic, but interesting nonetheless. In 1979, not enough midshipmen from Annapolis were signing up for the nuclear power program, so the top half of the class was ordered to Crystal City, Virginia, for a mandatory meeting with the admiral. We were shipped out on buses, herded into the government high-rise and closely guarded in windowless rooms for an entire day. There were about 50 of us packed into the room to which I was assigned, and access was so controlled we had to sign in and out simply to go to the restroom. During the course of the day, each "candidate" was interviewed by three senior naval officers, prior to meeting Rickover himself. My meeting with the admiral was terse. I entered his office, sat down on the chair in front of his huge desk (we were instructed not to allow our backs to touch the back of the chair, the seat of which purposely sloped forward), and with great fear and trepidation awaited his first question. "Why did you major in Soviet Area studies?" "Well, sir," I began to explain. Before I finished my answer, Rickover abruptly ended the interview, informing me that the Navy needed engineers, not people with leanings toward the arts. I was ordered to leave the room, and my file was summarily tossed into a large box behind the admiral's chair. A Navy Captain scurried out of a side room, emptying the box, and my interview was over.

For 33 years, Rickover ran the Navy's nuclear power program. He kept the standards high, clearly laying out what he expected from his officers. He had the fortitude to tell many individuals that they were not qualified for his program, and he was not hesitant to correct or fire officers who did not live up to his high standards. For many long years, he endured the critics, and built the finest nuclear powered fleet in the world.

The Christian leader needs to show more grace than that exhibited by the renowned admiral, but we can learn much from his tenacity, his moral courage, and his endurance. Of all the leadership principles, this one is most difficult. Generally, we are working with volunteers, and the concept that "we shouldn't criticize what anyone is doing, because they are not being paid for their work" is prevalent. Churches have a tendency to flounder in mediocrity because the tasks that need to be accomplished for quality ministry remain unfinished or poorly done. The good leader will, with grace, offer enough supervision and constructive criticism so that his or her ministry team brings honor and glory to the Lord. The courage that it takes to correct another comes from God. As the Bible says, *"perfect love drives out fear"* (1 John 4:18) and again *"in God I trust; I will not be afraid. What can man do to me?"* (Ps. 56:11). Esther, the Queen of Persia, clearly understood the task that lay before her when she courageously appealed to the King on behalf of the Jews in his kingdom (Esth. 4:14). Nehemiah showed great perseverance and fortitude in rebuilding the walls of Jerusalem in the face of hostile opposition. And Jesus clearly understood the task that was before Him when He went to the cross. The courage He exhibited while standing before the Governor of Judea is an example for all (John 18:33-37). In his letter to the churches, James writes, *"Blessed is the man who perseveres under trial, because when he has stood the test, he will receive the crown of life that God has promised to those who love him"* (Jas. 1:12).

With hard work it is possible to learn a lot about yourself and about others. It is possible to master the technical and tactical aspects of your trade. Leaders can learn to delegate as they become surer of themselves, and can learn how to make the right decisions in a timely way. Setting a good personal example, developing good communication skills, training people to form a good team, and understanding the limits of that team are all principles that can be mastered with hard work and with experience. Ensuring that assigned tasks are properly accomplished, however, involves the courage to correct the errors of another and to persevere continually in doing the right things. The other ten leadership principles primarily involve self-improvement. This one involves correcting the flaws and shortcomings of others. It is easy to get people excited about vision statements and programs, but far more difficult to lead them through the process of making a vision become a reality. Humans are lazy by nature. We have a tendency to slack off when no one is watching. But the effective leader knows how to supervise others and ensure that assigned tasks are accomplished.

A ship at sea illustrates the importance of completing one's work. There are innumerable tasks that must be performed in order to keep it seaworthy. These tasks are divided between five major departments and hundreds of sailors. A program called PMS, the Planned Maintenance System, organizes all of this work into a manageable possibility. The effects of one simple task left undone, however, can have disastrous consequences.

One of the requirements placed on a navel vessel before it can get underway is to test the engines, first in the forward direction and then in the astern. This process involves opening a large valve, allowing high pressure steam to flow to the appropriate engine. The valve is then quickly closed, ensuring that only a small amount of steam actually enters the turbine, minimizing movement along the pier. Once, while our ship was preparing to get underway, the Officer of the Deck called for a test of the forward engine. The valve was opened properly, and steam was admitted to the engine. But when the engineers attempted to close the ahead valve, it froze in the open position. Before emergency shutdown procedures could take effect, the ship had plowed along the pier for a couple of hundred feet, snapping all mooring lines and colliding with another warship moored to an adjacent pier. Fortunately, there were no injuries or deaths, but damage to the adjacent ship amounted to tens of thousands of dollars. The admiral, as one might expect, was furious, and a thorough investigation followed. The cause of the accident was a tiny cotter pin, shorn in half, on the ahead valve. One of the engineers had "gun decked" the required PMS check, indicating that the maintenance had been performed, when in reality it had not. The task was clearly understood by the person at fault, but it was not accomplished, and everyone suffered as a result. The sailors had been looking forward to a port call in a foreign city, but as a result of the casualty, the excitement of experiencing a new culture was replaced with a liberal and painful dose of engineering casualty control drills. Navy or Marine Corps leaders often come across as "hard-nosed" or "hard core" when they press for perfection in the small details, but it is for good reason; human lives are at stake.

The local church is as complex an organization as any military unit, and there are a myriad of tasks that must be accomplished in order for a body of believers to be successful in its outreach to others. Every member must be willing to take on some of the work and ensure its completion. If one person, charged with responsibility, fails to deliver, ministry is hampered. Simple things like failing to open doors on time, or Sunday School teachers absenting themselves from their classrooms can result in seekers never setting foot in the church again, and perhaps never hearing about the love of God. A good leader ensures that all of the painful details in his/her organization are faithfully completed. This often involves the personal courage to challenge those who tend to "slack off" when no one is watching. There may be some grumbling as a result, but in the long run, ministry will flourish. As one preacher stated, "If you want to call the shots, you're gonna take some shots." Military leaders have been known to resort to name calling and shouting to ensure that the little things are accomplished properly. Surely we, as servants of the Most High, can accomplish such tasks with dignity and tact.

Ensuring that assigned tasks are accomplished is one of the main themes coursing its way through Scripture. In the beginning, Adam was to take care of the garden. The salvation of the human race depended upon his faithfulness. When he failed in his mission, *'the LORD God called to the man, "Where are you?"'* (Gen. 3:9). When Adam refused to take responsibility for what he had done, the Lord relieved him of his duties, summarily removing him from the garden. Fortunately, God provided a second Adam (Ro. 5:15-19) who clearly understood what was required of Him, and accomplished it to perfection. The courage and perseverance of Jesus Christ in going to the cross brings salvation to all who believe. Because He understood the nature of His task, and ensured its completion, we will one day enter a new garden prepared for us from the foundation of the world (Rev. 22:1-2). What man was unable to do in his own strength, God accomplished in His. In response to what He has done, let us so live our lives in such a way that others may join us in His kingdom. For the church leader, that means ensuring that the necessary tasks of the church are understood, supervised and accomplished.

The American military is successful in training or in battle when there is good organization and planning, and when competent leadership ensures tasks are completed. Every mission in the Marine Corps is preceded by initial planning conferences, mid-planning conferences, and final planning conferences. Leaders at every level sit down and discuss how an action by one platoon or company will affect the entire mission. Following the planning conferences, all of the troops are given a pre-deployment brief in order that they understand the big picture. In the midst of the training (or battle), commanders conduct daily briefings in order to monitor progress and respond to crisis. Following a mission, leaders sit down and conduct a "hotwash," a debriefing where errors can be discussed and strategic and tactical improvements made in the event of future crisis.

An institutionalized leadership culture must be cultivated in the local church. A structure must be in place in order that lay leaders carry on the mission of preaching the gospel, even in the absence of a pastor. Too many churches flounder and become ineffective when pastors submit their resignations and move on to new callings. God works through the Church; He accomplishes His will through the men and women who make up the body of Christ, and He expects His servants to work together corporately, in the institution, in order to accomplish the mission. Boards and committees must function effectively, regardless of the personalities involved. There should be clear-cut job descriptions and expectations of all who serve. Meetings should start promptly with agendas published well in advance, and they should end on time with minutes distributed as soon as possible afterwards. The local church need not be as hierarchical as the military, but it is essential that there be a qualified individual in charge of every group or committee, in order to articulate clearly what needs to be done and to motivate others to accomplish assigned tasks.

Before any great vision comes to pass, leaders must organize their work, identify the people who will make it happen, and ensure that all of the baby steps needed along the way are taken. The words of Neil Armstrong from the surface of the moon, "That's one small step for man, one giant leap for mankind," clearly illustrate what we are trying to say. The grand vision of setting a man on the moon would not have happened if not for all of the little tasks that were supervised and accomplished before the great day of July 20, 1969. The same principle works in the church. Every task accomplished along the way will lead to great things for the kingdom of God and His Christ.

Principle Ten

Train your Marines (People) as a Team

So all the men of Israel got together and united as one man against the city.

Judges 20:11

Military training always focuses on teamwork. At Annapolis, we quickly learned that by working together we could do much better than working by ourselves. Some guys were better at making racks; some were better at shining shoes; some were better at shouting out the "chow calls" we had to make prior to each meal. When we learned to help others in the areas in which we were strong, others would help us in the areas where we were weak. As a result morale was higher and mission accomplishment more effective.

One of the most enjoyable moments I have ever had in the military occurred at the Coast Guard Academy in New London, CT. Our chaplains' class from Newport was there for a tour and for a chance to observe the training undergone by Coast Guard officers. (Navy Chaplains serve in the Coast Guard and Merchant Marine as well as in the Navy and Marine Corps). For fun, the instructors threw us into the high tech ship simulator and told us to get the ship away from the pier at New London, and safely navigate out of the Thames River into Narragansett Bay. Normally, chaplains "crash" the simulator quickly because it is something they have never done before. In our case, we kept the ship afloat through all sorts of high sea states, dangerous traffic, currents and even a loss of steering control. After about thirty minutes, the instructors stopped the drill and asked if there were former service personnel in the simulator. In fact, there were several of us, but the key to our success was that we very quickly formed a team that performed well under confusing situations. I took the Officer of the Deck job and gave steering and engine orders because it was something with which I was well acquainted. Another man, who served previously as a Radar Intercept Operator on a Navy jet, handled the communications, while others with some experience took the helm and lee helm. We functioned so well as a team that the instructors said we did better than some of the classes of Coast Guard officers. The prior experience had something to do with it, but the cooperative spirit that existed in our chaplains' class was the real cause for success.

The local church must also be a team. Members must be united in their efforts. Nothing is more destructive to gospel ministry than churches divided by controversy. Jesus said to His followers: *"I tell you that if two of you on earth agree about anything you ask for, it will be done for you by my Father in heaven. For where two or three come together in my name, there am I with them"* (Mt. 18:19-20). Paul pleaded passionately with the church in Corinth: *"agree with one another so that there may be no divisions among you and that you may be perfectly united in mind and thought"* (1 Co. 1:10). To the Ephesians he wrote: *"Make every effort to keep the unity of the Spirit through the bond of peace"* (Eph. 4:3). To the Philippians, his words were similar: *"I plead with Euodia and I plead with Syntyche to agree with each other in the Lord"* (Phil. 4:2). Peter writes: *"Finally, all of you, live in harmony with one another; be sympathetic, love as brothers, be compassionate and humble"* (1 Pe. 3:8). The Bible is filled with verses about how we should work together as a team, yet so often we find ourselves divided and conflicted, unable to get our minds beyond what is going on within the church walls. If our military was as conflicted as some of our churches, we would not exist today as a nation; we would have been annihilated in battle.

Christians are involved in spiritual combat. We need each other. By working together as a team, we accomplish far more than by acting as "lone rangers." Good church leaders recognize this principle and seek to build the best possible team. Jesus took twelve men from various backgrounds and trained them so well that within a few years they carried the gospel to the far reaches of the Roman Empire. Following the resurrection He *"opened their minds so they could understand the Scriptures"* (Luke 24:45). He explained the importance of His death and resurrection and the need for repentance and forgiveness of sins to be preached in His name. Later, Christ poured out His Spirit upon all people; and the Church, the team in which every Christian should be involved, was born (n. Acts 2). The gifts that God gave to His people on that day (and those He continues to give up to the present time) are numerous and diverse (n. Ro. 12:3-8; 1 Co. 12:12-31). He gives them, *"just as he determines"* (1 Co. 12:11). In the same way as military commanders know how to take the various assets at their disposal — infantry, artillery, tanks, tracks, engineers, etc. — and mold them together in such a way as to win our nation's wars; we, who lead others in spiritual combat, need to train the wonderfully gifted people who make up our congregations, and form ministry teams capable of bringing the gospel to bear on all aspects of life.

Our role is to discover the gifts of our people, plug them into ministries where they will be successful, and teach them how to help the local church succeed in its mission. The team concept must always be at the forefront of any agenda.

When we conduct our church meetings, a portion of the agenda should involve training. There is always room for improvement. Discussions over such things as "What does it mean to be a good deacon?" "How can one help with property maintenance?" "What kinds of fellowship or outreach events are we conducting?" "How do I visit someone in her home or at a hospital?" "Are there things that we are doing wrong as members of the Body of Christ?" Topics concerning personal spiritual growth, church growth, and evangelism are always of immense value. Lay persons need to develop an appreciation of the information contained in the church bulletin or newsletter. They should be involved with business meetings and pray for the mission of the church. As the Navy puts it, we are "one team, one fight." As a seasoned Vietnam veteran writes, "there are no lone patrols."[1] Good leaders recognize the team concept and train their people accordingly.

---

[1]Chuck Dean, *Point Man in Your Pocket* (Winepress Publishing, 1997), p. 12.

Principle Eleven

Employ your command (church) in accordance with its capabilities

> *"The general who wins a battle makes many calculations in his temple before the battle is fought. The general who loses a battle makes but a few calculations beforehand."*
>
> Sun Tzu[1]

Military commanders have a clear understanding of the capabilities of their units and of their men. As a Naval Officer, I have served in six different commands, each with a very different mission. My first assignment was with a fast combat support ship. The mission of this ship is to provide food, potable water, and fuel to other units in the carrier battle group. Although armed with a three inch naval gun, the fast combat support ship is not the type of vessel an admiral would call upon for anti-ship or anti-submarine warfare. In fact, in situations where intense combat is anticipated, the fast combat support ship best serves the mission by steering clear of the action.

---

[1]Sun Tzu, *The Art of War,* James Clavell,ed., (New York, NY: Delacorte Press, 1983), p.11.

My second command was on board a guided missile frigate. Its mission is to locate and, if necessary, destroy enemy submarines. Admirals use such ships to encircle carrier battle groups, providing a shield of protection against enemy submarines hundreds of miles in diameter. It would be foolish to rely on the guided missile frigate as a primary means of shore bombardment or anti-aircraft protection.

My third assignment was with the First Combat Engineer Battalion of the United States Marine Corps. The mission of the combat engineers is "mobility, counter-mobility, survivability and general engineering." Combat engineers lay mines and dig tank ditches. They are adept at clearing mines and obstacles that might get in the way of advancing troops. They ensure that the First Marine Division has sufficient potable water and electricity to complete its mission. Combat Engineers are neither tank drivers nor helicopter pilots.

In the same manner as a successful military commander knows how to employ his command in accordance with its capabilities, so the leader in God's kingdom knows how to employ his "troops" in accordance with its capabilities. Often, local churches attempt to do everything by themselves, acting as if they are the only ones involved in spiritual warfare. They want to save the entire world, but lack the resources. Smaller churches, in particular, need to specialize. It is silly for a small church to try and run a food pantry, a clothing closet, open their doors for every social group in the community, practice door-to-door evangelism, be involved politically, and run vibrant youth programs all at the same time. It is likely that church resources will be spread too thin, and ineffectiveness will reign in all areas. What is the make-up of your local church? Is a significant portion of your membership involved in education? If so, you will probably be more effective in reaching educators with the gospel than you will be at jail ministry. Are there many in your congregation who struggle to make a living, barely keeping food on the table? If so, you will probably be more effective at social-outreach programs than at reaching members of the local country club. How can your congregation best reach others for Christ? Good strategy involves studying those areas in which your people are gifted. In God's economy, it is likely that other churches in the community are gifted in those areas where you are weak. Great blessing will arise if churches support each other in areas where they are strong.

A Commanding Officer with whom I served at the First Combat Engineer Battalion gave a very impassioned speech upon his departure. He was convinced that warriors should critically evaluate themselves in order to ascertain their capabilities as well as their limitations. Once those capabilities were ascertained, leaders should build on them. Vision for the future involves working out of areas of strength. In this man's parting message, he encouraged battalion leadership to pursue a very expensive piece of military hardware, even though the logistics were not in place to take care of the gear properly. "Capability first, logistics second," the Colonel thundered, and he clearly made his point. If a church tries to build upon its weaknesses rather than upon its strengths, it will meet with frustration and failure. But if a church honestly evaluates its strengths and builds upon them, it will be successful. Effective programs will draw new members who, in turn, will share their gifts and abilities. This will begin to create a momentum that will be very difficult to stop, enabling the church to further expand its ministry into the local community. When churches work together, each operating out of a position of strength, a veritable force for good will wreak havoc upon the powers of darkness.

Part Three / Arming Yourself For Battle

Introduction

What does it mean to equip yourself for battle? How can we prepare for the spiritual warfare we face as believers in Jesus Christ? The sheer numbers of Biblical texts that address such matters are amazing. I developed the following fifteen-part curriculum while serving as a chaplain to the Marines of the First Combat Engineer Battalion. These teachings resonated well with the military personnel who attended my Bible studies. I suspect that anyone who is serious about putting on the full armor of God, who wants to do battle against the spiritual forces that wage war against our souls, against Christ, and against His Church, will find these thoughts very valuable.

Text Number One

The Ten Commands

"I am the LORD your God, who brought you out of Egypt"

Exodus 20:2

As a Junior Officer on board a large supply ship, I once found myself in a very perilous situation. We were returning to our homeport of Alameda, California, after a brief time at sea. The waters upon entering San Francisco Bay were particularly rough, and a very large wave knocked us directly into the path of a large oil tanker leaving the harbor. The Captain of our ship issued three commands: "right full rudder," "all engines back full," and "sound five blasts on the ship's whistle." The rudder order decisively turned the ship toward starboard, the engine order slowed her down, and the whistle warned the other vessel of impending danger. Each of these commands was obeyed instantaneously. Had any one of them been ignored, there would have been a terrible accident at sea, with great loss of life.

In like manner, God has issued ten important commands by which we should run our lives, but most Christians do not even know them. Do you? Would you know where to find them if given a Bible? Can you write them down in order, without first looking them up? Although our eternal destiny is not wrapped up in knowing or even in obeying the Ten Commandments, many Christians make shipwrecks of their lives because they do not follow what God has commanded. These are not ten "suggestions." Nor are they ten "pretty good ideas." They are commands, issued from on high. If you do not obey them your life will be filled with problems. You will enter into spiritual warfare virtually weaponless, a fence sitter who is both "in the world" and "of the world," missing out on the divine power needed to demolish the strongholds of the enemy. Your life will become miserable and ineffective. Why not take the time to arm yourself with all that God has provided? Learn and obey the Ten Commandments! If you do, your life will become much more meaningful. Intangible qualities such as joy and inner peace will strengthen your soul, and many of the worries that afflict Christians today will be eliminated from your own life. What follows is a listing of the Ten Commandments with some thoughts as to how they apply to everyday life. I have taken the liberty of paraphrasing them. Although Roman Catholic believers number these commands differently than most Protestants, the content is identical. Each of them, when obeyed, brings strength to the soul.

Command 1: You shall have no other gods before me.

Nothing is more important than your relationship with Almighty God: He created the heavens and the earth and fashioned you in His image. Placing God foremost in your thoughts is the intent of this command. What is the most important thing in your life? Is it to make a good living?

Jesus says, *"A man's life does not consist in the abundance of his possessions"* (Luke 12:15). Is it to raise a family? He says, *"anyone who loves his father or mother more than me is not worthy of me"* (Mt. 10:37). Is it to enjoy life? *"Whoever wants to save his life will lose it, but whoever loses his life for me and for the gospel will save it"* (Mark 8:35). Is it to be successful? *"'You have plenty of good things laid up for many years. Take life easy; eat, drink and be merry." But … "You fool! This very night your life will be demanded from you"'* (Luke 12:19-20). If success, family, or even life itself are more important than loving *"the Lord your God with all your heart and with all your soul and with all your mind"* (Mt. 22:37), you are in violation of the first commandment, and will find yourself ineffective in driving out the forces of evil that war against your soul.

The Commander-in-Chief, the President of the United States, is in charge of the Armed Forces of our nation. Admirals and generals do well to follow his lead. Those who ignore his commands or who have other agendas are quickly removed from power. This is even truer on a spiritual level. Our God is the only source of power, salvation, and true happiness. The kingdoms of this world, and everything in them, must bow before His authority. To enjoy life at it fullest, we must drink from His well. Nothing else will satisfy. *"Seek first his kingdom and his righteousness, and all these things will be given to you as well"* (Mt. 6:33).

Command 2: You shall have no idols.

Military Chaplains frequently lead services in noisy helicopter hangars, in front of M1A1 Abrams tanks, or on the forecastles of Navy ships. Often, the amenities found in civilian churches are completely absent, and that is not necessarily a bad thing. Crosses, stained glass windows, beautiful sanctuaries, candles, fine musical instruments, and lovely paintings can make for an inspiring setting, but none of these accouterments are essential for worship. The Bible tells us that *"God is a spirit, and his worshipers must worship in spirit and truth"* (John 4:24). An idol is something that gets in the way of worshipping the true and the living God. If "things" are needed before worship can take place, the enemy has gained a stronghold in our lives.

Human beings make idols out of each other: out of metal, plush and chrome; out of power, wealth, and influence; out of wood, stone and fabric. Sometimes these idols take the form of automobiles, clothes, or homes. Sometimes the idol is the college degree, the successful career, or membership in the club. It is easy for humans to worship at the altar of the golf course, to do obeisance at the ballpark, or to make vacation time the preeminent thing. While all are acceptable pastimes, they can become idolatrous when pursued more passionately than one's relationship with the Almighty. How critical for the servant of the Most High to resist making idols of created things; how important to keep our priorities straight![1]

Command 3: You shall not misuse the name of the LORD your God.

Of all of the commandments, this is the most widely misunderstood. On the surface, we take the name of the LORD in vain when we use it in a profane way: using the name of Jesus when we hit our thumb with a hammer or when we suggest that God would "damn" someone or something. (Who are we to presume such things)? On a deeper level, misusing the name of the LORD involves one's character, one's reputation, and one's walk as a Christian. To take the

---

[1]Some of the thoughts in this section come from: *Old Testament, Student Manual Genesis - 2 Samuel,* (Salt Lake City, Utah: The Church of Jesus Christ of Latter-day Saints, 1981), p. 128.

name of Christ in order to manipulate someone or to seal a business deal is the true thrust of this commandment. According to the Geneva standards, perfidy, the misuse of symbols for deceptive purposes, is an unlawful act of war. Wearing the enemy's uniform, or using the white flag or a Red Cross symbol in order to attack at close range, are all examples of this practice. Nothing delights the enemy more than for "Christians" to manipulate others, in very pious tones, using the name of Christ.

Command 4: Remember the Sabbath day by keeping it holy.

Disobeying this command leads to unimaginable stress. There are really two parts: the first involves taking time off from your every day endeavors in order to rest. Your body and your mind need to get away from the things you normally do in order to refresh and "recharge." Looking at the same desk, the same walls, and the same people day-in and day-out, without a break, will quickly lead to "burn out." The human body needs rest. Without it, you quickly become irritable and ineffective, playing right into the enemy's hand. It is important to take vacations. Get away from the routine; go on a trip; see something new. You will be amazed at how refreshed you will be upon your return. The Jews of the Old Testament understood this concept very well. The three major holidays of Judaism — Passover, Pentecost, and Tabernacles — were actually week-long vacations from ordinary life. Many Europeans today vacation with family for an entire month during the summer to rest and recuperate. We can learn much from them.

The second part of this command involves taking time to worship the Most High. God created you; He made you in His image. Make it a life's priority to be involved in the ministries of a local church. Worship there regularly. Arrange your schedule in such a way as to contribute tangibly to the gospel ministry. In so doing, you touch the future. Lives, including your own, will be changed; and a better society will result. Ultimately, Jesus is our Sabbath rest (n. Mt. 11:28; Col. 2:16-17; Heb. 4:1-12). When you bow your heart in meaningful worship, His grace, strength and peace will flow into your life.

Command 5: Honor your father and mother.

This is the first commandment with a promise. If you honor your father and mother you will live long in the land. The essence of the command is to obey all authority: your actual parents, leaders in business, government and industry, or elders in the Church. Life will prove far less tumultuous if you render respect to all who occupy positions of authority (n. Ro. 13:1-7; 1 Ti. 2:1-4; 1 Th. 5:12-13; and 1 Pe. 2:13-3:7). The enemy of our soul loves chaos and disorder.

Command 6: You shall not murder.

This commandment is of particular interest to those who serve in the military or in civilian police forces. These individuals are called to bear arms, and sometimes use them in the interest of national defense or civil order. A First Lieutenant in the Marines once dropped out of Army Ranger School because of the language used in training. An enlisted instructor informed the class that they were being programmed to become "cold-blooded, premeditated murderers." The language was neither appropriate nor endorsed by the school, but it does illustrate the tension faced by men and women whose duties may involve the use of deadly force.

The sixth commandment does not address outward behavior as much as it does the condition of the human heart. In the Sermon on the Mount, Jesus declares: *"You have heard that it was said … 'Do not murder …' But I tell you that any-*

one who is angry with his brother will be subject to judgment ... anyone who says, 'You fool!' will be in danger of the fire of hell" (Mt. 5:21-22). If there is hatred in your heart toward others, whether you kill them or not, you have committed murder in the eyes of God. The powers of darkness rejoice when Christians become filled with hatred. When a man cannot control his temper, the enemy becomes bold, and the light which should surround the people of God is obscured.

Killing in the line of duty is always tragic, but it does not constitute murder unless the element of hatred is involved. War, or the use of deadly force by civilian authorities, is often the lesser of two evils. Mowing down unarmed civilians or innocent children, however, is always murder. To kill an enemy soldier, who steps out of a bunker with his hands held high in surrender, likewise violates the command. John the Baptist did not condemn the professional soldier (Luke 3:14), neither did Peter (Acts 10), nor Jesus (Mt. 8:5-13). In none of these cases did the man of God require that the soldier abandon his profession.

In its essence, the sixth commandment forbids us to take the law into our own hands. The State is to carry the sword, and ultimately, all judgment belongs to God. To serve in the military or in a civilian police force is an honorable profession, but those who love the violence associated with such work will find themselves in grave danger of Divine judgment (n. Ps. 55:21; 68:30; 120:7).

Abraham Lincoln's second inaugural address, delivered in the midst of the Civil War, reflects the tensions inherent with the sixth commandment:

> "Both (sides) read the same Bible and pray to the same God, and each invoked His aid against the other ... The prayers of both could not be answered. That of neither has been answered fully. The Almighty has His own purposes."

Christians serve a Power far greater than the generals of this world. We must trust Him, even in the most baffling of circumstances.

Command 7: You shall not commit adultery.

One of the most satisfying of all human activities is sexual intercourse between a man and a woman who are united in marriage. But adultery, sexual contact outside the confines of marriage, is one of the most destructive. The book of Proverbs tells us,

> *"the prostitute reduces you to a loaf of bread, and the adulteress preys upon your very life. Can a man scoop fire into his lap without his clothes being burned? Can a man walk on hot coals without his feet being scorched? So is he who sleeps with another man's wife; no one who touches her will go unpunished"*
>
> (6:26-29)

In the New Testament, the words are equally strong. *"Flee from sexual immorality. All other sins a man commits are outside his body, but he who sins sexually sins against his own body"* (1 Co. 6:18). Heterosexual activity outside of marriage and all homosexual activity is wrong. Many military secrets have been given away because of the failure of men to resist a fleeting moment of sensual pleasure. Countless marriages have been destroyed as a result of sexual unfaithfulness. Reputations earned by women as "loose" or "easy" are psychologically destructive, and the hardness of men's hearts that rebel against God in this area is a pitiful sight. Those who commit adultery and remain unrepentant are of very little value in the battle against the spiritual enemies of our souls. The Scripture declares, "*those who live like this will not inherit the kingdom of God*" (Gal. 5:21).

Command 8: You shall not steal.

This command forbids taking things that do not belong to us. This includes property, money, time, rights, privileges and anything else. We steal by falsifying accounts, by avoiding the payment of taxes, by improper declarations of bankruptcy to avoid repayment of student loans, or by failing to offer a full day's work for a full day's pay. Servants of the Most High are not to be controlled by material things or by the accolades of others. We are content with how God has made us and with the things He has given us. Rather than steal from others, we work hard to make others look good, and we give financially to those who are in need. Such attitudes disarm the enemy and advance the message of God's kingdom. For the most part, *work* is the method God has provided for us to meet our needs. A military force that works hard will be effective in battle. Christians who put in an honest day's work bear testimony to their faith.[2]

Command 9: You shall not give false testimony against your neighbor.

This command involves telling the truth. Honest communication up and down the chain of command in a military unit is essential for mission effectiveness. Honest communication in marriage is paramount for its survival. Honesty from those who take the name of Christ ensures healthy growth in God's kingdom. But it is so easy to be dis-

[2]*ibid.*, p. 134.

honest, especially when we come to the house of the Lord. Like the Beatles' Eleanor Rigby, we find ourselves, "wearing the face that she keeps in a jar by the door."[3] Pretending to be spiritual, we occupy ourselves with gossip, juicy rumors, innuendo, and speculations about others that are not true. Occasionally we offer false testimony because we lack all the facts or because of various misunderstandings.

The congregation of the small Lutheran church I attended as a boy recited the following public confession every Sunday:

> O God, our heavenly Father, I confess unto thee that I have grievously sinned against thee in many ways; not only by outward transgressions, but also by secret thoughts and desires which I cannot fully understand, but which are all known unto thee. I do earnestly repent, and am heartily sorry for these my offenses, and I beseech thee of thy great goodness to have mercy upon me, and for the sake of thy dear Son, Jesus Christ our Lord, to forgive my sins, and graciously to help my infirmities. Amen.[4]

Many churches today continue to have a time of confession during worship, but a far greater number are slipping away from this time of self-evaluation and honesty.

In the military, there are times when deception and lies are strategically used against the enemy. This, too, has Biblical precedent. There are some very interesting Scriptural passages where falsehoods are used to advance the kingdom of God (n. Ex. 1:15-21; 3:16-18; 1 Sam. 16:1-3; 20:5-8; 2 Ki. 6:8-19; 1 Ki. 22:22; and 2 Thess. 2:11). The ninth com-

[3]Eleanor Rigby lyrics © Sony Beatles Ltd; Sony/atv Tunes Llc

[4]*Service Book and Hymnal*, (Minneapolis, MN: Augsburg Publishing House, 1958), p.248.

mandment is directed primarily toward guarding the basic right of the covenant member (a believer) against the threat of false accusation. It is not necessarily a prohibition against lying. In general, however, the servant of the Most High is one whose word is bond. We are honest in our dealings with others, even as we look for edifying things to say about them. The truth is something that the father of lies cannot handle.

Command 10: You shall not covet.

If at this point you believe there is a viable possibility of actually obeying the Ten Commandments, number ten should dispel all doubt. Coveting summarizes the previous nine. If you have difficulty submitting all aspects of your life to the Lordship of the Most High, you are coveting His authority. If you do not honor those in power above you, you covet what belongs to them. If you have hatred in your heart toward others, you covet their lives. If you look with desire in your heart toward the wife of another man or toward the husband of another woman (n. Mt. 5:28), you are coveting that which does not belong to you. If you lust after the material possessions of another, you have broken this command. If you slander someone, you have coveted a reputation. It is impossible not to covet. If we could live without coveting, perfection would be achieved. War itself is a result of covetousness. James writes:

> *"What causes fights and quarrels among you? Don't they come from your desires that battle within you? You want something but don't get it. You kill and covet, but you cannot have what you want. You quarrel and fight. You do not have, because you do not ask God. When you ask, you do not receive, because you ask with wrong motives, that you may spend what you get on your pleasures"*
>
> (4:1-3)

Buddhism recognizes this problem as well. The Four Noble Truths of this religion follow:

1. Suffering is universal.
2. The cause of suffering is craving (selfish desire, or coveting).
3. The cure for suffering is to eliminate craving.
4. Eliminate craving by following the Middle Way — the Noble Eightfold Path.[5]

Unfortunately there is not one Buddhist who can accomplish what the noble eightfold path requires. There is not one Christian or Jew who can keep the Ten Commandments. But the good news is this: Christians serve the One who has kept the Law perfectly – Jesus Christ, fully God, fully man, completely without sin. Jesus died on a cross for our sins and was raised again to life. His resurrection has destroyed any power that sin and death may have over our eternal destiny. God knows that we cannot eliminate coveting from our lives. He knows that we are unable in our own strength to keep the commandments. He wants our heart. He wants us to trust Him. When we do, the gift of everlasting life is ours. Out of gratitude, then, we struggle to obey His commands; and when we fail, we recognize the poverty of our spiritual estate and appreciate, even more, the work of our Lord. This is what Jesus means when He says, "*Blessed are the poor in spirit, for theirs is the kingdom of heaven*" (Mt. 5:3).

---

[5]See footnote 7, p. 165.

Text Number Two

The Greatest Command

"Teacher, which is the greatest commandment in the Law?"

Matthew 22:36

I have received a lot of advice in the course of my life: from parents at home, from employers, from seminary professors, from church officials, and from wizened servants of Christ. In the military, advice from one who is senior to you is construed as a command, and should be followed immediately. If the commanding officer of my unit issues a command, and then declares it to be the most important one he has ever given, I will pay particularly close attention, and redouble my efforts to comply. Christ has issued commands to His followers. If we are so passionate to obey the orders of our earthly commanders, how much more zealous should we be in following those of the Heavenly Commander? And Jesus has clearly spelled out the greatest commands.

When the lawyer asked Jesus, *"Teacher, which is the greatest commandment in the Law?"* (Mt. 22:36), he was hoping that our Lord would single out one of the Ten Commandments. By so doing, the legal experts of the day could bring scathing criticism against Him for making light of the other nine. As happened so frequently, however, Jesus stumped the critics. His response? *"'Love the Lord your God with all your heart and with all your soul and with all your mind.' This is the first and greatest commandment. And the second is like it: 'Love your neighbor as yourself'"* (Mt. 22:37-39). The answer was brilliant. The first and greatest commandment, which summarizes Commandments one through four, involves one's vertical relationship with the Almighty. The second one, which summarizes Commandments five through ten, involves one's horizontal relationship with fellow human beings. The command that Jesus gives is to love, and the word He uses is *agape*.[1] If Jesus Christ is the King of kings, and the Lord of all lords; if He is the Author and Finisher of our faith (Heb. 12:2), and the Captain of our salvation (Heb. 2:10); the commands He deems most important ought to be of paramount significance in our lives.

When Jesus first taught the great commandment, a religious lawyer approached Him and sought clarification. *"And who is my neighbor?"* (Luke 10:29). Perhaps we need to refine our terms and limit those to whom we are required to extend divine love. At this point, Jesus relates the parable of the Good Samaritan (Luke 10:30-37). By the time He finishes, the silence must have been deafening. For the Jew of Jesus' day, there was no such thing as a "good" Samaritan. Samaritans were bad![2] They were despised by the Jews. Racial tensions fomented great hatred between the two groups. Jewish leaders publicly cursed Samaritans in worship, offering prayers to God that they should have "no share in eternal life." A Jewish court of law would not accept the testimony

[1]See comments on agape love pp. 69-73.

[2]This makes our Lord's conversation with the Samaritan woman in the Gospel of John, chapter four, all the more compelling.

of a Samaritan, nor would a Jew accept their service.[3] Even the gospel writer John notes, *"Jews do not associate with Samaritans"* (John 4:9). How shocking that Jesus should tell the story of a *good* Samaritan! If He were to retell the story today, it could very easily be entitled: the parable of the Good Taliban, or the parable of the Good Communist. In any case, by the time Jesus finished telling the story, it was abundantly clear that the great command involves extending the love of God to all: to your enemies as well as to your friends (Mt. 5:43-48).

One of the highlights during my tenure as a pastor in upstate New York was an opportunity to attend the National Association of Evangelicals' "Washington Insight Briefing" in April 1994. A small group of pastors and lay leaders from all over the United States had the opportunity to meet with and listen to the President, five U.S. Senators, two Congressmen, one State Governor, and numerous other individuals, all influential in establishing policy for our nation. I particularly enjoyed a presentation by the by the late Rev. Richard Halversom, Chaplain of the U.S. Senate. At the time, Halversom was in his late 70's and walked with a cane. But his mind was as sharp as a razor, and his spirit overflowing with the love of God. For nearly an hour He held court with his evangelical audience, and reflected on some of the things he had observed over his years as Senate Chaplain. Two things, in particular, bothered him deeply about the witness of evangelicals in the nation's Capitol: the first was the type of letters Christian constituents sent to their Senators and Congressmen – angry letters, selfish letters, and single issue letters. Very rarely did a Congressman receive a positive letter, thanking him for a job well done. Halversom suggested

---

[3]Robert H. Stein,, *An Introduction to the Parables of Jesus,* (Philadelphia: The Westminster Press, 1981), p. 77.

that there was no better way to close off communication with the leaders of our land than to send letters such as these. The second issue that deeply bothered the Senate Chaplain was the reluctance of many Christian leaders to join the President at the White House for the National Day of Prayer. Even after repeated pleas from the nation's most powerful elected official, some Christian leaders refused to join President Clinton because of personal dislike for the man. Halversom suggested that the love of Christ would have done otherwise.

First Corinthians, chapter thirteen, offers an excellent description of the *agape* love about which Christ speaks. In a sermon entitled "The Greatest Thing in the World," the Rev. Henry Drummond, a nineteenth century Scottish clergyman, offers great insight into the text.[4] "What is the greatest thing in the world?" he asks. What is the *summum bonum*, the supreme good? What is the noblest object of desire? The supreme gift to covet? What is that pearl of Great Price, which if you had to give up everything else in order to purchase it, you would?

Is the greatest thing faith? We are encouraged throughout the Bible to have faith in God. We are told that salvation comes through faith in Jesus Christ (Eph. 2:8). But 1 Corinthians 13 declares, *"if I have a faith that can move mountains, but have not love, I am nothing"* (v. 2). Is the greatest thing knowledge? The ancient Greeks (and many who live today) treasured knowledge above all else, but 1 Corinthians 13 informs us that knowledge will pass away (v. 8). Is the greatest thing power? The ancient Romans (and many who live today) prized power above all else. But where are the armies of Rome? What has become of the empires of Charlemagne, of Genghis Khan, or of Napoleon? There is something far greater that operates in our world: a love that comes from

---

[4]*The Greatest Thing in the World,* Henry Drummond, (New York: Barse & Hopkins).

God, capable of destroying all enemy strongholds. Peter declares, *"Above all, love each other deeply, because love covers over a multitude of sins"* (1 Pe. 4:8). Paul writes, *"love is the fulfillment of the law"* (Ro. 13:10). Love fulfills the Ten Commandments, and is the essence of the great commandment. Love – the unconditional love of the Almighty – is the summum bonum, the greatest thing in the world. As Drummond analyzes 1 Co. 13, he divides the text into three parts: love contrasted (vv. 1-3), love analyzed (vv. 4-7), and love defended (vv. 8-13).

In verses one through three of 1 Co. 13, agape love is contrasted with other things that are very important. Famous singers, politicians, ministers, college professors and authors of great books can speak with eloquence in very moving ways, but it is quite possible to sway huge crowds and still have a heart that is callous and words that are brazen. We need people who love us and care about us more than pious words from some distant platform. Agape love is far better than prophesy or tongues. There are people who know the Bible inside and out and say they have great faith in God, but they do not care about their neighbor. Agape love is greater than a knowledge that puffs up. There are great philanthropists, men and women who give millions to charity, but they give with cold hearts. Sometimes it is easier to give a dollar to a beggar on the street than not to give it. Giving the dollar shuts him up; it takes his cry out of the giver's ear, but the motive is wrong. Love is far better than a cold-hearted philanthropy.

Verses four through seven of 1 Co. 13 analyze love. What is agape love? How can you recognize it? In ninth grade science class, many of us experimented with a prism and shined a light through it. At the other end of the prism, we were able to see the white light broken down into the seven colors of the rainbow. In analyzing divine love, nine elements are mentioned. *Love is patient*. It does not have a short temper or a quick fuse. *Love is kind*. We think of the great deal of time Christ spent in trying to make people happy. *Love does not envy*. It is very generous. Rather than seeking to have, it gives. *Love does not boast*. It is very humble. It talks more about the accomplishments of others than it does of oneself. *Love is not rude*. It is courteous. It is polite. It tries to do what is appropriate in social situations. *Love is not self-seeking*. It is unselfish. It seeks to help others before it helps self. *Love is not easily angered*. There is a time for anger, but it is controlled and well thought out. *Love does not rejoice in evil*. It is guileless. It looks for the best in every situation. And *love rejoices in the truth*. It is sincere.

Do others see these characteristics when they hold up the prism to your professions of love? Are these the characteristics that you see in others when they say that they love you? Love comes from God. Much in the same way that you cannot take the different colors of the spectrum and mix them together in a pot and produce light, you cannot work on these nine characteristics apart from God and come up with divine love. To love perfectly — to love your neighbor as yourself, or to love your enemy — you must open up your life to God. A human being is the prism through which the love of God flows. You cannot be an instrument of divine love unless you dwell in the presence of God through Jesus Christ.

Verses eight through thirteen of 1 Co. 13 defend divine love. Why is love the supreme possession? It lasts, the text tells us. It never fails. Prophesies have ceased. If you think of a book as great as the Holy Bible, and all of the prophesies that have been fulfilled; each of them have ceased. They are no longer prophesies, because they have been fulfilled. Tongues will cease. The language in which the New Testament was written, Koine Greek, is no longer spoken. It is gone, but love endures. The English language as we know it will one day vanish, but love remains. Knowledge will pass away. We no longer study the wisdom of the ancients. Very few people even care what Plato or Aristotle said so long ago. Their teachings may vanish, but the love of God remains. School children today know more science than Isaac Newton in his prime. Yesterday's newspaper ends up in the fire; it is old news. It passes away, but love continues. We defend this virtue of love, because it is the greatest of all virtues. We are told to have faith in God, but one day we will see Him face to face, and there will no longer be a need for faith. But love remains. Human beings cannot live without hope. Life, at some point, must get better. But one day, all of our hopes will be realized. As a young man, I had the hope of being married. In 1983, when I was united in marriage to my wife, that particular hope was fulfilled. But love still remains. As Christians, we look forward with great hope to the day we find ourselves in the presence of the Almighty. That will soon transpire, and the hope will be fulfilled. But love remains.

The eternal God is the source of all love, so when you share your life with others, do not merely offer joy or peace or rest or safety; that is but a thimbleful of what the Most High offers. The gospel, the good news of Jesus Christ, is all about the unconditional love of God, and the abundant life that results when a man or woman opens up his or her heart to embrace it. Agape love is the greatest power on earth, the only virtue that brings peace to the soul.

In looking at 1 Corinthians 13, Drummond concludes: "soiled and clumsy hands have touched a thing of exquisite beauty and holiness." Read this chapter regularly. Open your heart to the love of God and to the love of the Lord Jesus Christ, the One who died on a cross for you, while you were still in your sins (Ro. 5:8). Make it your life's passion to obey the greatest of His commands.

Text Number Three

The Great Commission

"go and make disciples of all nations, baptizing them in the name of the Father and of the Son and of the Holy Spirit, and teaching them to obey everything I have commanded you"

Matthew 28:19-20

My commissioning papers as an officer in the United States Navy read as follows:

> To all who shall see these presents, greeting: Know ye that, reposing special trust and confidence in the patriotism, valor, fidelity, and abilities of Roger Emory VanDerWerken, I do appoint him a Lieutenant, Chaplain Corps, United States Navy, as a Reserve Officer to rank as such from the Ninth day of January, nineteen hundred and ninety-six. This officer will therefore carefully and diligently discharge the duties of the office to which appointed by doing and performing all manner of things thereunto belonging.

> And I do strictly charge and require those officers and other personnel of lesser rank to render such obedience as is due an officer of this grade and position. And, this officer is to observe and follow such orders and directions from time to time, as may be given by the President of the United States of America or other superior officers, acting in accordance with the laws of the United States of America.
>
> This commission is to continue in force during the pleasure of the President of the United States of America, under the provisions of those public laws relating to officers of the Armed Forces of the United States of America and the component thereof in which this appointment is made.
>
> Done at the City of Washington, this ninth day of March, in the year of our Lord, one thousand nine hundred and ninety-eight and of the Independence of the United States of America, the two hundred and twenty-second. Effective: Date Accepted. By the President:

In accepting this commission, I swore an oath of allegiance which reads as follows:

> I Roger Emory VanDerWerken having been appointed Lieutenant in the U.S. Navy ... do accept such appointment and do solemnly swear (or affirm) that I will support and defend the Constitution of the United States against all enemies, foreign and domestic, that I will bear true faith and allegiance to the same; that I take this obligation freely, without any mental reservation or purpose of evasion; and that I will well and faithfully discharge the duties of the office on which I am about to enter, so help me God.

The passage of Scripture at which we are now looking is referred to as the "Great Commission." The words, you will note, are not entirely different from those printed upon my commissioning papers:

> *"Go and make disciples of all nations, baptizing them in the name of the Father, and of the Son, and of the Holy Spirit, and teaching them to obey everything I have commanded you. And surely I am with you always, to the very end of the age."*

As the President of the United States reposes special trust and confidence in my abilities as a citizen of his country to represent it faithfully wherever I might be sent, so Christ reposes special trust in me, as His child, to represent the interests of God's kingdom wherever I go. Jesus commissions all of His followers with the task of representing the kingdom of heaven. We are under His authority, and obedient to the orders of the great God who rules over us. My earthly commissioning papers remain in effect at the pleasure of the President; my heavenly commissioning endures until the "end of the age."

Christ issued the Great Commission shortly before His Ascension. In fact, the words of this commissioning may have been the last He ever spoke before leaving the earth. The Great Commission takes effect the moment any human being submits his or her life to the Lordship of Jesus Christ. I take my commissioning as a Naval Officer seriously; I want to be a good ambassador of my country. How much greater, then, is the attention I should give to the commissioning issued to me from on high?

The Great Commission involves several important points. First of all we are to "go." We are to take the battle to the enemy. We are to shine the light of Jesus Christ in the dark areas of this world. We do not passively sit at our desks and wait for the world to come to us; we "take it to the streets," challenging the very institutions of our world with the claims of our Lord. World War II was not won by sitting on the beaches of England, waiting for Nazi Germany to invade; the war was won by taking offensive action, invading the beaches of Normandy. Christians should become knowledgeable in the arts and in the sciences; we should study law, medicine, and politics, becoming the very best in our fields of endeavor while, at the same time, letting the light of Christ shine where God has placed us. Servants of the Most High need to get out of the Christian ghetto, and go into the world with the truths of God. Christian schools, Christian radio, Christian television, Christian magazines and newspapers are excellent ways to disciple the Body of Christ, but they do very little in reaching beyond the confines of the Church. To go into the world, we must understand it, and be able to speak the same language as those we are trying to reach.

The second part of the Great Commission involves making disciples. This includes evangelism and spiritual growth. Evangelism is the act of bringing good news to those who wallow in despair. Without Christ, people perish; they will never have inner peace, tranquillity or joy. Their lives will be marked by turbulence. Evangelism brings the good news of eternal life in heaven as opposed to eternal perdition in hell. John McCrae's famous poem, "In Flanders Fields" serves to illustrate the passion that servants of the Most High should have for evangelism:

In Flanders fields the poppies blow
Between the crosses, row on row,
That mark our place; and in the sky
The larks, still bravely singing, fly
Scarce heard amid the guns below.

We are the dead. Short days ago
We lived, felt dawn, saw sunset glow,
Loved, and were loved, and now we lie
In Flanders fields.

Take up our quarrel with the foe:
To you from failing hands we throw
The torch; be yours to hold it high.
If ye break faith with us who die
We shall not sleep, though poppies grow
In Flanders fields.

The Church will die (it will never die) if we fail to share the Good News of Jesus Christ. Those who have gone before us have handed us a bright torch, a message that brings life. If we fail to declare this message and fail to take up the quarrel with the Devil and his minions, the Dead will hold us accountable. As the Apostle Paul declares: *"Woe to me if I do not preach the gospel!"* (1 Co. 9:16). Evangelism, telling the story of Jesus, is an essential part in fulfilling the Great Commission, but more is required.

Making disciples involves spiritual growth as well as evangelism. Our mission is not complete when someone makes a decision to follow Jesus as Savior and Lord. In the military, the completion of boot camp is a great accomplishment, but it is only the beginning. So, too, with the Christian journey. Continual training is necessary to grow in the faith. We need to read the Bible, and understand how it fits together (theology). We need to learn how to pray, and how to follow the teachings of Jesus. This is a never ending process. Discipleship continues until the day we die.

While serving as an assistant pastor at a church in suburban Philadelphia, one of my responsibilities was to follow up on members of the church who had not attended for long periods of time. At one such home visit, I was informed by an elderly man that the sole purpose of the church was to "provide Sunday School programming for young people." Amazingly, this man was a retired Army Colonel. I responded (rather boldly, at that), "the entire mission of the Army is to get people through boot camp. After that, no further training would be needed." The Colonel got the point. Discipleship never ends. It is an ongoing process where young people are able to tap into the wisdom of their elders, and where older folks are inspired by the passion of their juniors. In so doing, we all become better servants of the Most High.

The third element of the Great Commission involves making disciples of all nations. Unlike God's covenant with the Jewish people in the Old Testament, our responsibility involves sharing the gospel with everyone: rich or poor, moral or immoral, religious or not. People from every racial background, language, and religion are invited to become disciples of the Lord Jesus. Church doors are never closed to anyone who has an interest in God. The beginning of the Calvary Chapel movement in the 1960's serves to illustrate. Many hippies of that day were attracted to Pastor Chuck Smith's preaching at a small local church in southern California, entering the sanctuary with bare feet and dirty clothing. Church elders were concerned that newly installed carpet would become soiled by such a crowd. Pastor Chuck responded, "if the carpet prevents these young people hearing the gospel, remove it." His comments marked a turning point in the church's ministry. Since then, thousands of Calvary Chapel churches have been planted throughout the world, bringing the message of God's love to all people.

Baptism is the fourth major element of the Great Commission, marking one's initiation into the Christian faith. There are many perspectives on how and when baptism should be administered, and unfortunately, the Bible offers little guidance on the subject.[1] But one thing is very clear: every believer should be baptized in obedience to Christ. My ordination is with the American Baptist Churches, and I appreciate the manner in which we celebrate baptism. Baptist ministers ask the candidate, "Have you accepted Jesus as your personal Lord and Savior?" This is followed up with, "Are you making a commitment, with God's help, to follow Him the rest of your life?" If the answer to both of these questions is "yes," the candidate is submerged backwards into the

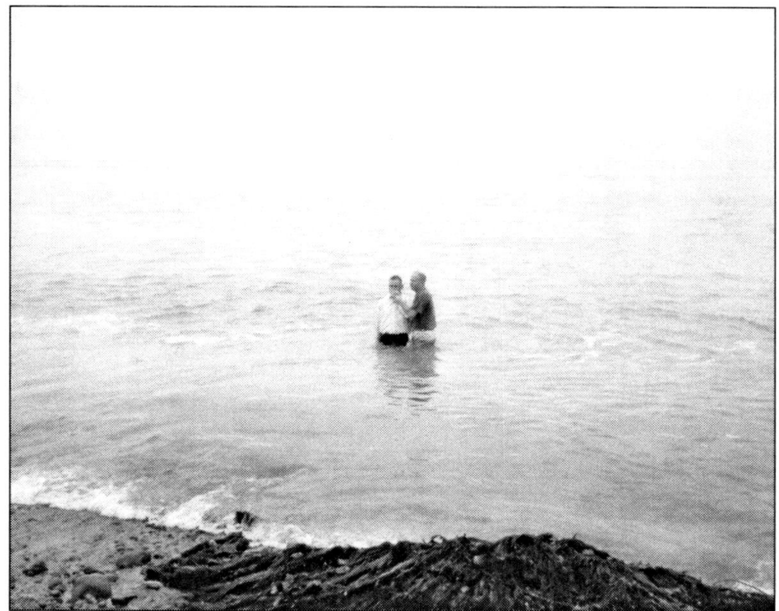

[1]See further comments regarding baptism on page 130.

water, and raised up again, a vivid picture of the death and resurrection of Jesus Christ, as well as a picture of the death, resurrection, and new life of the one being baptized.

The water washing the body is symbolic of the spiritual cleansing of one's heart. When we confess our sins, and ask for forgiveness, the Holy Spirit enters our lives and cleanses us from all of our sin. We baptize, as commanded, in the "name of the Father, and of the Son and of the Holy Spirit," and although no one completely grasps the nature of the Trinity, the baptismal formula uses "name" in the singular, but "Father, Son, and Holy Spirit" in the plural: one God, three persons. Whenever someone is baptized, a statement is made: "I believe in the great God of Scripture, and totally surrender my life to Him."

Finally, the Great Commission tells that we are responsible to teach those who have accepted Christ to obey everything He has commanded. Obedience to the lawful orders of those who are senior in a military chain of command is one of the great keys to success in battle. This principle is equally valid in our struggles against the world, the flesh, and the Devil. It is critical for those who enlist in the army of the Most High to obey the things Christ has commanded.

Text Number Four

The Whole Armor of God

"Finally, be strong in the Lord and in his mighty power."
Ephesians 6:10

The Apostle Paul closes his letter to the church in Ephesus with the exhortation, *"be strong in the Lord and in His mighty power. Put on the full armor of God so that you can take your stand against the devil's schemes."* He then proceeds to give us a shopping list of gear issued to every soldier in the mighty Roman army.

When I first checked in with the First Combat Engineer Battalion, I was issued the following equipment:

(1) Camouflaged Alice Pack in which to carry all of my gear
(1) Load bearing vest to carry canteens, smaller packs, weapons[1]
(1) Pair of men's gloves and liners for cold weather operations
(1) Tent shelter half and related gear
(1) Flak jacket to protect upper torso
(2) Canteens and (1) canteen cup
(1) Knit cap for cold weather
(1) Kevlar helmet
(2) Sets polypro long undergarments
(1) Entrenching tool
(1) First Aid kit
(1) Poncho and liner
(1) Gortex jacket and pants
(1) Field pack — for smaller daytime operations
(1) Sleeping bag system
(1) Gas mask

What I was issued was far more sophisticated than that received by the Roman soldier 2000 years ago, but the purpose of the gear is exactly the same: to equip the soldier for war.

The Christian is involved in spiritual warfare; his battles are not against flesh and blood. The enemy he faces is demonic and invisible, lurking behind every evil that is seen. To engage such a one without making use of God's armor is foolish, and whoever attempts to do so is totally ineffective in the battle for human souls. The Christian soldier must equip himself with the full armor of God on a daily basis.

Equipment used by Marines is not fool proof. On a trip to the desert training grounds of Twenty-nine Palms, Califor-

[1]A chaplain does not use or bear arms. Senior ranking Marines (E-6 and above) are issued a 9mm pistol and magazines. Junior ranking Marines are issued an M-16 rifle and magazines.

nia, in May 1999, a young man was killed when a ricocheting round from an M-16 rifle tore through his flak jacket. On numerous other occasions, Marines have been killed because their armament was not sufficient to protect them. God's armament, however, offers perfect protection against the spiritual enemies humans face.

Ephesians, chapter six, commands us to stand firm with a belt of truth buckled around the waist (v.14a). Marines wear load-bearing vests to which are attached ammunition magazines and canteens. If a Marine runs out of ammunition, he is unable to engage the enemy, and his life is endangered. If he runs out of water, he will dehydrate and be ineffective in battle. The load-bearing vest ensures that two of the Marine's most essential items for success in battle are within arm's reach. In like manner, the Christian soldier wears a belt of truth. He is honest, forthright, and a person of integrity. The truthful manner in which we conduct our business bears witness to the great God we serve.

In addition to the belt of truth, we also arm ourselves with a breastplate of righteousness (v. 14b). Marines don Kevlar-lined flak jackets prior to going into combat. When a weapon explodes in the vicinity of one of these warriors, the flak jacket protects vital organs from shrapnel and debris that is scattered over large areas of the battlefield. Likewise, the Christian dons a breastplate of righteousness. Righteousness is one's standing with God. If you are righteous, you will go to heaven and inherit the blessings of God's kingdom. If you are not righteous, you will go to an eternal place of torment. The book of Romans tells us that the righteous live by faith (Ro. 1:17), and that righteousness comes from God through faith in Jesus Christ (Ro. 3:22). To be successful on the battlefields of human life, we must place our faith in Jesus Christ. If we fail to do this, the horrible weapons employed by our hideous enemy will maim and destroy. By putting on the breastplate of righteousness, we are spared this destruction and promised an eternal home in the kingdom of our Lord.

We also fit our feet with *"the readiness that comes from the gospel of peace"* (v. 15). Marines wear combat boots, sturdy footwear laced high above the ankles. These offer great protection from the elements, keeping both feet and ankles safe. Of all the battle gear worn by Marines, the combat boot requires the most time to put on. Once the boot is laced up, however, the Marine is "ready for battle." When other nations ask for military help from the United States, Marines are generally the first to respond, and when those black leather boots march into an area where help was requested, good news breaks out: victory is on the way. Christians should always be ready to share the gospel (the good news) of Jesus Christ. Wherever God places us, we bring hope and peace to those suffering under the slings and arrows of the evil one. If we are living our lives in a way that honors the God who has sent us, others should rejoice that we are in their midst. As Isaiah the prophet writes: *'How beautiful on the mountains are the feet of those who bring good news, who proclaim peace, who bring good tidings, who proclaim salvation, who say to Zion, "Your God reigns!"'* (52:7).

We take up the shield of faith to extinguish the arrows of the enemy (v. 16). Marines do not carry shields, but they are very skilled at finding shelter in any type of terrain. A three inch hollow in the earth's surface offers sufficient cover to survive an enemy attack. When time allows, they are able to build bunkers and trenches, revetted with lumber and earth to protect from enemy armament. Christians take up the shield of faith, a faith that is grounded in the person and work of Jesus Christ. Only He is able to protect us from the enemy. Wherever we go, Christ, our great shield, goes before us.

Christians also strap on the helmet of salvation (v. 17a). The Kevlar helmet worn by Marines protects the head from "the fog of war." Nothing is more devastating than a head wound, and without a helmet, nothing is more exposed. Christ offers salvation (victory) to all who believe in Him, and when one receives this gift, he becomes a child of God (John 1:12), part of the Body of Christ, with Jesus Himself serving as head of the body (Eph. 5:23). For me, much of the "fog of life" cleared up when I put on the helmet of salvation. The journey through life's battlefields is significantly better because of the One who is sovereign over my very thought processes.

Finally, we are to take up *"the sword of the Spirit, which is the word of God"* (v. 17b). All of the "armor of God" mentioned up to this point is defensive in nature, but now we equip ourselves with a weapon. Every Marine is a rifleman, deadly accurate in the use of the M-16. Annually, he must qualify with his weapon at distances of 200, 300 and 500 yards, firing from four different positions: prone, kneeling, sitting and standing. The qualification involves firing at two different rates: slow fire, where three 5-round magazines must be emptied in 20 minutes, and rapid fire where two 5-round cartridges must be emptied in less than seventy seconds. If a Marine fails to qualify, his career will be short. When Marines are in the field, they are never to be separated from their rifle; they eat with it, they sleep with it, and they relieve themselves with their rifle close at hand. Although I totally disagree with the theology of the "Infantryman's Creed" (Perhaps someday I'll be in a position to change it), its passion gives valuable insight as to the importance of the most valuable piece of equipment issued to the Marine:

Infantryman's Creed

This is my rifle. There are many like it but this one is mine. My rifle is my best friend. It is my life. I must master it as I master my life. My rifle, without me is useless. Without my rifle, I am useless. I must fire my rifle true. I must shoot straighter than any enemy who is trying to kill me. I must shoot him before he shoots me. I will. My rifle and I know that what counts in this war is not the rounds we fire, the noise of our burst, or the smoke we make. We know that it is the hits that count. We will hit.

My rifle is human, even as I, because it is my life. Thus, I will learn it as a brother. I will learn its weakness, its strength, its parts, its accessories, its sights and its barrel. I will keep my rifle clean and ready, even as I am clean and ready. We will become part of each other.

Before God I swear this creed. My rifle and I are the defenders of my country. We are the masters of our enemy. We are the saviors of my life. So be it, until victory is America's and there is no enemy but peace.[2]

For Christians, a thorough knowledge of the Bible is a weapon of great offensive power. If we know the Word, and if we live by it, spiritual enemies will crumble before us. I try to read the Scriptures every day. I have read through the Bible on numerous occasions. I have read it in other languages. I read it in the morning; I read it in the evening. Sometimes I will use a devotional such as *Our Daily Bread* from the Radio Bible Class in Grand Rapids, Michigan. Sometimes I use

---

[2]It is believed that M Gen. William H. Rupertus, USMC, authored the creed shortly after the Japanese attack on Pearl Harbor in 1941. Marlon F. Sturkey, *Warrior Culture of the U.S. Marines*, 2001.

pocket-sized bibles graciously placed within military units by men and women of the Gideon's organization. Sometimes I'll read an entire book of the Bible in one sitting. On other occasions I'll read five Psalms and one chapter of Proverbs every day. (This practice will result in reading through the books of Psalms and Proverbs in one month.) I am always interested in how other people interpret the Scriptures.

The Bible testifies to its own power. The Psalmist declares: *"Thy word is a lamp unto my feet, and a light unto my path"* (119:105, KJV). The author of Hebrews writes, *"the word of God is quick, and powerful, and sharper than any two-edged sword, piercing even to the dividing asunder of soul and spirit, and … is a discerner of the thoughts and intents of the heart"* (4:12, KJV). As noted above, the words of Scripture sustained many POWs in enemy camps when almost all hope of survival was gone. The Bible is given to men and women sitting in brigs today, with the hope that the power of God's Word will change their lives. As men and women of God, serving in the great army of the Most High, it is paramount that we equip ourselves with the best that God has to offer. We must read His Word, abide by it, and let it dwell richly in our hearts. In so doing, the spiritual enemies we face will fall before us.

The last command in the book of Ephesians is: *"pray in the Spirit on all occasions with all kinds of prayers and requests"* (v. 18). Prayer is the communication that takes place between God and man. As any commander knows, if the lines of communication between headquarters and foot soldier are severed, the war is lost. It does not matter how well-equipped the soldier might be. If bread and bullets are cut off, the warrior cannot fight. Prayer – communication with God – is critical to the success of anyone serving in the army of the Most High.

Text Number Five

The Weapons of our Warfare

"For though we live in the world, we do not wage war as the world does. The weapons we fight with are not the weapons of the world. On the contrary, they have divine power to demolish strongholds. We demolish arguments and every pretension that sets itself up against the knowledge of God, and we take captive every thought to make it obedient to Christ."

2 Corinthians 10:3-5

The American Heritage Dictionary defines a stronghold as: 1) "a fortress," or 2) "an area of predominance."[1] As Christians, we do not want the enemy to have a stronghold in any arena of life: neither in the military, nor in our schools, our halls of government, or any other segment of human society. Some of the arguments and pretensions that the enemy uses include comments such as: 1) "It doesn't matter what you believe, as long as you are sincere. There are many roads

[1]*The American Heritage Dictionary of the English Language,* (Boston: American Heritage Publishing Co., Inc., Wm. Morris, Editor, 1975), p.1277.

that lead to God." (Could you imagine such a philosophy in the military? "It doesn't matter how you fight, as long as you give it your all?") 2) "We cannot see God. Why should we believe in something that our senses cannot perceive?" (We cannot see electricity or gravity either, but we do well to pay attention to their influence.) 3) "There is no God. Everything just evolved." (There is no William Shakespeare either. The tragedy called "Hamlet" came together by itself.) 4) "There is no judgment; there is no hell." (Who gives you the authority to make such pronouncements?)

In the name of Jesus Christ, we demolish these kinds of arrogant boasts. As salt and light in a world that can be unsavory and dark, we are a redeeming influence. But as we come against Satan and his minions, we do not resort to worldly techniques; we use divine power, dunamis,[2] to eliminate the strongholds of Satan, and this power is tapped into by simply obeying God's commands.

Life in the military is generally much more intense than life in the civilian world. We see human nature at its noblest and at its ugliest. Due to the youth of those who serve in the Armed Forces, and due to the close quarters in which we find ourselves, many of the subtleties so common to civilian life have yet to be cultivated. Things are taken at face value: what you see is what you get. As a result, a believer in Jesus Christ stands out from among his peers. Although living in a world where violence, drunkenness, filthy language, and adulterous behavior can be quite prevalent,[3] the Christian does not engage in this. Faithful, non-judgmental Christian

---

[2]Our English word "dynamite" comes from this Greek word.

[3]I might add that most who fall in these categories are very much aware of their sin, and are willing to talk about it, opening up great opportunities for gospel witness. (In the parable of the Pharisee and the Tax Collector, Luke 18:9-14, it was the man who recognized his sinful estate, not the religious leader, who went home justified before God).

living in an intense military environment brings about scores of conversions. The Scriptural teaching – living in the world but not waging war as the world does – begins to make a lot of sense. Doing what is right, reinforced by the power of God, brings down enemy strongholds.

Combat Engineers are proficient with the M-16 rifle and the 9mm Beretta pistol, but their specialty is explosives. They are experts in the use of plastic explosives, fuses, blasting caps, detonation cord, TNT, dynamite, and ammonium nitrate. They can destroy any obstacle in their path. Bomb craters, barb wire configurations, tank ditches, fallen trees, mines or blown bridges — all of which slow down troop movement — can be overcome by the capable combat engineer. In addition, the engineer can blow up enemy strongholds: buildings, bridges, bunkers and the like. Marines, in general, will destroy anything that gets in the way of their mission. They will persevere until every enemy has been taken captive and made obedient to the will of the nation. They will use any weapon at their disposal to make this happen: ships, landing craft, helicopters, fixed winged aircraft, field guns, machine guns, grenade launchers, missiles and even the K-Bar knife. These are the worldly weapons used by military units to win battles and defeat the enemy, but they are not the kinds of weapons the Christian employs as he takes on spiritual enemies.

When the Apostle Paul speaks of "weapons of the world," he refers to moral shortcomings: sexual immorality, jealousy, envy, rage, drunkenness, lying, and gossip (Pro. 6:16-19; 1 Co. 6:9-10; Gal. 5:19-21). Roman Catholic Christians speak of seven "deadly" or "capital" sins: pride, avarice, envy, wrath, lust, gluttony, and sloth.[4] Humans naturally

[4]*Catechism of the Catholic Church,* (New York: Catholic Book Publishing Co., 1994), p. 457.

gravitate toward these kinds of behavior, especially under stressful situations, but it is not how the Christian responds. Our weapons are different. When someone smites us on one cheek, we do not hit back (Mt. 5:39). When someone does us wrong, we do not resort to gossip. There is no need to go to the bar and get drunk in order to "connect." We do not need to laugh at filthy, racist jokes or look at the pornography of our friends in order to "relate." God's weapons, His Divine protection and love, are sufficient to "wage war" in this world. His weapons bring down enemy strongholds, protect us from the contamination of this world, completely disarm spiritual forces that oppose the Most High, and bring victory to those in bondage. As we engage the arguments and pretensions that set themselves up against the knowledge of our God, may we not be ashamed to use the weapons with which the Most High has equipped us. They, indeed, have divine power, capable of demolishing enemy strongholds.

Text Number Six

The Greatest of All Weapons

"This, then, is how you should pray ..."

Matthews 6:9

One of the most interesting and least known billets for an enlisted man in the United States Marine Corps is the Gunnery Sergeant who is assigned as Division Officer for newly-recruited chaplains at the Naval Education and Training Command in Newport, Rhode Island. Can you imagine the challenge of taking ministers, scholarly men and women from hundreds of faith backgrounds who have spent most of their lives in academic and ecclesiastical circles, and transforming them into military officers? The "Gunny" for my class was a man by the name of Henry Johnson. He was assigned to the Chaplain School with no idea what his responsibilities might be, but there could not have been a better man for the job. Gunnery Sergeant Johnson was well-read, respectful, and eloquent in his own Marine Corps way. He knew how to speak in a manner that was not offensive to men and women of the cloth, but he also knew how to "run a tight ship," and whip inexperienced chaplains into a state of high military readiness. In two short months, our class of fifteen had doffed their suits and ties, and had learned the proper way to wear and care for various military uniforms. (Navy chaplains serve in the Marines, the Coast Guard, and the Merchant Marines, as well as in the Navy, and each of these branches has several different uniforms). We learned how to march, how to salute, and how to recognize the different officer and enlisted rankings found in each of the branches of the Armed Forces. Johnson took a group of out-of-shape, overweight fellows (my class was all men), and soon had us well within Navy standards. He coordinated our efforts to learn swimming, shipboard damage control, and firefighting. By the end of two months we were a very different group of people.

Prior to entering Navy Chaplain School, I knew that I would be assigned to a Marine battalion at Camp Pendleton, California, so I listened with rapt attention every time the Gunny spoke about his branch of service. One thing he said really stuck with me: "Every Marine is a rifleman." Regardless of military occupational specialty (MOS), he knows how to shoot. Cooks, tank drivers, intelligence specialists and construction shop workers are deadly accurate on the rifle range. They shoot standing up, seated or from prone positions, from 200 yards, 500 yards, or from any distance in between. Marines know their weapon inside and out. They can take it apart and put it together in the dark. They sleep with it, they eat with it, and it never leaves their sight when training or on the battlefield. The M-16 rifle is the weapon of choice, and when a Marine masters it, it builds self-confidence, confidence in the team, and ensures victory on the battlefield.

It is often said that the best defense is a good offense, and that we should attack our enemy where he is most vulnerable. For the believer in Jesus Christ, prayer is the greatest weapon. Prayer puts us in communication with the Commander-in-Chief, and hits our enemy where he is most vulnerable. Satan does not have the privilege of regular communication with the Almighty. But we do, and when we pray regularly and effectively, it builds self-confidence and worth. We become better team players, and are ensured victory on the spiritual battlefields of life. Jesus said, "*men ought always to pray, and not to faint*" (Luke 18:1, KJV). In the same manner as a Marine is able to use his weapon in any situation, so the Christian is able to pray at any time, tapping into a divine power capable of demolishing enemy strongholds (2 Co. 10:4).

In the Sermon on the Mount Jesus says, *"This is how you should pray."* He then proceeds to teach His disciples what is commonly known as "The Lord's Prayer," or the "Our Father." Committed to memory by Christians all around the world, the prayer is often recited without even understanding its basic concepts. Shakespeare writes: "My words fly up, my thoughts remain below. Words without thoughts never to heaven go."[1] A prayer that is honest, coming from one's heart is a far greater spiritual weapon than parroted words without thought. As we study Jesus' model prayer, we learn how to address the Almighty, how to praise and glorify His name, and how to make our requests known to the Most High.

Our Father which art in Heaven.... The opening word of the model prayer is exceedingly important. "Our" is a possessive pronoun. We pray as a community. We are not alone; there is more to the equation than "me and Jesus." When we pray, we are speaking to God on behalf of hundreds of people who are in our spheres of influence, and they are praying for us. By ourselves we can do very little, but as a team we can change the world. A military unit that does not train together is ineffective in battle. Spiritual warriors pray together; we need each other.

In the model prayer, Jesus tells us to address God as "Father," and although the Most High is neither male nor female (John 4:24), it is not prudent to change the words of Scripture. A good earthly father provides, protects, and loves. Our Heavenly Father does far more, transcending even what we can think or imagine.

God lives in heaven; we are on the earth, but God is also present in our midst. He sees our joys, understands our trials, and never forsakes us. But ultimately, He resides in the

---

[1]*The Complete Works of William Shakespeare,* (New York, NY: Walter J. Black, Inc.) *Hamlet,* Act 3, scene 3, p. 1152.

heavens. One day we will see God face to face, and join Him in that place where the streets are lined with gold, where there is no more pain, sorrow, suffering or death. One day we will reside in the heavens, and experience His love to its fullest. Until then, as we speak to the One who dwells there, we are reminded of the place He has prepared for us.

Hallowed be thy name: This is the first of five petitions in Jesus' prayer. "Hallowed" means holy. May the name of God be held in high esteem. May His name be honored in all that we do.

As a chaplain, I wear exactly the same uniform as every other Marine in the battalion, with the exception of a small cross on the left collar. In the course of a day, I often hear very juicy epithets used to describe the most mundane things, salty language which Marines and sailors are so accustomed to using. When the offending party suddenly realizes that the chaplain is standing right next to him, profuse apologies are often made (as if we have never heard such words before!). The real offense is against God, and I often remind the embarrassed Marine that even though the chaplain may not always be present, God is. It is shameful to hear the manner in which some believers speak. Believing that they are "cool," or "blending in with the crowd," they come across as great hypocrites. A real man or woman is not afraid of what others think, not ashamed to live up to the Biblical standard of refraining from unwholesome talk (n. Eph. 4:29).

On one occasion, during a field exercise, I walked into the tent of my battalion commander, just as he was letting loose a horrible expletive to describe his innermost feelings. Upon seeing the chaplain, the CO turned red in the face, and we both chuckled about the timing of the incident. I asked him if he knew the difference between obscenity and profanity. He said that he did not. "Obscenity," I informed him, "is when, for the lack of vocabulary, a man uses bodily parts and functions to express himself." We both chuckled again. (Fortunately, my commander had a great sense of humor.) "Profanity is something far worse; it takes the name of God and runs it through the mud. I am glad, sir, that you do not use profanity."

Hypocrisy is far worse than either obscenity or profanity. Men and women who call themselves Christians and then take advantage of people by using the name of God for financial gain or for other purposes, have not honored God but blasphemed Him. When we pray, the name of God is to be hallowed. We who take His name ought to live our lives in such a way that proclaims it.

Thy kingdom come. Thy will be done in earth, as it is in heaven. In this, the second petition of the Lord's Prayer, we are asking God that His will be done and not our own. We like being in charge; we enjoy sitting on the throne, but Christ's prayer reminds us that God is in charge. When we submit our will to His, we have victory in the battles of life. In asking God that His will be done, we remember our calling to be servants to the One who rules over the heavens and the earth.

God commands us to be salt in an unsavory world; He commands us to be light in a world that is filled with darkness (Mt. 5:13-14). When we are obedient, God's kingdom breaks through the darkness. The more obedient we become, the more we will see the hand of God at work. This is what Jesus meant when He said, "*the kingdom of God is within you*" (Luke 17:21). As servants of the Most High, we honor all people; we treat them with dignity and respect. We follow the sexual ethics that are taught in the Bible. We work hard for the money we earn and are not greedy. As we obey the Lord, there will be a day coming when we will see Him in the fullness of His kingdom, in a "*new heaven and a new earth, the home of righteousness*" (2 Pe. 3:13).

Give us this day our daily bread. The third petition of the Lord's Prayer reminds us that God is in charge. He supplies us with all of our needs; we need not worry. Military personnel often spend a significant amount of time worrying about getting promoted. "If I get this ribbon or medal," they say, "my chances for promotion are so much better." God wants us to live in the present. Do your job! Do it to the best of your ability! It is good to dream, to think about the future, and to plan for it, but do not be consumed with worry. In the Sermon on the Mount, the words of Jesus are as relevant today as they were 2000 years ago: *"do not worry about tomorrow, for tomorrow will worry about itself. Each day has enough trouble of its own"* (Mt. 6:34). Jesus' words remind us to focus on the mission at hand, to accomplish one thing at a time. In so doing, we will experience victory on a daily basis; God will meet our every need.

And forgive us our debts, as we forgive our debtors (petition #4). God has forgiven us our sins. They were taken care of at the cross. Once and for all, the penalty was paid (Heb. 7:27). If God has delivered our souls from Hell, ought not we, His forgiven ones, let go of the harmful things others have done to us? Many of God's people are filled with bitterness and have no victory in their lives because they are not able to forgive. Forgiveness does not mean you allow people to walk all over you, but it does mean you will let go of the hurts perpetrated against you. Forgiveness does not mean you will not report what has been done to the proper authorities (you may elect not to), but it does mean you will leave resolution of the matter in their hands. It is a good thing that our salvation is not based on our ability to forgive others. If it were, very few of us would get to heaven. The joy and life we are able to experience in this world, however, is directly proportional to our ability to forgive those who have harmed us. A man who has an unforgiving spirit is like one who holds a burning coal in his hand: the only one who gets burned is holding the coal.

And lead us not into temptation, but deliver us from evil. Christ has delivered us from evil. He destroyed the Devil, sin and death in one fell swoop. As the Scriptures remind us: "*You have been set free from sin and have become slaves to righteousness*" (Ro. 6:18). This fifth and final petition of the Lord's Prayer reminds us of what God has done and what is required of His people.

Do you struggle keeping sexual passion under control? Why, then, do you spend your time looking at pornographic magazines, X-rated movies, and seedy web sites? Do you struggle with greed? Why are you spending so much money playing the lottery? Is arrogant pride your issue? Why, then, is it so important that you receive praise for everything you do? So often we become our own worst enemy. We pour gasoline on fires that already burn within. This petition reminds us of things we should not be doing, of people with whom we should not be associating, and of places we should avoid. Temptations abound, but we thank God that He does not lead us into them. By remembering who God is, and what He has done, we flee those dangers that seek to destroy the soul.

For thine is the kingdom, and the power, and the glory, forever. Amen. The closing words of the Lord's Prayer are not found in all of the ancient manuscripts, but the prayer as most commonly recited includes these words. They are fitting and consistent with Biblical theology. By offering these thoughts in a spirit of prayer, we remember that God is in charge; all power and praise belong to Him. NFL football fans get very excited on any given Sunday. Citizens can place great hope in political leaders. Musicians and movie stars stir deep emotions. Military officers place great faith in delivery systems and in the tonnage of modern-day weapons, but God is in charge. He holds the future in His hands, and one day we will stand before Him in judgment. He will not ask us how successful we were, how much money we earned, how often we attended church, or to how many philanthropic causes we contributed. On that day, His question will be, "What did you do with my Son?" Christ promises a kingdom to all who place their faith in Him. The closing words of this great prayer remind us that the ultimate victory in life, the salvation of our souls, is achieved by trusting the Lord Jesus Christ.

Text Number Seven

The Attitude of a Soldier
(The Beatitudes)

"Now when he saw the crowds, he went up on a mountainside and sat down. His disciples came to him, and he began to teach them"

Matthew 5:1-2

Wherever a United States Marine goes, his presence is noted. His hair is short and neatly trimmed. His clothing is clean, and his shirt is tucked in. Male Marines do not wear earrings on or off duty. Neither do they use illegal drugs. Marines are polite in their dealings with others, frequently using "sir" or "ma'am" when addressing a stranger. Their uniforms are impeccable, and the salutes are sharp. If you ask a Marine how things are going, a likely response will be, "outstanding!" There is an attitude that causes the Marine to stand out among his peers. It is a learned behavior, a result of very intensive training.

Jesus, likewise, seeks to cultivate a certain attitude among His followers. His teachings found in the "Sermon on the Mount" have been highly influential throughout the ages. What a thrill it must have been for the crowds to have heard this incredible man share from the depths of His soul at that remote Galilean hillside so long ago. As recorded in chapters five through seven of the Gospel of Matthew, the teachings of Jesus Christ come from the heart of God. All who read and follow will benefit greatly.

At the outset of the Sermon on the Mount, Jesus teaches human blessedness. The first twelve verses of Matthew chapter five, referred to as the beatitudes, constitute a formula for happiness, peace, and joy. One might say that these are the "attitudes" to which a child of God adheres in order to live "the blessed life." There are eight of them. If the desire of your heart is to honor the King of kings, the beatitudes need to be part and parcel of your innermost being.[1]

In looking at each of the beatitudes, one notices they fly directly in the face of what the world would constitute success or happiness. Some Christian teachers even suggest that

---

[1]Recommended reading on the beatitudes: *The Divine Conspiracy, Rediscovering our Hidden Life in God,* Dallas Willard, HarperSanFrancisco, 1998. *The Cost of Discipleship,* Dietrich Bonhoeffer, The MacMillan Company, 1937.

the beatitudes be relegated to some future "kingdom age." But they apply now. In our prayers to God, we ask: *"your kingdom come, your will be done on earth as it is in heaven"* (Mt. 6:10). This is something we want now. God's kingdom is for the present, as well as the future.

In following the beatitudes, Christians may not achieve the success or fame that the world offers, but we walk closer to the heart of God. As foot soldiers in His army, we prefer to do the will of our Commander-in-Chief. As the Scripture declares: *"No one serving as a soldier gets involved in civilian affairs — he wants to please his commanding officer"* (2 Ti. 2:4). The success the world offers may bring temporary happiness, but it is often fleeting, leaving only emptiness of soul as it departs. The success God offers runs deep, and endures forever.

Beatitude 1: *Blessed are the poor in spirit ... theirs is the kingdom of heaven.* Much of basic training in the military — be it Plebe Summer, Boot Camp, the Basic School, Flight School, or any other initiation — involves the application of overwhelming amounts of mental, physical, and spiritual stress. Long periods without sleep, grueling physical and mental testing, ever-changing scenarios, and senior personnel who are always "in your face" ultimately build strong individuals who will function well in stressful wartime environments. One of the key points learned by anyone who has ever graduated from Boot Camp is that everyone has a breaking point. No one can make it on his own. Only after a person has been "broken" can he be trained to become a valuable member of the Armed Forces.

The same principle applies in God's kingdom. The Most High seeks those who are *spiritually* broken – men and women who recognize their own sinfulness and unworthiness – to serve as His soldiers. When we acknowledge our spiritual poverty, God begins to work in our lives. The Christian who believes that he has it "all together" is of little value in spiritual warfare. Only those who are *poor* in spirit receive the blessing. There is no room for "holier-than-thou," "self-righteous" attitudes. The man or woman who comes to God with a broken spirit is the one who finds salvation and enters heaven's gates.

Beatitude 2: *Blessed are those who mourn ... they will be comforted.* One of my most difficult moments as a chaplain was to comfort the mother of a Marine who had died in a vehicular accident in the line of duty. Mom had never been to California, but now she had to gather funds together and make the trip west only to see her twenty-year-old son lying in a casket. For four days I was her escort. We went to the site of the accident; we visited with friends of the deceased, and we met with officers who were in the young man's chain of command. The most emotional moment of the entire visit was viewing her son's body at the local funeral home. Standing next to the Lance Corporal's casket, in his dress blues, tears streaming down his face, was the young man's Company Commander. The Marine Captain was mourning the loss of one of his men.

God does not call us to be stoics. There are many occasions that warrant our tears. It is important to mourn with those who are mourning. In fact, one of the worst things we can do to someone who has suffered loss (and loss does not always mean death; It can mean divorce, trouble with the law, failing health, etc.) is avoidance. Those who are able to mourn with others will also be comforted during their time of loss.

Beatitude 3: *Blessed are the meek ... they will inherit the earth.* The mighty weapons of war in the arsenals of the United States have not made us a great nation. Conversely, the values for which we stand have made us what we are today. Concepts such as liberty, justice, and an equal chance for all, resonate around the world. Immigrants come here because of the freedoms we enjoy, not because of our aircraft carriers, ballistic missile submarines, and Tomahawk cruise missiles. The "meeker" values are those that stand the test of time. The same is true on a personal level. It is the humble person, the respectful person, the polite person, the one who places others before self who will make the most lasting impact in our world. They will inherit the earth.

Beatitude 4: *Blessed are those who hunger and thirst for righteousness ... they will be filled.* God's people are concerned about doing things right. We do not take short cuts; we learn our subject matter and practice our professions in a manner that brings honor and glory to God. That may involve standing against the current of popular opinion. Dr. Martin Luther King, Junior's crusades against segregation in the 1960's were very courageous. They were successful, because the cause was right, and the evil of the status quo seared the conscience of the nation.

Beatitude 5: *Blessed are the merciful ... they will be shown mercy.* Mercy is the opposite of justice. By nature, human beings seek justice. When we have been wronged, the offending party is to be punished: "eye for an eye, tooth for tooth." But when we wrong someone else, mercy is the desired quality. To be sure, justice is important. God has created a Paradise, a Heaven, where sin cannot enter. If sin were permitted, justice would flee. Seeing as all have sinned against God, and that "*the soul who sins shall die*" (Eze. 18:20, NKJV), justice demands that all be denied entrance to the kingdom God has created. This is what makes the cross so important: on it, the Son of God paid for our sins. Divine justice was satisfied the moment Christ cried, "*it is finished*" (John 19:30), and breathed His last. God now extends mercy to all who place their trust in the person and work of Jesus Christ; and we, the beneficiaries of such mercy, extend it to others. The gift of mercy is a powerful spiritual weapon; it disarms our enemies, makes huge inroads into the Kingdom of God, and results in mercy being extended to us, as well.

The Versailles treaty following WWI and the Marshall Plan following WWII make for an interesting case study. Versailles sought to punish the aggressors. Allied signatories wanted justice for the wrongs perpetrated against them. As a result, the Axis nations were plunged into abject poverty. Out of the ashes rose Adolf Hitler. Playing on nationalistic pride, Hitler built a war machine that ultimately led to a Second World War, far more destructive than the first. In it, the Allied nations were once again victorious, but this time chose to rebuild Europe under the Marshall Plan rather than punish perpetrators of the war. As a result of this act of mercy, Western Europe has enjoyed the blessings of peace ever since.

Within the Christian community, there is significant debate over the issue of capital punishment. Based on such passages as the ninth chapter of Genesis, verse six: "*Whoever sheds the blood of man, by man shall his blood be shed; for in the image of God has God made man,*" many cannot understand why some are opposed to the death penalty. Beatitude number five sheds light on the matter. If someone has taken a life, putting the murderer to death does not even the score. What possibly could bring justice to one who lies in the grave? Does not justice, especially in situations such as these, rest with God? "*Vengeance is mine; I will repay, saith the Lord*" (Ro. 12:19, KJV). Ultimately, we all "*stand before God's judgment seat*" (Ro. 14:10). If, from the cross, Jesus declares "*it is finished,*" should not His work begin to satisfy our longings for justice, especially in those areas where it is beyond the realm of human possibility to exact it? We are always grateful to God for the mercy extended to us, and mindful of our responsibilities to extend it to others.

Beatitude 6: *Blessed are the pure in heart ... they will see God.* Blessed are those who do not have hidden agendas. Blessed are those who do not deceive their fellow human beings. Blessed are those who are open and honest, who do not wear masks of hypocrisy. They will see God.

Beatitude 7: *Blessed are the peacemakers ... they will be called the sons of God.* I am a military chaplain, a man of peace living in a culture of war. In one sense, this is the role of every Christian. We live in a world that often takes its stance against the teachings of the true and the living God. Our role is that of evangelist: that of bringing God's peace to others around us, a peace that arises as a result of a right relationship with God, a peace "*which transcends all understanding*" (Phil. 4:7). The greatest peacemakers lead others into a saving relationship with Jesus Christ. This is the motive of my heart, and the primary reason I serve as a chaplain. When people lay claim to the peace that God brings on a vertical level, it results in peace in many other areas of life, as well. On a day to day basis, I help diffuse problems that arise between individuals. When one or more of the parties involved have the peace of God in their hearts, it helps in the mitigation. If I serve long enough in the Chaplain Corps, perhaps one day I will even find myself in a situation where I might help diffuse a dispute between nations and avoid the curse of yet another war.

Beatitude 8: *Blessed are those who are persecuted because of righteousness ... theirs is the kingdom of heaven.*

There are many Christians who are persecuted because they deserve it. They act weird; they do not interact with the prevailing culture. Out of fear of "contaminating" themselves with the world, they isolate themselves from it. Often they are engaged in "culture wars" that have little relevance to the teachings of Christ, and when these saints face the inevitable persecutions, they walk around like martyrs. Then there are other Christians who so accommodate themselves to the world system that if charges brought up against them of being a Christian, no evidence would be found. At the slightest whiff of persecution for their faith, they change their point of view.

In this beatitude, Jesus speaks of being persecuted for doing the right things: for doing a job the right way, for being honest, for protecting the dignity of another human being, for standing up for truth. Such a person is blessed, and the kingdom of God belongs to him/her.

Text Number Eight

The Qualities of a Soldier

(The fruit of the spirit)

"Since we live by the Spirit, let us keep in step with the Spirit."

Galatians 5:25

There is a certain kind of "fruit" expected of the men and women who serve in the United States Marine Corps. Every Marine is expected to be an alert sentry and an accurate shot with the M-16 rifle. All are required to achieve certain standards of physical fitness. Semiannually, Marines must run three miles in less than 27 minutes, do three pull ups from a dead hang and forty sit ups in two minutes. (To achieve a perfect rating, the Marine must do 20 pull ups, 100 sit ups, and complete the three mile run less than 18 minutes. Most come very close to a perfect score). If they fail to accomplish these minimum standards they will be administratively separated from the Corps. There are certain weight standards to which all Marines adhere. Hygiene and grooming is precisely prescribed as is the clothing worn on liberty. There is zero tolerance of illegal drugs. Anyone testing positive for even a small amount of marijuana is quickly separated from "America's 911 force." This is the "fruit" that distinguishes a Marine from the rest of American society. An unproductive Marine will have a very short career.

There is a certain "fruit" expected of the Christian, as well: the fruit of the Spirit. Believers in Jesus Christ are to exhibit the following characteristics: love, joy, peace, patience, kindness, goodness, faithfulness, gentleness and self-control.

The ***love*** talked about in this passage is "agape" love; it comes from God. (See pp. 69-73). Agape treats others with dignity and with respect regardless of how others treat you. In his wonderful little book, *Stress, Power, and Ministry,* John Harris states that there are "only two emotional attitudes through which human life can be radically determined. They are love and fear." "Love," he says, "is the positive principle of life. Fear is the death principle in us."[1] Christians, of all people, are motivated by love. As the Bible says, *"There is no fear in love. But perfect love drives out fear, because fear has to do with punishment. The one who fears is not made perfect in love"* (1 John 4:18).

Abraham Lincoln exhibited this particular quality in executing the office of President. As Dr. Martin Luther King, Jr. notes in his book, *Strength to Love:*

> When he was campaigning for the presidency, one of Lincoln's archenemies was a man named Stanton. Stanton used every ounce of his energy to degrade him. He uttered unkind words about his physical appearance. When Lincoln became President he chose Stanton as Secretary of War. There was an uproar in the inner circle. "You are making a mistake. Do you know this man? Are

---

[1]John Harris, *Stress, Power, and Ministry,* (Alban Institute, 1977),p. 32

> you familiar with all of the ugly things he said about you?" "I am aware of all the terrible things he has said about me, but I find that he is the best man for the job." After the assassination, of all the great statements made about Lincoln, Stanton referred to him as one of the greatest men that ever lived and said "he now belongs to the ages."[2]

Lincoln's example should inspire all of us who take the name of Christ.

Joy is a quality that runs deep; it perseveres even when external circumstances are difficult. The Greek word for joy, "charis," is a root for the English "charismatic." A charismatic person is one who exudes joy: she is someone you like being around. Many Christians tend to repress strong emotions and feelings of joy, but God's joy is precisely what our world needs.

Joy is not to be confused with happiness. When I was a young boy, living in upstate New York, I hired myself out to a farmer who was in the hay business. July and August were the busy months, and I had the privilege of being the "mow man." The mow man stood at the very top of the hay loft and stacked the 75# bales that came off of the elevator one after the other. A kicker wagon held approximately 150 bales, and on a good day we would unload ten wagons. Temperatures outside might be in the 90's, while temperatures in the top of the mow were much higher. There were all sorts of bugs living in the hay mow: spiders, birds, and even an occasional raccoon. Hay seed would fly as the bales fell from the elevator, and the air was filled with dust particles. But most of all, there was sweat. Quarts of perspiration would

---

[2]Martin Luther King, Jr., *Strength to Love,* (New York: Harper & Row, Pub., Inc., 1963), p. 39.

flow from the poor unfortunates who joined me in the endeavor. What a relief when a wagon was unloaded and we were able to climb out of the mow and go to the well not far from the barn! The old hand pump, after it was sufficiently primed, drew water from the well; and soon, refreshing cold water came from the depths. The old rusty cup that hung on a chain was filled and quickly drained by thirsty workers. One cup followed another, and soon our thirst was slaked. That was joy! The situation of being in the hay mow was not a particularly happy occasion, but in spite of the circumstances, we were able to draw from a deep well and find refreshment. So it is with the Christian. Men and women who are filled with the Spirit can find joy during the hard times of life, a joy that refreshes and sustains.

The ***Peace*** mentioned in this section of Scripture is internal. It is not the kind of peace that our military seeks to maintain, a peace that often utilizes threat power to maintain stabile relationships between nations in the international community. The peace spoken of in this passage is tranquillity of the soul. We find comfort being made in the image of God, realizing that our sins are forgiven. *"Peace I leave with you;"* Jesus said, *"my peace I give you. I do not give to you as the world gives. Do not let your hearts be troubled and do not be afraid"* (John 14:27). A man by the name of Henry Drummond tells the story of two artists commissioned to do a picture depicting true peace:

> One painted a landscape with a mountain lake. The background was one of beautiful green hills, with tall slender pine trees reflected in the mirrored surface of the lake. The second artist did a very turbulent scene; a violent waterfall crashing down on jagged chunks of granite. Alongside the waterfall was a slender birch with its fragile

> branches reaching just over the crashing foam. In the branches was a bird's nest; in it, lying calmly, glistening from spray and foam of the waterfall was a small bird fast asleep. That was his rendition of peace.

Although we live in a violent, chaotic world; as servants of the Most High, we enjoy peaceful lives. There is, however, a day coming when Christ will return and set up His Kingdom upon the earth. This will be a time when His peace will reign universally. Until then, we are instruments of His peace, living in a world that is crying out for deliverance.

Patience is an attribute valued by every Marine warrior. A Marine is able to hide in the bush all day, waiting for the appropriate time to engage the enemy. The Greek word for patience means "long suffering," and as Christians, we are able to endure adverse situations and difficult individuals for long periods of time. We do not need instant gratification. We wait patiently for the proper situation in which to act or speak. Without patience, it is easy to come across as abrasive and judgmental. There is a time to speak and a time to remain silent (Ecc. 3:7). How much better to wait patiently for the "teachable moment," than to force your words upon someone who is not ready to hear. Teresa of Avila, 1515-1582, wrote the following:

Let nothing trouble you,
Let nothing scare you,
All is fleeting,
God alone is unchanging Patience,
Everything obtains.
Who possesses God
Nothing wants.
God alone suffices.

Kindness is a quality much needed in our broken world. Jesus was kind wherever He went. Many Marines with whom I work can often be quite vile in their conversations. When a junior Marine makes a mistake, he is often rebuked with a string of expletives from those who are his seniors. The net result of this is: 1) either the junior loses all respect for those above him in the chain of command, or 2) he begins to develop the very same characteristics in his own leadership style. I have noticed that the Marines who have the most successful careers are those who treat their subordinates with kindness, while still maintaining stern discipline.

There is an old story about an 18th century vagabond in England who came to a roadside inn, with a sign above the door reading: "George and the Dragon." The vagabond knocked, and the innkeeper's wife opened the door a crack and peered out. "Could ye spare some victuals?" Glancing at the man's shabby clothes, she shouted "No!" and slammed the door in his face. Nonplused, the man knocked again. "What now?" the woman screeched. To which the vagabond replied: "D'ye suppose I might have a word with George?" Kindness goes a lot further than door slamming.

Goodness means that you always do the right thing, regardless of popular opinion or peer pressure. The Indian leader Mahatma Gandhi once said, "In matters of conscience, the law of majority has no place." The old hymn declares, "If none go with me, still I will follow." The Parson in Chaucer's *Canterbury Tales* declares:

"If gold rusts, what then will iron do?
For if a priest be foul in whom we trust,
No wonder that a common man should rust."[3]

---

[3]Geoffrey Chaucer, *The Canterbury Tales,* (Great Britain: Penguin Books Ltd, 1974), p. 32.

John Wesley, the great English evangelist and founder of the Methodist church writes:

> Do all the good you can, By all the means you can,
> In all the ways you can, In all the places you can,
> At all the times you can, To all the people you can,
> As long as ever you can.[4]

If, in human warfare, our soldiers are involved in evil-doing, the nation's integrity is at stake. If we go to war with the wrong motives, we lose face in the international community and will ultimately suffer defeat. As a nation, we must do the right things, standing up for justice and truth wherever they may be found.

The same is true in spiritual warfare. Servants of the Most High must be good. We do not allow ourselves to be corrupted by the things of this world. Conversely, we offer a wholesome example to others around us. If we are not good, if we do not practice what we preach, our message is undermined. Hypocrisy – preaching about goodness, but failing to measure up – has kept more people away from our houses of worship than any other single issue. Quality ministry, compassionate pastoral care and just plain goodness are far more important than the size of the church or the number of programs it runs.

Faithfulness is a quality that is characteristic of a believer. Would you consider your car faithful if it started every time you needed it, except on those occasions when you needed to go to the emergency room? Would you consider the paperboy faithful if he brought the daily news only on those days when it did not rain? Would your bank consider

---

[4]*Christian History,* (Carol Stream, IL: Christianity Today, Inc., vol. II, no. 1, 1983), p. 6.

you faithful if you made every mortgage payment, except for those months when the electric bill was higher than usual? Obviously, faithfulness is a very important quality. When the going gets tough, servants of the Most High must not be deterred from their mission.

In warfighting, faithfulness is key to success. What would happen if the cooks were unfaithful in delivering meals to those on the front line? Or if the utilitymen decided that potable water was not needed for a few days? Or if the logisticians were unfaithful in supplying ammunition to the combatants? The war effort would be curtailed or lost! What do you think happens in the local church when a Sunday School teacher, an usher or a deacon fails to show up on time (or fails to show at all)? Jesus issues a clarion call to faithfulness when He says, *"let your 'Yes' be 'Yes,' and your 'No,' 'No'; anything beyond this comes from the evil one"* (Mt. 5:37). Christians are called to be faithful; we are men and women who follow through on the promises we make.

Gentleness is not a quality one would expect to find in a Marine, yet it is very touching to watch these warriors drive every month to a local homeless shelter in order to feed the hungry, or serve as surrogate parents in an elementary schools. Many of these young men continually seek opportunities to help others who are in great need. There is a spirit of gentleness that permeates the ranks of these mighty men, and although you will never see it in their relationships with one another or on the battlefield, it is very evident in their dealings with the less-fortunate and oppressed peoples of our world.

Sometimes Christians fail to be gentle. Theodosius was the Emperor of Rome from A.D. 379-395. Despite his Christian faith, he once slaughtered 7000 citizens of Thessalonica in the city's hippodrome. A star charioteer had been arrested for homosexual rape and was not allowed to appear in one of the popular sporting events. The crowd rioted, and several police officers were murdered. In seeking vengeance, Theodosius called for another such event, and when the stadium was filled, he barred the gates and ordered the massacre of innocent spectators. Less than a week after the tragedy, the Emperor sought to worship at the cathedral in the city of Milan. Ambrose, the bishop of Milan, refused Theodosius entrance until he had done public penance for his crime. Protesting that if he had been guilty of homicide, so had King David, the man after God's own heart. Ambrose replied with the famous words: "You have imitated David in his crime, imitate him in his repentance."[5] The stinging rebuke corrected the Emperor for his lack of gentleness.

Jesus came gently to us. He was born to simple parents in a remote region of the world. He rode into the city of Jerusalem on the back of a donkey. He came gently then, and comes gently into our hearts today. He will not force Himself upon us. We, His servants, are to imitate this gentleness.

The Scriptures tell us that Jesus will come again, but the Second Coming will not be gentle. Like a Divine Warrior, His eyes will be *"like blazing fire."* He will be "*dressed in a robe dipped in blood,*" and the "*armies of heaven*" will follow Him into battle. At that time He will *"strike down the nations ... rule them with an iron scepter,"* and tread *"the winepress of the fury of the wrath of God Almighty"* (Rev. 19:12-15). Until then, servants of the Most High live peaceably among the nations of the world, sharing the gospel message with grace and dignity. We set apart Christ in our hearts, and gently offer the reason for the hope that lies within us to anyone who asks (1 Pe. 3:15). There may be times for "holy bold-

---

[5]Stephen Williams and Gerard Friell, *Theodosius, The Empire at Bay*, (New Haven: Yale University Press, 1994), pp. 67-69.

ness" as we sharpen our understandings of the faith, and when we communicate with those who are hostile to it, but gentleness, ultimately, is a characteristic of those who take the name of God.

Self-Control is the last fruit of the Spirit. The Greek "egkrateia" means "to master the ego." This is a perfect definition, because most of us love to be in charge. Mastering the ego is a perfect corrective. We enjoy fame, glory, and attention. Commanding Officers frequently remind their juniors to "check their egos at the door." Marine leaders often conduct "hotwashes" following major operations, and invite company commanders, platoon leaders and staff officers together in order to discuss how improvements can be made the next time a similar evolution is performed. "Check your ego at the door" means that you are not going to complain about how someone else made you look bad. Positively, it means personal agendas and the desire for recognition are put aside for the greater good.

In 1975, Arthur Ashe played in the Masters tennis tournament in Stockholm, Sweden, against Ilie Nastase. Nastase was a volatile player who frequently lost control on the courts. On this particular day, Nastase was in especially bad form, 'stalling, cursing, and taunting Ashe like a madman. Finally, Ashe put down his racket and walked off the court. "I've had enough," he told the umpire. "I'm at the point where I'm afraid I'll lose control."' Ashe was winning the match, and the official told him that to walk off the court was to default. "I don't care," Ashe said. "I'd rather lose that than my self-respect." The next day, the tournament committee met and made a very wise decision. They disqualified Nastase for his bullying tactics, and awarded the crown to Ashe.[6]

---

[6]Charles Pasarell, "Unforgettable Arthur Ashe, *Readers' Digest*, v. 143, Sept. 1993, pp. 35-40.

Christians are to exercise self-control. We are to keep our egos in check, honor God with our lives, and prefer others to ourselves. When we do, victories come our way. The Scriptures declare, *"Like a city whose walls are broken down is a man who lacks self-control"* (Pro. 25:28).

Text Number Nine

Promotion to Chief

"put off your old self, which is being corrupted by its deceitful desires ... be made new in the attitude of your minds"

Ephesians 4:22-23

In the U.S. Navy, the transition from First Class Petty Officer (E-6) to Chief Petty Officer (E-7) is quite dramatic. There is an extensive initiation ceremony that the candidate undergoes, and once the initiation is complete, the old dungaree work uniforms and "crackerjack" dress uniforms are put away, and the new khaki uniforms and formal dress blues are put on. The new chief does not want to go back to the old uniforms, and with great excitement looks forward to new ways of doing things. In like manner, the new Christian, upon accepting Jesus Christ as Lord and Savior has been initiated into a new life. Often, baptism serves as the rite of passage. The old ways are to be put off, and a new way of behaving put on.

In this passage of Scripture we are told to *"put off your old self, which is being corrupted by its deceitful desires ... and to put on the new self, created to be like God in true righteousness and holiness.* There are four major behavioral patterns that the Apostle Paul tells us to "put off." These four ways of behaving come naturally to us; they are part of our sinful nature. If the Christian acts according to the flesh, the forces of good make no inroads into enemy territory. But if we put off bad patterns of behavior and put on that which honors God, we will be armed with powerful spiritual weapons capable of demolishing enemy strongholds.

In Ephesians chapter four, verse 25, the Christian is told to put off falsehood and put on truthfulness. The end does not justify the means. The Christian is to be honest in his dealings with others, even when the truth can be quite painful. By being honest, non-Christians will understand that believers are persons of integrity, men and women who can be trusted. The word of a Christian is good. Others believe what we say. The Scripture informs us that the Devil is a liar, the father of all lies (John 8:44), and when we fail to be honest, we become accomplices to his work, regardless of how noble the cause. Preachers, especially, need to be honest, in and out of the pulpit. Often, in order to emphasize a point, truth gets exaggerated, or sources are not checked before claims are made. Unfortunately, the ultimate fruit of such "preacher's excess" is lack of credibility.

In verse 26 we are told to put off the unrighteous, uncontrolled anger with which so many of us struggle and to put on an anger (if it is appropriate at all) in which we do not sin, an anger that is righteous by nature, under tight control and concluded in a timely manner. Uncontrolled rage is a tool of the Devil, totally ineffective in any endeavor.

In verse 27, we put off stealing and put on hard work. The opposite of stealing is not simply the cessation thereof, but the commencement of something that will be very beneficial to others. By substituting hard work (as the new way of life demands) for stealing (the pattern of behavior so characteristic of the old), the Christian accomplishes something productive for society, and generates income with which he will be able to help others who are in need. In short, the opposite of stealing is giving. Believers should be the best workers on the job, honest and reliable in all that they do, and also the best givers when human need arises. "Idle hands or an idle mind," as the saying goes, "is the Devil's workshop."

In verse 29, the Scripture informs us to put off *"unwholesome talk" and put on words that are "helpful for building others up according to their needs."* As my mother used to tell me, "if you can't find anything good to say about someone then don't say anything at all." For the most part, it is easy to find something good to say. Humans are made in the image of God, and each of us, in some way, reflects the divine glory. Look for those qualities in others. You may be surprised at what you find. In the process, you might just make a friend and an ally in the Lamb's war against the powers of darkness. There is no room in our vocabulary for destructive gossip and foul language.

In addition to the four bad attitudes listed above that we are to put off – lying, anger, stealing, and gossip — the Apostle gives us a shopping list of other negative characteristics that should be shed. We are to rid ourselves of bitterness, rage and anger, brawling and slander, and every form of malice (v. 31). These are to be replaced with kindness, compassion, and forgiveness. If a believer does not begin to do this, he may not lose his salvation, but he will bring much grief to the Holy Spirit and become nearly worthless in the battle for the hearts and souls of men and women who are looking for meaning and purpose in life.

Text Number Ten

Ribbons and Medals

(Add to your faith...)

"His divine power has given us everything we need for life and godliness ..."

2 Peter 1:3

Marine Corps Boot Camp is renowned all over the world for its ability to transform a young man or a young woman from a civilian lifestyle to that of a hardened Marine. The three month "camps" are held either in San Diego, California, or Paris Island, South Carolina. While at Boot Camp, recruits undergo a grueling regimen of physical and mental testing that weeds out those who are unable to keep up, and strengthens those who remain. Course curriculum includes Marine Corps history, customs and courtesies, uniform regulations, the uniform code of military justice, weapons handling, swim qualifications, and close order drill. Near the end of Boot Camp, a defining moment takes place in the life of a recruit, when he or she knows that the transformation to United States Marine has been complete. The event is called "The Crucible" — a 72 hour nonstop event where the young men and women are tested to their limits.

The event begins at 2:00 a.m. (0200 hours). Recruits march with fully-loaded packs to a predetermined bivouac, where camp is set up in the dark without the help of a drill instructor. Once camp is established, a very demanding training regimen begins. This includes such things as engaging multiple targets at unknown distances with the service rifle, participating in fierce one-on-one combat using pugil sticks, and casualty evacuations through rugged terrain with and without the use of stretchers. In addition, day and night infiltration courses are negotiated, and the bayonet assault course is mastered. Several other team oriented leadership reaction drills take place, including the crossing of wilderness streams and the safe negotiation of enemy mine fields. Every recruit has the opportunity to exercise leadership for at least one of the events. Throughout the three-day period, participants are sleep-deprived (they are lucky to get 3-4 hours sleep per evening) and food-deprived (they are given 2 1/2 MRE's: Meals, Ready to Eat). At the culmination of the event, after nearly fifty miles of terrain has been traversed on foot, a large hill called the "Reaper" is ascended. At the top is an alleyway lined with flags from every state in the Union. Patriotic music is played, tears flow, and the eagle globe and anchor – the symbol of the United States Marine Corps – is pinned on. The recruit is now a Marine, and the real journey begins.

During the course of a career, the Marine accumulates various awards and medals, which are added to the eagle globe and anchor that was earned at boot camp. One of the men with whom I became acquainted during my time at the First Combat Engineer Battalion was First Sergeant Michael Miller. Miller is a decorated veteran who first entered the Corps in 1969. At the 1999 Marine Corps Birthday Ball, I noticed that he wore more medals than anyone else in the battalion. I sat down with the First Sergeant and asked him to tell me about each of the awards he had received during his time of service. Listed in order of precedence (from the least important to the most important award) are the nineteen medals which decorate his full dress uniform:

1) *Kuwaiti Liberation Medal, Kuwait for* participation in Desert Shield/Desert Storm
2) *Kuwait Liberation Medal* from the Kingdom of Saudi Arabia for participation in Operation Desert Shield/Desert Storm
3) *Republic of Vietnam Campaign Medal* for participation in the Vietnam conflict 1970-1971
4) *Republic of Vietnam Civil Action Unit Citation* for participation in the Vietnam conflict 1970-1971
5) *Republic of Vietnam Gallantry Cross Unit Citation* for participation in the Vietnam conflict 1970-1971
6) *Sea Service deployment ribbon with four bronze stars* for leaving home, family and friends on five occasions for six months or more, defending the nation's interests.
7) *Southwest Asia Service Medal* for participation in Desert Shield/Desert Storm
8) *Vietnam Service Medal with two stars* for participation in two major combat engagements during the Vietnam conflict
9) *National Defense Service Medal with one star* for service to his country during two major conflicts (Vietnam, Desert Shield/Desert Storm)
10) *Selected Marine Corps Reserve Medal* for his time as an active Reservist (1971-1982)
11) *Good Conduct Medal with a silver star* for good conduct while serving on Active Duty (six separate awards)

12) *Meritorious Unit Commendation* for service with the First Reconnaissance Battalion during the Vietnam Conflict
13) *Navy Unit Commendation with one star* for service to country during the Vietnam and Desert Shield/ Desert Storm conflicts
14) *Combat Action Ribbon* for involvement in an exchange of fire during the Vietnam conflict
15) *Navy Achievement Medal with one bronze star* Awarded twice: 1) for service as monitor at USMC Headquarters in Quantico, Virginia. (A monitor provides career advice to fellow Marines), and 2) for service as Staff Non-Commission Officer in Charge of the Marine Corps mounted Color Guard at the Logistics Base in Barstow, California
16) *Navy Commendation Medal Awarded* for outstanding service as Gunnery Sergeant with the 2nd Battalion of the 7th Marine Regiment
17) *Meritorious Service Medal Awarded* while serving with the Indoctrination and Instruction unit in St. Louis. (Miller's involvement with the local community, especially in coordinating the "Toys for Tots" program was of particular note)
18) *Purple Heart* Awarded as a result of a shrapnel wound from an enemy grenade, Vietnam conflict, 1971
19) *Bronze Star with a combat "V"* Awarded for successfully extracting a wounded officer via helicopter from a Vietnamese rice paddy in 1971

The life of a Marine begins when the eagle, globe and anchor is pinned on at the end of Boot Camp. As a successful Marine continues his or her career, the types of ribbons and medals earned by First Sergeant Miller are added to the uniform. The process is somewhat similar for the servant of the Most High. There is a defining moment when a transition has been made from the kingdom of darkness to the kingdom of light. This is followed by the addition of virtue to one's character.

For God's servant, the defining moment occurs when a decision is made to trust Jesus Christ as Lord and Savior. Tears often accompany the decision, along with great zeal and excitement for the cause. Life, now, begins to make sense. Faith in Jesus is the beginning of a new journey. The Bible tells us, *"without faith it is impossible to please God"* (Heb. 11:6). The book of Romans, in its entirety, describes how one is made "right" in the eyes of God. As the Apostle Paul concisely summarizes: *"The just shall live by faith"* (Ro. 1:17, KJV). These words energized Martin Luther, the founder of the Protestant Reformation, and inspired John Wesley to begin the Methodist Church. "Justification by faith" is clearly spelled out in both Old and New Testaments (n. Hab. 2:4; Gal. 3:1; Heb. 10:38). Abraham is called the father of many nations (Gen. 17:5) because he believed God and was declared righteous before Him. Many Christians can tell you the precise moment when they first trusted Christ, but they will also admit that the simple act of placing their faith in Him was only the beginning of the journey. Faith is the foundation; faith is where we begin; faith is the transformation, but as James so clearly states: *"faith without works is dead"* (2:20, KJV).

Outsiders often perceive Christians as such morally upright people they feel intimidated, but nothing could be more tragic. Like everyone else, Christians are seriously flawed people. The only difference is that our sins have been forgiven. Nearly every Bible hero has tragic character flaws, and it is often best *not* to imitate their lifestyles. Abraham tried to pass off his wife as his sister (Gen. 12:13). Jacob was a deceiver and a conniver (Gen. 25:31; 27). Moses had a horrible temper (Ex. 2:12; Nu. 20:9-12). King David committed adultery and arranged for an innocent man to be murdered (2 Sa. 11). Peter denied knowing the Lord (Mt. 26:75), and Paul was party to cold- blooded murder (Acts 8:1). The one thing that each of these men held in common was that they came to know the true and the living God. They believed in Him, and through their faith, experienced the forgiveness of sin. As God worked in their lives, the character flaws began to disappear as well.

So it is with each of us. We begin first with faith. If we do not believe that Jesus died for our sins on a cross, that He rose again from the dead, and that He is coming back again to judge world, we are not "right" with God and will have no part of His Kingdom. But if we believe, God begins to mold and shape our moral character. A man who begins his spiritual journey with poor morals will see improvement. One who had high moral standards before coming to know Christ will likewise find improvement. As we grow in Christ, the attributes listed in this passage Scripture will take root in all of us. In the same way as the military man puts medals on his chest as the career progresses, so the Christian adds virtue, knowledge, self-control, perseverance, godliness, brotherly kindness, and love, to the faith which was given at the beginning of the journey.

Each of these attributes have already been discussed. *Virtue* is mentioned under leadership principle #1: "Know yourself and seek improvement" (p. 163). *Knowledge*, an important trait of the effective leader, is discussed under leadership principle #2: "Be technically and tactically proficient" (pp. 171-179). *Self-control*, a fruit of the Spirit, is addressed in text number eight: The Qualities of a Soldier (p. 318). *Perseverance* is mentioned under Article II: "I will never Give Up" (pp. 77-92). *Godliness* (or holiness) is discussed under leadership principle #5: "Set the Example" (pp. 197-209), and both *brotherly kindness* (phileo love), and *love* (agape love) are mentioned under Article I: "I am a Christian Soldier" (pp. 69-73).

Upon accepting Jesus Christ as Lord and Savior, upon placing our trust in His leadership, we become the children of God. Our leader has overcome the world, the flesh and the Devil. Christ delivers us from hell and places each of us firmly in the kingdom of God. Just as the military man adds medals to his uniform as a result of faithful service to his Commanding Officer, so we add the above characteristics to our lives out of gratitude for what the greatest of all Commanders has accomplished on our behalf.

Text Number Eleven

Semper Paratis

"Always be prepared to give an answer to everyone who asks you to give the reason for the hope that you have."

1 Peter 3:15

The motto of the United States Coast Guard, "Semper Paratis" (always ready), reflects the type of work that Coast Guard sailors are called to do: to rescue those in peril on the sea, at any hour of the day, in any type of weather. Being prepared for any contingency is the goal of every branch of the Armed Forces.

The cutting edge of the Marine Corps is the Marine Expeditionary Unit (MEU). The MEU consists of a Ground Combat Element (GCE), an Air Combat Element (ACE), and a Combat Service Support Element (CSSE). Hardware for the MEU includes: four amphibious ships loaded with M1A1 Abrams tanks, light armored assault vehicles (LAVs), amphibious assault vehicles (AAVs), Armored Combat Excavation Vehicles (ACEs), personnel landing craft (LCACs), helicopters, Harrier aircraft, a whole arsenal of weapons, and over 3000 Marines prepared to go into harm's way on a moment's notice. In fact, the guiding policies of the Marine Corps expect the MEU to be on site within 48 hours of the outbreak of hostilities anywhere in the world, and remain there for as long as 30 days until reinforcements can arrive. Like the Coast Guard, U.S. Marines are always ready to get into harm's way.

The training performed by Marines prior to a MEU deployment is astounding. They learn how to handle explosives; how to guard buildings, camps, ships, piers, and docks; how to properly search personnel and seize illegal paraphernalia; and how to master urban sniper techniques. By the time Marines deploy, they have participated in simulated mock battles using laser-activated MILES gear and M-16 rifles equipped with lasers. (More recent technology makes use of "simunitions" — M-16 rounds filled with red or blue dye). They study urban warfare, desert warfare, jungle warfare and mountain warfare. Marines learn how to carry out boat raids with zodiac craft, as well as mechanized raids with larger amphibious vehicles. The men who make up the MEU are instructed in non-lethal methods of crowd control, using foam guns, net guns and rubber bullets. Marines have studied assault climbing — rappelling from towers and cliffs — and they have completed close quarters combat training. They have learned to fight in daylight and in darkness. They can jump from helicopters into enemy territory, or emerge from submarines onto enemy coasts. They are able to fight alongside the U.S. Army in division-sized maneuvers, or stealthily attack the enemy in units as small as fire teams. In short, these men are prepared for just about any situation.

In this text, Peter reminds the servant of the Most High, *"Always be prepared to give an answer to everyone who asks you … the reason for the hope that you have."* We have the words of eternal life; the Lord of glory lives in our hearts! This is even more important than the defense of our nation. Am I prepared to share the words of life with others? How do I speak to a large group of people about Christ? How do I engage others in one on one conversation? How do I share good news with someone who is hurting, with someone who is in the hospital, or in trouble with the law? There may be times when a full frontal assault is possible, when you are able to bring out the spiritual tanks and the artillery, because the foundations of the Christian faith are being openly challenged. Take advantage of such opportunities, but always respond with gentleness and respect. There may be times you should be more subtle in your approach, presenting the gospel with stories that will suddenly grip the hearer with truths about the kingdom of God. There may be times to remain silent, while awaiting the proper moment to speak.

The average Marine is not an expert in all of the areas listed above. Some are far more gifted in certain proficiencies than others, but every Marine knows how warfare is to be waged. The same is true for God's servant. Our message needs to impact every area of life: the university, the halls of government, the work place, the neighborhood, the jail or the local hospital. And no one is perfectly equipped to bring truth into each of these environments, but we do need to know how the war is being waged, and be supportive of the war effort. As a body of believers, we are prepared — any time, any place, under any circumstance — to take on the powers of darkness with the armor of light.

Marines, trained to be vigilant in watch standing, have memorized Eleven General Orders for Sentries:

General Order 1: To take charge of this post and all government property in view.
General Order 2: To walk my post in a military manner, keeping always on the alert and observing everything that takes place within sight or hearing.
General Order 3: To report all violations of orders I am instructed to enforce.
General Order 4: To repeat all calls from posts more distant from the guardhouse than my own.
General Order 5: To quit my post only when properly relieved.
General Order 6: To receive, obey and pass on to the sentry who relieves me all orders from the commanding officer, officer of the day, and officers and noncommissioned officers of the guard only.
General Order 7: To talk to no one except in the line of duty.
General Order 8: To give the alarm in case of fire or disorder.
General Order 9: To call the corporal of the guard in any case not covered by instructions.
General Order 10: To salute all officers and all colors and standards not cased.
General Order 11: To be especially watchful at night, and during the time for challenging, to challenge all persons on or near my post and to allow no one to pass without proper authority.[1]

---

[1]*Marine Battle Skills Training Handbook, Book 1, PVT-GYSGT, General Military Subjects,* (Arlington, VA: Marine Corps Institute, November 1994), p. 1-9-3.

Marines understand what it means to be "ready." The general orders speak volumes about taking responsibility, and about the importance of being alert. They address the need to work as a team and to communicate. The orders inculcate respect for authority, and the importance of asking for help when unsure of oneself. We, who serve in the army of the Most High, likewise take responsibility for the things of God's kingdom. When truth is challenged, we stand up and defend it. We communicate and rely on the strengths of others. As the Apostle Paul writes, "*we demolish arguments and every pretension that sets itself up against the knowledge of God, and we take captive every thought to make it obedient to Christ*" (2 Co. 10:5). In short, we are always ready to share the hope that lies within us.

Text Number Twelve

Civilian Affairs

"No one serving as a soldier gets involved in civilian affairs— he wants to please his commanding officer."
2 Timothy 2:4

At the 1994 National Association of Evangelicals conference in Washington, DC, Rep. Guy Vander Jagt, of Michigan mentioned something that has stuck with me over the years: "People say that there are two things you should not speak about in public. One is politics and the other is religion. But I say, what two more important things are there to talk about? One affects your temporal destiny, and the other affects your eternal destiny." I take a deep interest in both, but have found that there are certain invisible lines over which one should not cross. Although often misinterpreted, the Bible clearly teaches that there is to be a separation of Church and State: *"Give to Caesar what is Caesar's, and to God what is God's"* (Mt. 22:21) is a pretty clear statement.

In many ways the separation of Church and State is similar to the differentiation of powers that should exist between the State Department and the Department of Defense. One of the biggest mistakes of the Vietnam War was micromanagement of the war effort. Government officials, who knew nothing about war, were telling soldiers how to fight. As a result, our nation was embroiled in a conflict that dragged on for years and affected an entire generation of young people. The converse is also true. The military does not dictate to civilian authorities how to run the government. General MacArthur, one of the most brilliant tacticians in history, got himself into a lot of trouble by crossing this line on a couple of occasions. When he ran for President, while still serving as Commanding General in the Pacific theater, a lot of confusion ensued. When he openly defied the President of the United States over political matters, he found himself without a job.[1]

The distinctions between Church and State are similar. The Church, a spiritual warfighting unit, does not dictate to the State how to conduct its day-to-day business. A preacher should take a leave of absence from the pastorate if he/she decides to run for a highly visible public office. In like manner, the State does not tell the Church how to conduct its business. When government controls how people worship, it crosses the line. Such behavior completely violates the First Amendment of the U.S. Constitution, which soldiers in the military so valiantly swear to support and defend.

Soldiers serve at the pleasure of the Commander-in-Chief, regardless of political persuasion. They are allowed to have strong opinions, but not permitted to express them while wearing their uniform in public. It is appropriate for men and women in the Armed Forces to register with a political party, and very important that they exercise the right to vote, but they should not actively campaign for either Democratic or Republican causes. When high-ranking mili-

---

[1]*The American Caesar,* pp. 616-620; 756-781.

tary personnel cross that line and invest their energy in political causes, loyalty gets called into question, regardless of how noble the intentions. Soldiers are called to defend the Constitution of the United States against all enemies, foreign and domestic. When someone from another political party becomes the "enemy" while on the campaign trail, it is difficult to turn off that passion when the campaign is over.

Along those same lines, the Church is not a political organization. We do not dictate to the State; we serve as its moral conscience. Our goal is to bring the gospel to bear on all aspects of life, regardless of who is in office. Like the soldier in human warfare, the Christian in a highly visible leadership position should not become a political animal. When the Church at Pierce Creek in Binghamton, NY, took out a full-page ad in the *USA Today* warning Christians that a vote for Bill Clinton was a "plunge down a path of immorality," it crossed the line.[2] A far more appropriate action would have been to offer Biblical critique on the candidate's proposed policies, rather than attack a candidate or a party. God is neither a Democrat nor a Republican, but His churches frequently find themselves too closely aligned with one party or the other. When this happens, politics becomes a stumbling block (n. 1 Co. 1:23), and the Church turns into yet another pesky, bureaucratic lobbying group irritating our legislators in Washington. In our witness to others, the testimony of Jesus should be the only thing that brings offense. In everything else, "*If it is possible ... live peaceably with all men*" (Romans 12:18, NKJV). The role of the Church in the political arena is summarized best in Paul's first letter to Timothy:

---

[2]*Christianity Today,* (Carol Stream, IL: Christianity Today International, vol. 36, December 14, 1992), p. 64.

> *"I urge, then, first of all, that requests, prayers, intercession and thanksgiving be made for everyone — for kings and all those in authority, that we may live peaceful and quiet lives in all godliness and holiness. This is good, and pleases God our Savior, who wants all men to be saved and to come to a knowledge of the truth."*
>
> (1 TIM. 2:1-4)

The Church does not dictate to the State; She bears witness to it. We do not mandate prayer in the public school, because the public school belongs to Caesar. We encourage Caesar to be sympathetic to the spiritual needs of students, but we cannot dictate. The Church, however, belongs to God, and if we want to have a real impact in the lives of young people, our energies must be invested in strengthening it – not wasted in some feeble attempt to usurp the role that God has given to the State. If we confuse these two spheres of influence or attempt to blur the distinctions, the results can be devastating.

TEXT NUMBER THIRTEEN

THE LORD IS MY BANNER

"He will raise a banner for the nations"

ISAIAH 11:12

For much of my time as chaplain at the First Combat Engineer battalion, I was the oldest man in the unit. When I was first selected for the Chaplain Corps in 1998, I had a long discussion with my detailer (the detailer is the person who assigns where you will be stationed), as to what would constitute a successful chaplain career. He indicated that a tour of duty with the Marines, one at a Naval Air Station, and one on board a large deck ship would be an excellent start for a junior chaplain. My immediate response was, "you'd better assign me first to the Marines, because I'm not getting any younger." (I was 42 at the time). That was one of the best decisions I ever made in my life, because the physical training I underwent with the Marines tested me to my very limits. I am looking forward to the day when my physical regimen will be far less strenuous.

By far, the Marine's most difficult physical training is the "conditioning hike," or "the hump." (For a more detailed account, see pp. 197-198). There were many times I simply wanted to quit; I wanted to take advantage of my position as chaplain and ride in one of the trucks following behind the battalion. There were times I thought about finding important "administrative tasks" to do on the day of the hike. I am glad to report, however, that I completed every single conditioning hike during my two and a half year assignment with the Combat Engineers. Often, the banner held up high by the company guidon bearer was the only thing that kept me going.

The guidon for the Headquarters and Service Company is a red flag 28 inches long by 21 inches high. Four inch gold letters are sewn on the red background indicating the company, battalion, and division represented. The golden eagle, globe and anchor, symbol of the Marine Corps, fills the center section. The flag is mounted on an eight foot pole, topped with a triangular-shaped, chrome-plated pike. This simple device brings enormous encouragement to the members of the unit it represents. During conditioning hikes or other grueling events, the guidon bearer marches alongside the company commander at the head of the unit, holding the emblem aloft for all to see. There were many occasions, when in the midst of a grueling conditioning hike, I would lift up my head, see the banner of my company flying high and proud at the front of the formation (I was usually struggling somewhere in the back), and be inspired to persevere. The banner was especially motivating when flying high at the top of a hill looming before me. Without the banner, and without Marines alongside, I would have quit. I would never have achieved the physical conditioning expected by the commanding officer, and would have been ineffective in battle.

In the book of Exodus, one of Israel's greatest military victories is described in vivid detail. Moses stood at the top of a hill with the staff of God stretched out toward the heavens. As long as the Israelites, led by the field commander Joshua, were able to see the outstretched arms of their leader, victory was theirs; but when Moses' arms dropped to his sides, the Amalekites would win. To ensure defeat of their bitter enemy, Aaron and Hur propped up the arms of Moses until *"Joshua overcame the Amalekite army with the sword"* (Ex. 17:13). When the battle was over, Moses built an altar to God and declared, *"The LORD is my banner"* (Ex. 17:15). The banner that Moses held aloft inspired the military men at the base of the hill, but the One who inspired Moses was God. Hundreds of years later, the prophet Isaiah picked up on this theme. Knowing that God would one day bring victory to all people, Isaiah writes:

> *"A shoot will come up from the stump of Jesse (Jesse is the father of King David); from his roots a Branch will bear fruit. The Spirit of the LORD will rest on him— the Spirit of wisdom and of understanding, the Spirit of counsel and of power, the Spirit of knowledge and of the fear of the LORD— and he will delight in the fear of the LORD. He will not judge by what he sees with his eyes, or decide by what he hears with his ears; but with righteousness he will judge the needy, with justice he will give decisions for the poor of the earth. He will strike the earth with the rod of his mouth; with the breath of his lips he will slay the wicked"*
>
> (Is. 11:1-4)

Isaiah could see the future. In his mind's eye, he sees Jesus and writes, *"the Root of Jesse will stand as a banner for the peoples; the nations will rally to him, and his place of rest will be glorious"* (Is. 11:10).

Jesus is the great warrior. He has defeated sin. He has defeated death. He has defeated the Devil. He holds up a banner and cries out, "come, follow me." Lift up your eyes to the hills and trust Him, for He alone brings victory. Moses carried the banner for such a One, and others helped him. Our faith demands that we, too, hold up a banner for this King, offering hope to others who struggle along the hills and valleys of life, burdened down with heavy loads and downcast looks. A guidon bearer for the Lord? There is no higher calling. Trust Him; love Him; do not be ashamed to cry out, "the LORD is my banner."

Text Number Fourteen

The Granddaddy Of All Parades

"Blessed is the king who comes in the name of the Lord!"
Luke 19:38

As the old saying goes, "Everybody loves a parade," and a military parade is no exception. The best parades occur at a change of command. When the Commanding General of the First Marine Division relinquishes power, hundreds of VIPs are invited to the parade field. The First Marine Division Band plays patriotic music as guests are seated, and the grounds are graced with the flag of every State in the Union. The latest military hardware surrounds the parade field, and men from every battalion serving under the General's command are present in their finest uniform. Each unit conducts close order drill, off-going and on-coming commanders give speeches and then, the command, "Pass in Review," is given. At that point in the ceremony, every unit represented smartly marches past their old and new commanders, doing an "eyes right" as they pass the reviewing stand. The audience applauds politely each time a new battalion is announced.

The word "parade" comes from a Latin word meaning "to prepare." As the men and women march before their unit commander, they proudly and publicly declare their readiness for any contingency. Without specifically stating it, the parade that takes place at a change of command ceremony tells the new commander, "we are prepared, if necessary, to go to war."

The greatest of all parades took place nearly 2000 years ago in the city of Jerusalem. Jesus told His disciples to find a donkey to ride. They followed His orders, procured a young animal, and watched as their Leader mounted and entered the city. Spontaneously, Jerusalem went wild. Men, women, and children who lined the streets tossed palm branches and articles of clothing before the donkey as it made its way up the city streets. They shouted out: *"Blessed is the king who comes in the name of the Lord!" "Peace in heaven and glory in the highest!"* Religious leaders felt threatened by this man. *"Teacher, rebuke your disciples,"* they cried (Luke 19:38-39).

Palm Sunday was a parade. Christ was the Commanding General, passing in review of all creation. At this particular parade, the Son of God openly declared that He was prepared for the ultimate battle. Five days later He hung on a cross, dead. Seven days later He was alive again, victorious over sin, over death, and over the Devil. Before the great battle that played out on the cross at Calvary, the world had little hope. Upon its conclusion, creation experienced a new beginning.

Near the end of the book of Revelation there is yet another great parade. Once again, Christ is at the head of the army, but this time He is not riding on a donkey. He is riding on a white horse. As the writer John proclaims:

> *'His eyes are like blazing fire, and on his head are many crowns. He has a name written on him that no one knows but he himself. He is dressed in a robe dipped in blood, and his name is the Word of God. The armies of heaven were following him, riding on white horses and dressed in fine linen, white and clean. Out of his mouth comes a sharp sword with which to strike down the nations. "He will rule them with an iron scepter." He treads the winepress of the fury of the wrath of God Almighty. On his robe and on his thigh he has this name written: KING OF KINGS AND LORD OF LORDS'*
>
> (REV. 19:12-16).

The armies of heaven who follow this mighty warrior are men and women like you and me. We become part of this army when we trust our lives to the General who rides at the front. Palm Sunday was the parade where Christ prepared Himself for the battle that took place on the cross. Revelation, chapter nineteen, is the parade where Christ prepares His army for the end of this world order, and for the establishment of a new heaven and a new earth. We live in between these two parades, at a time when the Almighty asks each of us, "are you prepared to stand before Me?" 'Are you ready to "pass in review" before the Creator of heaven and earth?'

Trust now in Christ! He is the One who has crushed the serpent's head, who forgives us of our sins, and who prepares us for the world to come. Do not delay in signing up! In so doing, you become a servant of the Most High, victorious in the battles of life. But you must personally enlist. It is, after all, an all-volunteer force.

Text Number Fifteen

The Greatest of All Symbols

"For the message of the cross is foolishness to those who are perishing, but to us who are being saved it is the power of God."

1 Corinthians 1:18

All formations at a Marine Corps base are presided over by the National Ensign. The adjutant calls the battalion/ regiment/division to attention on the parade deck. This is followed by the command, "March on the Colors." When the colors – the flags of the Marine Corps and of the United States – arrive at their appointed place, the entire unit renders a hand salute as the National Anthem is played. After honors are rendered, the command, "Post the Colors," is given, and the flags are placed at an appropriate location overlooking all of the business that transpires. When the ceremonies are complete, the command, "Retire the Colors" is given, and the unit is dismissed to carry out the plan of the day.

The flag of the United States is held in reverence by nearly all who have served in the U.S. military. It is the most important symbol of our country and of our Armed Forces. Whether onboard a ship at sea, flying high on the masthead, or at a shore station, where it is proudly raised and lowered with great ceremony, it is held in honor by all. Military personnel who board U.S. warships render salutes prior to boarding and again upon debarking. On shore bases, when "colors" is sounded, all activities stop and salutes are rendered as the symbol of the American republic is hoisted or lowered from the flagpole. The flag is given as a gift to those who have honorably served their country for twenty or more years. It is tenderly draped over the caskets of veterans who have died. Although theologically, the words border on idolatry, the following tribute to the flag — read frequently at the retirement ceremonies of military personnel — stresses the importance given to this great symbol of the United States:

"Old Glory"

I am the flag of the United States of America. My name is "Old Glory." I fly atop the world's tallest buildings; I stand watch in America's halls of justice.

I fly majestically over great institutions of learning. I stand guard with the greatest military power in the world. Look up and see me! I stand for peace - honor - truth - and justice. I stand for freedom.

I am confident - I am arrogant - I am proud. When I am flown with my fellow banners, my head is a little higher - my colors a little truer - I bow to no one! I am recognized all over the world. I am worshipped - I am respected - I am revered - I am loved - and I am feared!

I have fought in every battle of every war, for more than 200 years: Gettysburg, Shiloh, Appo-

> mattox, San Juan Hill, the trenches of France, the Argonne Forest, Rome, the beaches of Normandy, the deserts of Africa, the cane fields of the Philippines, the rice paddies and jungles of Guam, Okinawa, Korea, Vietnam, Guadalcanal, New Britain, Peleliu, and many more islands, and the score of places, long forgotten by all but those who were there with me, I was there.
>
> I led my soldiers - followed them - I watched over them, they loved me. I was on a small hill in Iwo Jima, I was dirty, battle worn and tired, but my soldiers cheered me! And I was proud.
>
> I have been soiled, burned, torn, and trampled on the streets of countries that I helped set free. It does not hurt, for I am invincible. I have been soiled, burned, torn, and trampled on the streets of my own country, and when it is by those with whom I have served in battle, it hurts.
>
> But I shall overcome for I am strong! I have slipped the bands of earth and from my vantage point on the moon, I stand watch over the uncharted new frontiers of space. I have been a silent witness to all of America's finest hours.
>
> But my finest hour comes when I am torn into strips, to be used as bandages for my wounded comrades on the field of battle, when I fly at half mast to honor my soldiers, and when I lie in the trembling arms of a grieving mother, at the graveside of her fallen son.
>
> I am proud ... my name is "Old Glory." Dear God ... long may I wave.[1]

The flag is a symbol of freedom. It stands for "life, liberty and the pursuit of happiness." It stands for a people who are willing to work together "to form a more perfect union,

---

[1]Howard Schnauber, Fort Collins Public Library Local History Archive, 1994.

to establish justice, to ensure domestic tranquillity, provide for the common defense and promote the general welfare of ourselves and of our posterity." It stands for free speech, a free press, and freedom of religion, for the right to bear arms, the right to a quick and speedy trial by one's peers, and the right to assemble freely. As the flag towers over every significant event in the military, we are reminded of those values for which our country stands.

An even greater symbol than the flag is the cross. Beautiful, ornate crosses decorate our places of worship, adorn our cemeteries, overlook our interstate highways, and are perched on the peaks of high mountains. Some people wear the cross as jewelry, but many have forgotten its meaning.

The cross was an instrument of torture and death. The violent criminal was executed on it: his arms and legs were nailed to its timbers, and a sign, spelling out the crime with which he was charged, tacked above the head. The entire assembly was then raised high above the ground, and its base dropped into a hole with a loud, shuddering thud. The condemned man hung suspended above the earth, without food or water, exposed to the elements, until he died.

Jesus was put to death on such an instrument of torture. The Bible tells us that He died on it for our sins, an innocent man charged with wrong-doing in a bogus kangaroo court. Jesus carried the cross along the Via Doloroso (the way of sorrow) to Golgotha, the place of the skull. He was crucified there for deeds He had never done.

The Scripture declares, "*the message of the cross is foolishness to those who are perishing.*" Just as the American flag has no real meaning to those who do not understand the values for which it stands, so the cross has no meaning for those who do not understand what happened on it. The men who put Jesus to death did not know who He was. They mocked Him; they blindfolded and beat Him while saying: "*Prophesy!*

Who hit you?" (Luke 22:64). They made a crown of thorns, pressed it so hard upon His scalp that it drew blood, while lustily shouting out: *"Hail, king of the Jews!"* (Mt. 27:29). Political leaders, as well as one of the criminals who was crucified at His side, cried out with sneering voices: *"He saved others; let him save himself if he is the Christ of God, the Chosen One"* (Luke 23:35).

Many, even today, see the crucifixion as foolishness. "Why did the Son of God die?" "If He is God in the flesh, why did He not destroy those who sought to take His life?" But this is the very essence of the gospel. Christ came to die, and *"to us who are being saved it is the power of God."* As the American flag has meaning for those who appreciate the freedoms represented by it, so the cross represents the power of God to those who have been set *"free from the law of sin and death"* (Ro. 8:2).

Our world promises death. As a result of our sins, we die – both physically and spiritually. Separated eternally from the love of God, we are promised a place of torment and perdition. But Christ came to save us. When He cried out from the cross: *"My God, my God, why have you forsaken me?"* (Mt. 27:46), He took God's wrath upon Himself. He died on that day, both physically and spiritually, in order that we might live. *"For Christ died for sins once for all, the righteous for the unrighteous, to bring you to God"* (1 Peter 3:18). More importantly, on the third day, He rose from the dead, forever destroying the grip that sin and death have on members of the human community.

Most Americans greatly appreciate the freedoms of our country; for them, the flag has great meaning. The cross, likewise, has enormous significance for those who have been set free from the bondage of sin. The cross is a symbol that stands for life, a life that is abundant and eternal, a life that Christ offers to all who place their trust in Him. When you, the reader, acknowledge the sinfulness of your ways, when you place your faith in the One who died in your place, when you believe that God raised Him from the dead, and when you ask Him to take control of your life, the message of the cross begins to make sense. At that moment you have become a servant of the Most High God, and the real journey begins.

About the Author

Chaplain Roger VanDerWerken, CDR, USN, is an ordained minister with the American Baptist Churches, USA. He grew up on a farm in upstate New York, and graduated from Schoharie Central High School in 1974. From 1974-1975 he was a Rotary Exchange student to the Netherlands. In 1975, he was accepted to the United States Naval Academy in Annapolis, Maryland, graduating with honors in 1979. From 1979-1981, he served as the Communication's Officer on board the USS SAN JOSE (AFS-7), and from 1982-1984, as the Main Propulsion Assistant on the USS RAMSEY (FFG-2).

In October 1979, through reading the Bible, and as a result of several profound religious experiences, VanDerWerken became a follower of Jesus Christ. In 1984, he resigned his Navy commission in order to receive theological training at the Westminster Theological Seminary in Philadelphia, PA, earning a Master of Divinity degree in 1988. From 1989-1991, he served as the Associate Pastor of the First Baptist Church of Glenside, PA, and from 1992-1998, as the Senior Pastor of the Memorial Baptist Church in Cortland, NY.

In October 1998, VanDerWerken reentered the Navy, serving as Chaplain for the First Combat Engineer Battalion, First Marine Division, until June 2001. This was followed up with a tour as Protestant Chaplain of the Marine Memorial Chapel at Marine Corps Base, Camp Pendleton (2001-2004). From 2004-2005, he participated in the Navy's Funded Graduate Education Program, receiving a Master of Theology degree in the ethics of warfare from the Jesuit School of Theology in Berkeley. Following his year of school he served as a Chaplain on board the aircraft carrier USS RONALD REAGAN (CVN 76) from June 2005-June 2007. His next assignment took him to the Naval Air Weapons Station in China Lake, California (July 2007- January 2010) where he served as Base Chaplain. He is currently stationed at the Marine Corps Base in Quantico, Virginia. VanDerWerken has also authored *Captain's on the Bridge: the Book of Revelation from a Military Perspective* (Selah Publishing Group, 2007).

Chaplain VanDerWerken and his wife Jacque have been married for twenty-six years. They have three children, Christina (25), Beth (22), and Jordan (20).